GROWING UP IN A CULTURE OF RESPECT

Inge Bolin

Growing Up in a Culture of Respect

CHILD REARING IN
HIGHLAND PERU

University of Texas Press ◆ Austin

Publication of this book was generously supported by Larry and Louann Temple; Allison, Doug, Taylor, and Andy Bacon; Margaret, Lawrence, Will, John, and Annie Temple; the Temple-Inland Foundation; and the National Endowment for the Humanities.

A portion of the royalties for this book will go to the Chillihuani herders to safeguard against times when crops are lost and sickness strikes.

Library of Congress Cataloging-in-Publication Data
Bolin, Inge.
Growing up in a culture of respect : child rearing in highland Peru / Inge Bolin. — 1st ed.
  p.   cm.
Includes bibliographical references and index.
ISBN 0-292-70982-x (cloth : alk. paper) — ISBN 0-292-71298-7 (pbk. : alk. paper)
1. Quechua children—Peru—Chillihuani.   2. Quechua Indians—Social life and customs.
3. Quechua Indians—Rites and ceremonies.   4. Herders—Peru—Chillihuani.
5. Chillihuani (Peru)—Social life and customs.   I. Title.
F2230.2.K4B63   2006
305.23´089´983230853—dc22

                                                    2005023647

With love and admiration I dedicate this book
to my Mother and to the memory of my Father,
to Ron, Greg, Andrea, Leith, and Liam,
and to the herders of Chillihuani,
who introduced me to their culture of respect.

Preface   ix
Acknowledgments   xiii

Introduction   1
    Raising Children in Poverty   1
    Village Structure, Living Conditions, and Subsistence Strategies   2
    Fieldwork and Research Methods   6
    Change: For Better or for Worse   10
    Central Ideas of Chapters   14

Chapter 1. From the Womb to the Cradle   16
    Pregnancy and Its Prevention   16
    Giving Birth   19
    Caring for the Newborn   24
    Unuchakuy—An Ancient Rite of Baptism   27
    When Things Go Wrong at Birth   29
    Sick Infants   30

Chapter 2. Early Childhood   33
    Learning to Care in a Culture of Respect   33
    Enculturation and Socialization   36
    Becoming Part of the Adult World   43
    Children's Rights and Responsibilities   47
    A Typical Day with a Chillihuani Family   52
    Disabled Children   57
    When Death Comes Too Soon   59

Chapter 3. Children at Play and Work   62
    Developing Creativity through Play   62
    Games Children Play   67
    Children at Work   71

Chapter 4. The Many Faces of Learning   82
   Laying the Foundations for Creative and Holistic Thinking   83
   Schooling in Chillihuani   85
   A New School Curriculum   88
   Mathematics—The Favorite Topic of Chillihuani Children   90
   Weaving and Mathematics   98

Chapter 5. Rituals and Ceremonies on Top of the World   109
   Pukllay—An Ancient Way to Play and Celebrate   110
   Suyay Ch'isin—The First Night of Rituals   115
   Ch'allaska in Honor of the Family Herds   122
   Dancing amid Thunder and Lightning   128

Chapter 6. Adolescence: A Time of Many Challenges   135
   Gender Complementarity and Cooperation   138
   An Adolescence Free from Stress?   141
   Approaching Adult Life   143
   Rondas Campesinas: Strengthening Solidarity and Self-Defense   147

Chapter 7. Building a Society of Respect   150
   What Makes for a Happy Childhood?   151
   Learning the Skills for Life   155
   Adolescents' Integration into Adulthood   156
   What Does It Take to Build a Society of Respect?   159

Notes   161
Glossary   179
Bibliography   187
Index   205

The puzzled tone in the voice of Aníbal Durán, school principal in Cusipata, rings in my ears as I remember him explaining that the children of the Chillihuani herders, who descend to the valley to continue their schooling, are always at the top of the class. "They are curious, self-confident, and always respectful," he adds. The other teachers agree. Yet for outsiders this is hard to believe. The families of these children are llama and alpaca herders who live in small adobe huts without electricity or running water. Their isolated village has neither streets nor stores, newspapers nor mail service, and only a few families own a book. Far from the mainstream of society, the Chillihuani herders feel more at home among the high peaks of their snow-covered mountains than among the population in the valley.

"It's a puzzle," the principal and teachers repeated throughout 1984–1985, when I studied the organization of irrigation among agriculturists along the hillsides of the Vilcanota Valley. Herding children made news in specific areas of study and in other activities as well. Since mathematics is the favorite topic of virtually all children in Chillihuani, it was not surprising that a fifth grader from the small school of 164 children took second place in a provincial math competition that included several larger towns. When Alicia, the third daughter of the healer Juan Mamani and his wife Luisa, lived in Cuzco with a *comadre* (godmother, Sp.), she held second place in her grade after only one year in the city. The children of Chillihuani won all the dancing contests in the district of Cusipata for three consecutive years. These and other achievements are unexpected, as competition is not encouraged in this egalitarian society high in the Peruvian Andes.

Yet despite the achievements of the members of this society, their superb organizational skills, respectful behavior, and the successful upbringing of their children, these high-altitude pastoralists have been subjected to a negative stereotype. Outsiders tend to judge them on the basis of their simple living conditions and adherence to tradition. The herders live in small adobe huts, wear homespun clothes, speak Quechua, the language of their Inca ancestors, and chew *coca* leaves. (*Coca* leaves, which have been sacred to the Incas, are still used in rituals and social interactions and release important nutritious elements when chewed.)

When I first met the herders who had descended to the valley to exchange their goods at the Sunday market in Cusipata, I realized that the stereotype had been imposed out of total ignorance. I was struck by the elegant and respectful demeanor of the highland herders. Their culture and religious ideology also stirred my interest. Whenever I participated in fiestas in the valley, my friends and *compadres* (godparents, Sp.) explained that celebrations and rituals are much more traditional in Chillihuani, where they reach back to Inca and pre-Inca times. Others spoke about powerful shamans who live close to the permanent snow.

Life in Chillihuani sounded intriguing. I liked the people I met on the rare occasions when they descended from their high mountains, and I desperately wanted to visit their village. But I did not dare to ask, knowing that high-altitude communities close themselves to outsiders and harbor a "legendary distrust of strangers" (Flannery, Marcus, and Reynolds 1989:5).

When I returned to the Andes in 1988, my *compadre* Antolín introduced me to Juan Mamani, one of the healers from Chillihuani. As we talked about the upcoming fiesta, he spontaneously invited me to celebrate the ancient Pukllay fiesta with him and his family in his remote village.

Chillihuani was more than I had ever imagined. Fourteen years after I had first set foot in the Andes, where I had traveled widely and was engaged in anthropological research and applied work in a variety of places, I did not expect to encounter such a unique village, unique in terms of people's respectful behavior, their wisdom and worldview, and their strong adherence to tradition.

Chillihuani stands apart not only from villages in the valley but also, in some ways, from other herding societies I have known. Visitors, such as the priest who ascends to many high mountain villages once a year, and merchants who travel with their llama caravans through the settlements along the high routes from as far as Bolivia, stress that Chillihuani's herders are more respectful and cling much more to ancient traditions than do people elsewhere. They also take more pride in their appearance. Teachers who have worked there throughout the years agree with these comments. They say that the children are also much better behaved, more curious, and more creative in their approach to different tasks than children elsewhere. Several teachers stated that all this makes it worthwhile to endure long ascents and difficult living conditions in this remote village.

Strong adherence to traditional values and unwritten moral laws fosters solidarity among the herders within an atmosphere that, despite extreme poverty, radiates energy and exuberance, especially during fiestas. This does not mean that sorrow is absent, or that conflict never arises. Problems do exist and conflict does flare up at times, but it is resolved with remarkable efficiency. Chillihuani does not fit the stereotype of the downtrodden Andean village so often referred to in the literature.

During the first years of my research among the high-altitude herders I focused primarily on rituals of respect as they are practiced during fiestas and in everyday life (Bolin 1998). Throughout these years I observed that children demonstrate respectful behavior at an early age, and I decided to study in greater depth the ways by which respect, the key value of this herding society, is instilled in children. When I asked the healer Juan Mamani and his wife Luisa what is most important in the upbringing of their children, both replied simultaneously, "We must always teach them respect."

Children constantly amaze me by the manner in which they combine politeness and responsibility toward family and community with curiosity and surprising scholastic abilities. It is equally intriguing to observe how parents socialize their children by combining their youngsters' individual needs with those of a community that depends on capable and compassionate young people to assure the survival of all in a marginal environment.

Childhood in high-altitude communities in the Andes differs considerably from childhood in mainstream society. In these remote regions, children's culture is not separate from that of adults. There are no children's stories, songs, or dances. Children participate in the adult world from an early age and soon become important members of society. They learn virtually everything they need to know through observation. It has been revealing to follow young children through adolescence—which is not a time of social and emotional upheaval but rather is considered the best time in people's lives—as they take over many of the rights and responsibilities of adults.

As one lives with Chillihuani families, it soon becomes evident that the ways children are raised in this village are highly beneficial to both family and community. Still, there are puzzling issues that are not easily understood by outsiders. I tried to get a deeper understanding of the strategies that are used to bring children to respect their social and physical environment, to be self-sufficient at a young age yet at the same time cooperate harmoniously within the community. I also tried to make sense of the ways children achieve within their society and beyond while always remaining dignified, respectful, and non-competitive. To come to grips with these seemingly contradictory questions, I focused on the following central issues:

Given a marginal environment with periods of hunger, disease, early death, and extreme poverty, what can parents offer their children that will put them on their way to becoming contented and well-adjusted individuals — honest, hardworking, and always ready to lend a helping hand? How can parents make children realize from an early age that they must acknowledge with gratitude what they receive to sustain their lives and that they must give, in return, to comply with the unwritten law of reciprocity?

Since children's culture as we know it does not exist in Chillihuani, where children are rapidly integrated into the world of adults, how do their personalities develop given the lack of a "childhood"?

As Chillihuani children learn almost exclusively by observation, how do they come to master complex tasks, such as playing an instrument or weaving intricate patterns into cloth?

How is it possible that in an egalitarian society, where the competitive attitude is minimal, children excel at work and play within their society and beyond its borders?

In Western society mathematics has been labeled a phobia for both students and their parents. Why would the boys and girls of Chillihuani be fascinated by mathematics and excel in that subject even before entering school? How is this interest in mathematics awakened and maintained?

In Chillihuani, both children and their parents consider adolescence to be the best time in their lives, while in North America it is seen as a time of conflict, rebellion, and power struggle between parent and child. What child-rearing strategies produce adolescents who are gentle and non-aggressive, yet self-confident and courageous even in the face of great danger?

In the chapters that follow I try to shed light on these issues as I present the concerns and strategies of the Chillihuani herders about child rearing and the maintenance of a dignified society. These people know that the perpetuation of their culture depends on the contribution children make in support of their families and for the benefit of the community. They understand that the continuation of life in their high mountains requires ancient ways of instilling respect in every new generation. The behavioral norms they show us are significant not only for their own community, but also for people elsewhere who want to build a society of respect on our all-too-disrespectful and rapidly disintegrating globe.

Many people and some organizations supported the research that led to the writing of this book. The study in Chillihuani was built on my previous research on the organization of irrigation in the Vilcanota Valley of Peru that was funded by the Wenner-Gren Foundation for Anthropological Research, the German Agency for Technical Cooperation, and the Canadian Fund for the Support of International Development Activities (University of Alberta). I value the support I received from Malaspina University College that reduced my teaching load by two courses, and I thank interlibrary loan for their efforts in finding all the books I needed. I much appreciate the help I received as research associate in 1992 and at other times from the Centro de Estudios Regionales Andinos Bartolomé de las Casas, in Cuzco, Peru.

Theresa May, editor-in-chief of the University of Texas Press, has been great to work with given her warmth and efficiency. I also thank her staff and the reviewers of my book for their thoughtful comments and the great care they took in their work on this manuscript.

My research in Chillihuani started in 1988 and thus took place while the Shining Path was still active in Peru. The years that followed were also difficult for the people in high-altitude regions due to extreme weather conditions that severely affected the meadows and destroyed the crops in several consecutive years. I would like to thank the organizations I contacted—the German Red Cross, the Landkreis Böblingen, the Wirtschaftsministerium of Stuttgart, the Lions Club of Leonberg, and Change for Children in Edmonton—for helping Chillihuani and my other study communities with essential grassroots projects throughout these devastating times. I would also like to thank Malaspina University College for funding a much-appreciated nutrition project for the children of Chillihuani and Cusipata. My family, especially my parents, and many friends, among them Gerda Teichert, Anneke and Peter van Kerkoerle, Kate Khan, Erika Ramirez, and Gunther Kuhn helped with many emergency projects. In Peru, my students Karoline Guelke, Karen McCoy, and Denis Berger assisted various communities, and Bob Atwal and others from the Malaspina Anthropology Club spent three weeks during exam time collecting money so the whole village of Chillihuani could buy seed potatoes after the harvests had been destroyed in two consecutive years. The many wonderful students I have taught at Malaspina University College deserve my deepest appreciation, not only for their steady help when need arose in Peru, but also for their keen interest in Andean culture and for the many stimulating discussions we have had over the years.

For thought-provoking conversations about Andean culture and insightful comments, I would also like to thank my friends and colleagues of various disciplines, among them Olive Dickason, Reinhild Boehm, Nancy and Ginger Gibson, Ross Crumrine, Rachel Cooper, Johnny Payne, Wade Davis, Daniel Gade, David Cahill, and Margrit Gauglhofer. I was trained in physical and cultural anthropology and am not a child psychologist so I am grateful to the authors I mention in this book, especially Jane Healy, for clarifying certain issues and giving a wider perspective to my observations in Chillihuani.

For intellectual stimulation and warm hospitality, I owe my Peruvian friends and colleagues, among them Lucho and Renata Millones, Antolín Maza, Jorge Flores Ochoa, David Ugarte, Jesús Guillén, Linda Ochoa, Solón Corazao, the Durán Zevallos family, Anton and Regia Ponce de León, Dina Pantigozo de Esquivel, César Palomino Díaz, Rosas Quispe, Genara Lizarraga, and their families. The late Manuel Chávez Ballón, Oscar Núñez del Prado, Aníbal Durán, and Manuel Orihuela have been great and will be remembered forever.

The members of the NGO that I founded in Cuzco in 1992 to deal with Andean medicine, nutrition, and ecology, called Yachaq Runa, were extremely helpful at every stage of my research and applied work. They labor relentlessly for the forgotten sectors of society and are a great inspiration in all matters. The soul of this organization is former school principal Ana Caviedes Ochoa, whose experience has been invaluable. José Cáceres, who was instrumental in bringing the faculty of medicine at the National University of San Antonio Abad in Cuzco to life, and Teresa Rivero have been great sources of knowledge. Other esteemed members include biologist Alfredo Tupayachi; José Soto; Juan Pablo Canchari Auccapuma; dentist Annushka Malpartida; teacher and lawyer Luz Marina Coronel M.; the late Juan Mamani and Naty Huamputupa, two healers who were dedicated to their last minute; and six outstanding healers from Cusipata and Chillihuani—Catalina Durán, Pascuala Villa, Modesto Quispe, Ricardo Illatinco, Teresa Mamani, and Braulio Quispe.

My family shares my fascination with the Andes and has been a constant source of inspiration and support. My parents, Eugen and Berta Bach, have been busy volunteers for decades, helping with many grassroots projects during the most devastating economic times in the Andes. My son Greg and daughter Andrea assisted me in the Andes and at home in many important ways. They and my husband Ron read this manuscript and gave valuable advice. I very much appreciate the help Ron gave me so many times when I had problems with the computer. My family's support for my Andean endeavors will never be forgotten.

I will always treasure the herders of Chillihuani, who accepted me into their village under the clouds, allowed me to participate in their manifold activities, and shared with me their concerns and their happiness. These people taught me that despite immense obstacles, one can raise children in an atmosphere of harmony and respect, thereby maintaining a dignified society.

GROWING UP IN A CULTURE OF RESPECT

Introduction

Raising Children in Poverty

It has been sixteen years since I first ventured to Chillihuani, a village of dispersed settlements of small adobe houses perched against the barren Andean landscape. At first it was difficult to comprehend how survival could be possible within this steep, marginal environment, with its extreme weather conditions and only the most basic tools available in the struggle to subsist. It was even more difficult to imagine how children could grow up to be healthy while living in dire poverty, exposed to the vagaries of a severe climate without a heating system, running water, or any other convenience.

As time went by, however, I noticed that below the poverty and the constant struggle to survive lies a wealth of wisdom and experience, a great deal of creativity, and a wide variety of talents. I came to realize that material poverty does not prevent these people from gaining a deep understanding of the most essential concerns of human existence, such as compassion for other forms of life, including the animate and inanimate spirits of nature. In fact, respect for these entities is what really holds the society together in the face of obstacles that seem insurmountable.

I soon learned that given great material poverty and an unforgiving environment, the maintenance of a dignified society depends to a large degree on the raising of children who perpetuate the values of that society. Child-rearing practices in the high Andes have, however, not been well documented. Historical accounts touch on this topic only occasionally and superficially. Even today, due to a lack of trust in outsiders, remote villages tend to close themselves off from mainstream society. Access to marginal regions is difficult as well because of high-altitude stress, extreme weather conditions, and inaccessible terrain.

Child rearing has never been an easy task anywhere. In fact, this age-old practice is fraught with considerable problems in many parts of the world, regardless of a society's culture or socioeconomic condition. Western society often assumes that problems associated with child rearing are rooted in poverty, leading to deviance or despair. Given this view, it is difficult to comprehend how children who grow up in a marginal environment and under most simple living conditions turn out to be valued community members who adhere to a strong work ethic, have a highly cooperative spirit, exhibit self-confident and respectful demeanor, and show very good scholastic achievements when given a chance. Yet this is the case in Chillihuani, a village of llama and alpaca herders that reaches the permanent snow of the Peruvian Andes.

The people of the high Andes are ideologically quite different from mainstream society, since the high-altitude herders do not separate the natural from the spiritual environment. They believe that not only do humans and animals have spirits, but so do the many features of nature, such as the earth, mountains, springs, lakes, rocks, and meadows. They all are imbued with life and require nourishment, love, and respect. Throughout the years I witnessed how these deep-seated beliefs and values are perpetuated from one generation to the next. I observed how respect translates into rights and responsibilities, as it reminds people of their duties vis-à-vis others and life in general and of the recognition they deserve in return. Thus, by giving and receiving respect, a cycle of reciprocity is created that links people to one another and to all parts of nature in a way that facilitates the survival of all. As the earth remains healthy, it provides for everyone and guarantees a successful life. The Chillihuani people believe that a successful person is one who, in their words, "leads a life of dignity and compassion."

Village Structure, Living Conditions, and Subsistence Strategies

In order to understand the people of Chillihuani—their attitudes and the ways by which they socialize their children—one must know their community and the land that grants them a living and provides spiritual guidance and support.

Chillihuani is located high above the Vilcanota Valley, between 3,800 and 5,000 meters (12,464 and 16,400 feet) above sea level in the district of Cusipata, province of Quispicanchis, department of Cuzco, Peru (see map). This high-altitude environment still allows its residents to subsist on pastoralism and horticulture. Several narrow paths lead to this village, but efforts are underway to extend a rudimentary road from the valley further toward Chillihuani. During the rainy season much of the region becomes impassable. The higher ranges of this dispersed village of 350 families (about 1,600 inhabitants) are within the most mountainous and rugged regions of southern Peru, where condors, pumas, and vicuñas can still be seen. In a day's walk, starting

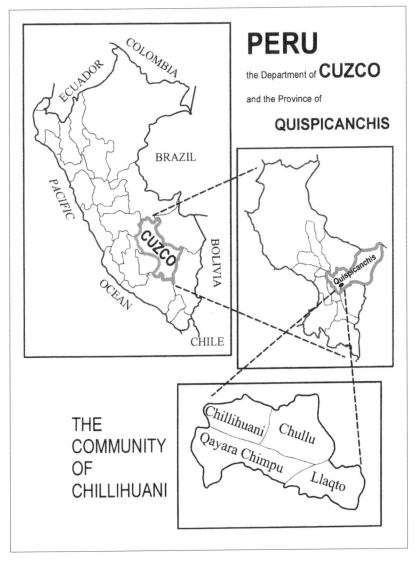

PERU, the Department of CUZCO and the Province of QUISPICANCHIS

THE COMMUNITY OF CHILLIHUANI

from the center of the village, one can reach Apu Ausangate, which at 6,384 meters (20,940 feet) above sea level is the highest and most sacred mountain of southern Peru.

Homesteads in Chillihuani and other parts of the high Andes are dispersed throughout the high mountains (Figure A).[1] The seasons are strictly defined. The dry season, or winter, lasts from May to October. The rainy season, or summer, goes from November to April. Temperatures vary more between day

FIGURE A. The steep hills, dispersed settlements, and towering mountains of Chillihuani do not keep the herders from meeting regularly for communal purposes.

and night than between summer and winter. They may rise to 20 degrees Celsius in daytime and fall to −15 degrees Celsius at night. Carl Troll observed that temperatures may drop sixty degrees Fahrenheit within several hours (1968:17). Air pressure at an altitude of 5,000 meters (16,400 feet), which is at the line of permanent snow, amounts to about 50 percent of the pressure at sea level.

Due to its high altitude, rugged environment, and isolation, this village has been less affected by mainstream attitudes and ideologies than more accessible villages. Neither has this herding society experienced servitude to a *hacienda* (landed estate), as have the people in lower villages. In the remoteness of Chillihuani, ancient ideologies are still alive in the minds of its people and are expressed in everyday life and sacred rituals.

As one ascends to this village of herders, remains from Inca and pre-Inca times crop up on both sides of the path. The archaeological evidence is set in stone: well-built settlements, irrigation canals, beautifully worked stones, and intriguing symbols engraved in rock—such as the double-headed snake, the insignia of the powerful Inca Pachacutec Yupanqui, who carried the same name as do many of the herders, suggest that this region may have been important in the ancient past. (See Bolin 1998 for details.) In addition, the presence of bones, skulls with trepanations, and, until recently, mummies, testifies that despite its remoteness, Chillihuani was not a forgotten place. The herders recount that "in the caves we had mummies, dried people who were sitting with their knees bent and covering their cheeks with their hands."

To reach Chillihuani from the Vilcanota Valley, one must pass through several ecological zones—*keshwa* (between 2,400 and 3,300 meters above sea level) and *suni* (between 3,300 and 3,910 meters above sea level)—before entering the *puna* (3,910 to 4,340 meters above sea level) and the high *puna* (above 4,340 meters) (Gade 1975:104–106), where Chillihuani is located. The village consists of four *suyus* (sectors): Chullu, Qayara Chimpu, Llaqto, and Chillihuani. *Suyu* Chillihuani carries the same name as the village itself. The division into four parts and the term *suyu* itself are reminiscent of Inca times. The Inca Empire was called Tawantinsuyu.[2]

The village center consists of a few adobe structures with thatched or corrugated iron roofs. These include the school, the municipal buildings, the house of the Women's Committee, and the health station.[3] The herder families live in small adobe houses with little or no furniture. From the center of the village, settlements reach into all directions for sixteen kilometers (ten miles) toward the permanent snow. The dispersed nature of the settlements, each of which consists of one to three adobe huts, gives the flocks enough room to graze during the day and return to their own corrals at night.

On March 21, 1957, Chillihuani was officially recognized by the Peruvian government as a peasant community with 350 families. The inhabitants, most of whom are illiterate and monolingual Quechua speakers, refer to this village as their *ayllu,* a Quechua term with a variety of definitions.[4]

The pastoralists subsist on their herds of alpacas, llamas, and sheep, as well as guinea pigs, and on potatoes and other tubers, such as *oqa* (*Oxalis tuberosa*), *ulluku* or *lisas* (*Ullucus tuberosus*), and *maswa, añu,* or *isaño* (*Tropaeolum tuberosum*), which they cultivate on steep hills at different altitudes and in different ecological microzones to minimize the risk of crop failure due to frost, hail, floods, and drought. Some vegetables grow in sheltered areas. The total area of Chillihuani, including the pastures, amounts to about 7,000 hectares.[5]

The herders also collect algae (*qochayuyu* or *llulluch'a*) from mountain lakes; mushrooms (*qoncha; setas,* Sp.) that grow in high regions mainly after lightning storms; and the fruit of the spiny *roq'a* plant (*Opuntia*), also referred to as *tuna de la altura* (Sp.).

Trees are few and only grow in the lower part of the village. Among native trees we find the *capulí* (*Prunus serotina*), which do not bear fruit at this altitude; the *kishwar* (*Buddleia incana*) and *kehuiña* (*Polylepis incana*); and the eucalyptus tree (*Eucalyptus globulus*), which is native to Australia (Tupayachi Herrera 1993).

Although the staples of the food supply consist of potatoes and other tubers, this society is referred to as a pastoral society, i.e., a society of herders. The Chillihuani people identify themselves as pastoralists, since they consider animal husbandry quite prestigious and their herds provide many of the items they require in their daily lives. Alpacas, llamas, and sheep provide wool for clothing, blankets, carrying cloths, ropes, and slings. Male llamas and alpacas carry loads to and from the fields and sometimes to other high-altitude villages. The animals' meat, blood, and skins are used by the herders or are bartered in the valley for necessities they cannot produce themselves. The dung is needed to fertilize the fields and serves as fuel in its dried form. The animals' hides serve as mattresses and pillows; their tendons are used for sewing and for stringed instruments. Fat is made into candles. Bones serve to make the weaving tool *tullu ruki*. Apart from the fact that the herds contribute much to subsistence, they are also significant in both cultural and religious terms.[6] Just as Pachamama, the Earth Mother, is honored every day for providing food for the people, so are the animals given love and respect for their help and companionship. (See Chapter 5.)

Fieldwork and Research Methods

The first time I asked myself about the kinds of child-rearing strategies that are required to raise a society of well-adjusted and dignified children, adolescents, and adults was in 1977, in the Amazon jungles of Loreto, along the Rio Tahuayo. The elegance and dignity of these people, and their generosity and helpfulness, were astounding. At that time I did research in primatology and could not pursue this intriguing question. Eleven years later, I was again confronted with the same surprise as I ventured for the first time to high-altitude Chillihuani. I am glad I got a second chance.

Fieldwork in Chillihuani has been both difficult and rewarding. The difficult part lies in the extreme weather conditions that can destroy harvests and bring about hunger, sickness, and frequent deaths when the knowledge of the healers is insufficient. On the other hand, fieldwork is also a fascinating experience. I will never forget the interesting conversations, the intriguing fiestas, and people's resilience in the face of terrible disasters. From the moment I arrived, I felt at home among the families of herders and the village at large. Yet it took me years to understand the overall ideology of the herders and to grasp the meanings of the metaphors and ancient symbolic patterns that guide these people's lives. After almost a decade and a half, I am still grappling with some of these issues as I continue my research and applied work in this village under the clouds. But work and research are not the only reason why Chillihuani keeps calling me back. There is an intrinsic harmony in this village, combined with the herders' dignified demeanor, their profound joy of living, and the melding of an enigmatic past that in some ways continues into the present. This special atmosphere has also seized others who have accompanied me to this village.[7]

One of the reasons why fieldwork is so rewarding is the fact that these people still adhere to the ancient Inca greeting "*Ama llulla, ama suwa, ama qella*" (Don't lie, don't steal, don't be lazy). In accordance with *ama llulla* (don't lie), all are careful to tell the truth. They answer questions about past and present events with precision. They feel that facts must be stated in the appropriate way. Whenever I misunderstood what was said or done, people immediately corrected me in a friendly but decisive manner.

Ama suwa (don't steal) is taken seriously as well. Theft is virtually unknown in this village and is further discouraged by a variety of strategies discussed in Chapter 6. Throughout many years of fieldwork, I never lost anything, though I left my equipment and other things unattended at all times.[8]

The herders are equally concerned about *ama qella* (don't be lazy). They speak proudly about their work on the fields, and about *faena* (communal work, Sp.). Work is even believed to be part of the afterlife, as people wish for good pastures, plentiful harvests, and a healthy flock of animals when they must depart for *hanan pacha,* the Andean heaven, literally the "upper world."[9] The strong work ethic is combined with respect for the deities and sometimes with fear of their powers. The deities cooperate in the subsistence activities as they provide the villagers with fertile earth, rain, and sun to make things grow.

The primary objective of this book is to describe and analyze child rearing in the cultural context of Chillihuani, with special emphasis on the issues listed in the preface. I did not engage in psychological testing of any kind, but instead observed the children, their parents, and their other caregivers in natural settings. My observations were complemented by dialogues with children and community members of both sexes and all ages. The examples I have used from other investigators in the Andes and elsewhere show similarities and differences in child rearing and their impact on children's development. No anthropological study had been done in Chillihuani prior to my arrival.

Interviews were held in the form of dialogues, which simultaneously satisfied my interests and those of my herder friends who were curious about customs in other parts of the world. Sometimes I received different answers to the same question, which is to be expected since people tend to view situations in a variety of ways and cultural practices differ to some degree even between families. To learn about a wider range of perspectives regarding the issues at hand and to clarify contradictory statements, I met with groups of people to discuss the observed events and analyze their symbolic significance. Researchers Flannery, Marcus, and Reynolds found in the course of their fieldwork among llama herders of Ayacucho that "it is one thing to collect a series of concepts in an American Indian language; it is quite another thing to have their underlying meaning revealed by someone who spent his entire youth thinking exclusively in that language" (1989:xii). I also agree with Victor Turner that one must try to discover how the indigenous people themselves feel and think about their own rituals (1969:11). For this reason I made sure that the local people spoke for themselves on many occasions, not only in the course of my fieldwork, but also in this book. I was unable to observe a few activities, in which cases I relied on the description of key informants and elders.

The herders have very good memories and remember details of discussions we had years ago. They are also well versed in oral history and are quite articulate. Given the negative stereotype of highland Indians, people in valley towns and in the city were surprised when listening to my tapes. I was especially amazed by old people's positive outlook on life after having endured grim poverty for so long in an unforgiving environment. These people speak with honesty and sophistication, adding wit and humor to their accounts. They showed me that even under the most challenging conditions, life is what you make of it.

I am grateful to the herders for being so forgiving, especially at the beginning of my studies when I was ignorant of their behavioral etiquette and thus unwittingly disrespectful with regard to the moral norms of this society. For example, after a thundering horse race close to the permanent snow, I was eager to discover who was the winner of this spectacular race. I persisted in asking until the healer pointed to the winner, who then looked to the ground in embarrassment. In a society where respect is paramount, no one sets himself above others. I also used to ask people at what ages their children had started to engage in certain activities. Here my questions were equally out of place, since many people did not keep count of the year of their children's birth, and children are not driven to do certain things according to age.

Old people and most women are monolingual Quechua speakers. Young and middle-aged men and those young women who attended school speak some Spanish. Children who have been able to continue schooling beyond grade six in the valley speak good Spanish and often express themselves in as eloquent a manner as they do when speaking Quechua. Village elders estimate that about 30 percent of the villagers are bilingual. I taped most interviews, music, and singing, as well as our joking sessions (*chansanakuy*). It was interesting to note that despite our very different cultural backgrounds, our senses of humor are very much the same.

The Indians of the high Peruvian Andes refer to themselves as *runakuna* (the people), or *runapunakuna* (the people of the high *puna*). They speak *runasimi*, the Quechua language. Quechua was not a written language in Inca times; therefore we find considerable variation in orthography. My spelling of Quechua is based on the 1995 Quechua-Spanish dictionary published by the Academia Mayor de la Lengua Quechua. For an occasional clarification of concepts, I used the *Diccionario Quechua Cuzco-Collao* (1976), by Antonio Cusihuaman, and the *Diccionario Kkechuwa-Español* (1968), by Jorge A. Lira. I have added the English "s" to designate the plural, since Quechua does not have an equivalent suffix and the Quechua suffix -*kuna* (as in *wasikuna*, meaning houses) cannot be used in all cases where the plural is warranted. Quechua words and expressions are typed in italics. Spanish terms are in italics, followed by "Sp." Quechua quotes from documents, as well as names of people and places, have for the most part been left in the customary spelling as it appears on the relevant documents and maps. My sources for Latin names of animals and plants are not always consistent. The principal sources for Latin names of plants are Daniel Gade (1975) and Antonio Brack Egg (1999); for animals it is the dictionary by the Academia Mayor de la Lengua Quechua (1995).

I am responsible for the translation of all documents and communications that required translating. Spanish-speaking herders and experts of the Quechua language assisted in translations from Quechua to Spanish and/or in the clarification of complex ideas expressed in Quechua. Possible errors in facts and interpretation, of course, remain mine.

Having lived in Chillihuani off and on between 1988 and 2004 (1988, 1990, 1991, 1992, 1994, 1996, 1997, 1998, 1999, 2000, 2001, 2002, 2004), my descriptions are based on accumulated observations and experiences over the years. Thus, for example, Anali, one of my godchildren, was three years old when I met her for the first time. Now she is seventeen. It is not always easy to establish the ages of the people in Chillihuani, since in the past only a few families kept track of the year in which they were born. But everyone knows the season when the births took place. Part of my research was carried out before 1996, while the Shining Path (Sendero Luminoso) was active in Peru. It is probably due to Chillihuani's inaccessibility that this region was not directly hit by the problems of that time.

Although I know most of the families in Chillihuani and was allowed to observe their customs and lifeways, I usually lived with any of the four healers and their families, who therefore enter more frequently into the discussion of specific events. The people of Chillihuani are pleased that I wrote a book on child-rearing practices in their village. Most people insisted that I use their photos and their proper names in the book. Others were not quite sure, in which case I used pseudonyms. Indians of the Andes use two last names, their father's and their mother's. I have sometimes used only the first of the two names, since both were not always given.

Although this book focuses on child-rearing practices, it also describes and analyzes community activities, fiestas, and ideological issues. These are important, since children grow up in a cultural milieu where they observe family and village activities and become participants in due time. As I compare situations that exist in Chillihuani with those in Peruvian towns and cities and the Western world, I use the term "modern" to describe these latter two societies, since neither cling to traditional ways of life.

Change: For Better or for Worse

In 1997 I concluded my book *Rituals of Respect: The Secret of Survival in the High Peruvian Andes* by expressing the belief that the magnificent culture of the Chillihuani herders will continue for a long time, given people's pride in their culture and customs and their determination to survive in their high mountains. The herding way of life in the Andes has continued and adapted to turbulent conditions for more than 6,000 years, since the llama was first domesticated. Llama herding has evolved "in response to countless sociopolitical changes around it . . . it has adjusted to the rise and fall of the Wari state in the Ayacucho Basin (AD 600–800), the expansion of the Inca empire (AD 1450–1532), the Spanish conquest of the sixteenth century, and the war of Peruvian independence from Spain (AD 1824)" (Flannery, Marcus, and Reynolds 1989:2). Legend tells that the first Incas originated in Lake Titicaca and made their way to Cuzco, from where they founded an immense empire that included the present countries of Peru, Bolivia, Ecuador, southern Colombia, northern Chile, and northern Argentina. In some cases the memories of the Andean people go back to Inca and pre-Inca times (see also MacCormack 1991:179).

Throughout their empire, the Incas created "enormous structures in stone and adobe, earthquake-resistant architecture, outstanding irrigation works, and superb agricultural terraces. They knew about astronomy, practiced brain surgery, and organized their empire in ways unlike any other known society. Tawantinsuyu became the largest native empire that ever arose in the New World" (Bolin 1998:4).

In colonial times, significant events took place in the provinces of Quispicanchis and Canchis, at the very margins of Chillihuani. Thus, in the early 1780s, Gabriel Condorcanqui, who was born in Tinta as a direct descendant of the Inca royal lineage, took the name Tupac Amaru II and together with his wife Micaela Bastides led a revolution against the exploitation of native peoples by colonial authorities. Against their intentions, the uprising turned into the bloodiest rebellion of the colonial epoch (Sallnow 1991:285), with both native peoples and the Spanish suffering devastating losses. Tupac Amaru II and his family were killed in the most cruel manner on the large central plaza of Cuzco. But in the memories of people throughout the region, they live on as heroes.[10]

Despite these upheavals, the ancient herding way of life has maintained essential elements from times long gone. Given Chillihuani's remote location, social change has been much slower than in more accessible regions. Yet for the last fourteen years, and especially since 1997, I have witnessed changes in Chillihuani that have brought along both beneficial and devastating results for the community.

The people of Chillihuani assert that prior to 1988, the village had never received assistance in its efforts to develop basic amenities. The only projects that reached this village had been a church, built in 1938 using the labor of the local people, and a small school, also built with communal labor.

On my first visit to Chillihuani in 1988, adobe walls destined to be a health station had been built in the center of the village. Given the subsistence way of life, this project could not be brought to conclusion, nor could other urgent projects be started. Formerly people could survive in their marginal environment, but extreme weather conditions caused by global warming had destroyed harvests and caused death among many herd animals, making survival difficult throughout wide regions of the Andes. During such dreadful times I would have felt uncomfortable if the sole reason for my presence had been to study rituals and child rearing. It was gratifying to be able to assist the villagers, with the help of individuals and organizations, in their struggle to survive (Bolin 1992:14).

Thanks to the funds provided by the organizations I contacted, environmentally safe projects were implemented.[11] With communal work and the help of the Yachaq Runa group of Cuzco, which I founded to deal with Andean medicine, nutrition, and ecology, the community built a health station, three first aid stations, a building for the Women's Committee, three drinking water

projects, and a water reservoir, and organized several seed projects, a refor-
estation project, a project to curb hunger and malnutrition, several health and
food campaigns, a greenhouse project, a fish project, and a library project.
To protect the delicate environment, people started to use solar cookers to
cook meals and sterilize medical instruments. Solar water heaters and solar
lighting systems for the health station and the school were also much appreciated by the local population (Bolin and Bolin 2003). Three of the Chillihuani
healers and two young herders joined the Yachaq group (see Pantigozo de Esquivel 1995). The group members appreciate the Chillihuani herders for their
knowledge and excellent cooperation, and the herders, in turn, learn about
other ways of healing from the various Yachaq members, who come from different regions of the Sierra. Aspects of modern medicine, such as courses in
hygiene and family planning, are taught in various villages along the Vilcanota and Urubamba Valleys by the Yachaq healers, nurses, and physicians. We
implemented a variety of grassroots projects in those regions as well. Finally,
in 2000, the province made a move and helped Chillihuani build a new school
with four rooms. Then, in 2002, Marcial, the mayor of the district capital of
Cusipata, who used to teach in Chillihuani, honored our request for more
drinking water projects, a washroom for the health clinic, and the repair of
the water reservoir. In 2004 we provided the school with solar lighting. All
of these projects were considered priorities by the local population and were
much appreciated.[12]

Yet the community has suffered various setbacks. Among these was the
sudden death of Ignacia, the president of the Women's Committee. She was
a generous person and a great organizer who knew how to make the most of
the scarce resources. Soon thereafter the esteemed elder Roberto Yupanqui
Qoa, whose memories of his ancestors reached back to Inca times (see Bolin
1998), died as well. In October 1999, Juan Mamani, the tireless and much-
appreciated healer, fell to his death from a steep cliff.

The extreme climatic conditions between 1997 and 2000, which destroyed
harvests and killed more than 30 percent of the herds, forced increasingly
more people to leave the village in search of work in agriculture; in households in larger urban centers such as Sicuani, Cuzco, and Quillabamba; and
in logging and gold washing in the jungle regions of Madre de Dios. The exhausting work and tropical diseases caused many people to fall ill. Sometimes
death followed.

In 1996, after the danger of the Shining Path had passed, a variety of religious sects infiltrated the Vilcanota Valley. Some of the Chillihuani villagers
descended to the valley to engage in a food-for-work relationship with spe-

cific religious groups. In September of 1998 representatives from one of the sects ventured to Chillihuani for the first time. In 1999, when I participated in the Pukllay fiesta in the heights of the village, the Chillihuani herders celebrated this ancient event with enthusiasm and serenity. Irrespective of torrential rains, hail, and landslides, they danced and made offerings of respect to the deities and their fellow humans in their adobe huts and between the borderlines of the *suyus*. But a small group of twelve people followed the leader of a sect to a different place in the high mountains, where they burned the sacred paraphernalia used in ancient rituals. This small group did not come to the Pukllay dances either. Influenced by sect members, who promised food and other amenities, these herders stopped chewing the *coca* leaves that provided them with much-needed calcium, vitamins, and minerals and instead started to chew gum, which slowly rots their teeth.[13] There is no money in Chillihuani for toothbrushes and toothpaste, let alone dental bills. *Coca* leaves also suppress feelings of hunger, thirst, cold, and fatigue and figure importantly in rituals and social interactions. Alan Ereira (1991) notes that *coca* leaves and cocaine are as different as rye bread and rye whiskey.

Many Andean people understand little about the basic premises of these religious sects, and they are not always sure which group carries out what activities. It is quite clear, however, that the propagators of various sects are competing with other sects who work in the same or neighboring villages, causing much conflict and even casualties.

The few Chillihuani herders who joined the sects confided that they were not allowed to follow any of their previous beliefs and rituals or sing traditional songs, dance, and tell stories from the time of their ancestors. Some local people were offered a salary by religious groups to go from house to house to convert villagers. Although only a few people joined the sects, the elders feared that the strong solidarity of the village was in jeopardy. They wondered what kind of culture would develop, given the many different beliefs and conflicting attitudes, and what would happen to their fragile, high-altitude region when the earth, water, and mountains were no longer acknowledged and respected as they have been since time immemorial. The village elders continue to hope that the people who abandoned their Andean culture and beliefs will come to their senses and return to the ancestral religion that has thus far assured respect and solidarity within their community.

When I returned a year later, in 2000, some converts had gone back to their Andean religion, which contains some elements of Catholicism and otherwise reveres nature in all its forms. By 2001, other people had exchanged the Chiclets they had started to chew for the traditional *coca* leaves that provide them with important nutrients. They again wore their ponchos and *llikllas*. In February of 2002, the elders reported that all of the families participated again in the ancient Pukllay celebration that honors Andean culture and religion.

The shock waves discussed above have introduced change but have not destroyed the most significant characteristics upon which Chillihuani society is built. This points to both great resilience on the part of its people and their determination to keep their culture intact. The chapters that follow show that now, as in the past, the people of these high mountains are concerned that their families and community continue to live in dignity as they instill the respect they have received from their ancestors in their children for generations to come.

Central Ideas of Chapters

In order to understand a society, it is necessary to consider how people live their lives, starting at birth. One must understand how children are accepted into this world and how the birth of a child can bring not only much joy, but also sadness when things go wrong.

As we accompany a young family throughout pregnancy and birth, Chapter 1 illustrates people's joys and concerns regarding these events. Natural childbirth techniques, the use of ancient Andean medicine, postpartum activities, and cultural beliefs throughout and following birth will be discussed. Although boys and girls are loved and treated equally, in the high Andes people pray for the firstborn to be a girl, contrary to many other countries where the firstborn is hoped to be a boy. Rituals for the newborn include *unuchakuy*, which introduces the child to godparents and to a sacred mountain that takes the role of a godparent, protecting the child throughout its life.

Wrapped in a swaddling cloth, an infant is always in close contact with its mother or other caregivers, as we will see in Chapter 2. Infants are raised in a permissive way and childhood is usually a happy time as children grow up in a world of adults. As they learn to honor the manifold forms of life by which nature presents herself, as kinship ties connect them with people from outside the family circle, and as they receive their rights and responsibilities, we witness the many ways by which respect is instilled in young children.

The permissive attitude toward infants and small children continues as they are allowed to playfully explore their environment and assist their families in everything they can. Chapter 3 defines how play and work merge into one entity. Creativity is stimulated as, in the absence of store-bought toys, children work at creating their own playthings. They meet with further challenges and get prepared for life as they begin to help in the fields and take their family's herd to pasture.

The great variety of stimuli children are exposed to at play and work impacts their further learning and performance in school. Chapter 4 reveals why children who are deprived of the tools and experiences believed instrumental to success in "modern" societies are actually well prepared for life, excelling in mathematics and rising to the top of the class when they continue schooling in the valley. The reason why children excel in a society that has no appreciation for a competitive attitude is also examined.

Chapter 5 discloses how fiestas, ceremonies, and rituals provide children with further opportunities to learn organizational skills, to become more familiar with metaphors, and to understand the significance of respect. It analyzes the importance of rituals during the ancient fiesta of Pukllay and shows how respect and reciprocity connect people not only to their fellow villagers, but to all life in the cosmos.

By the time they reach adolescence, Chillihuani children have established a framework of knowledge that accommodates new experiences in an organized way. Chapter 6 explores why these children feel neither lost nor unhappy or awkward during adolescence, and why physical changes are welcome. This chapter also discusses the challenges, rights, and responsibilities the adolescents assume at this stage in their lives, when they start to participate in various local institutions that convey knowledge, pride, and a strong sense of adventure.

In conclusion, Chapter 7 brings together the key issues that make childrearing practices in the high Andes so effective. Comparisons with child rearing in other settings shed light on ways of living that can benefit children and societies everywhere.

CHAPTER 1

From the Womb to the Cradle

In the high Andes, people must live in widely dispersed settlements to provide enough pastureland for their animals. Yet they are gregarious, they love company, and they are especially fond of children, whose births are greeted with great joy. Unfortunately little is known about pregnancy, birth, and the socialization of children in these remote regions. Documents on Inca and pre-Inca societies give us at most sketchy information (J. Rowe [1946] 1963:282), and not much more is known about these events from present-day herding societies. This is in part due to the fact that remote villages close themselves off to outsiders. Also, in the past it was usually men who investigated Andean culture, and they had little if any access to female spheres of activities. Valuable research has been undertaken on birth rituals, death, and disease in high-altitude societies (e.g., Allen 1988:19–20, 229–230; Bastien 1985:49–51, 85–101; and others), but pregnancy and birth as such have received only cursory attention.

Pregnancy and Its Prevention

Children are welcome after a couple has joined in *rimanakuy*, the traditional Andean marriage (see Bolin 1998, Chapter 8). Prior to marriage, a degree of promiscuity is not frowned upon as long as this does not result in pregnancy. Women do not take the birth control pill or use other preventative methods common in mainstream society, since these are neither affordable nor trusted. Instead, people rely on traditional knowledge to prevent conception. Some women deposit the plant *oqhe qora* (*Descurainia titicacensis Walp*) in boiled water and drink small amounts three times a day during menstruation. *Oqhe qora* is also used in combination with the herb *alqo kiska* (*Xanthium catharticum*). One of the healers suggested that juice made from parsley taken for two days for breakfast at the beginning of menstruation can prevent conception since it cools the body, but he cautioned that this does not work with all women.[1]

Another belief is that guinea pig soup, taken three times on the day after giving birth, prevents conception for several years. Some Chillihuani villagers assert that the water in which the plants *añu* or *maswa* (*Tropaeolum tuberosum*) are boiled also serves to prevent conception. Some healers are aware of the rhythm method, but there are few calendars in the village, and menstruation is not regular in many women. Abstinence during times of greatest fertility is not much adhered to. The herb *ruda* (Sp.; *Ruta graveolens L.*) is abortive in concentrated form but is considered damaging to the body if not taken in the appropriate way.[2]

When a child is born to a young woman who is not involved in a permanent relationship, her parents convince the young people to get married, or they raise the child themselves.[3] As young people start to live together after *rimanakuy,* the Andean marriage, or *casarakuy,* the Catholic wedding, which consists of primarily Andean and some Christian elements (see Bolin 1998, Chapters 8 and 9, for details), faithfulness to one's partner is expected and most often adhered to. This is the time when children are welcome, whether a young couple still resides with either set of parents or has already established a new household. The situation of Julia Illatinco Qoa and Lidio Yupanqui Quispe illustrates how young people establish a family in married life.

Julia and Lidio fell in love in the high *puna,* where they took their alpacas and llamas to pasture. It took some time, however, until Julia's parents allowed Lidio to marry their daughter. Only after Lidio had proven himself to be reliable and hardworking did he become accepted into Julia's family. Young men know that parents care very much about their daughters and demand utmost respect from suitors (Bolin 1998:104).

For the first year following *rimanakuy,* the young couple lived with Julia's parents; then they moved in with Lidio's parents. Lidio's parents were grateful that the young couple resided with them, since Lidio's father was recovering from a fall in the high mountains where he had tried to retrieve a young alpaca that was stuck on a steep ledge. After his recovery, he helped the young couple build their own small adobe house out of earth and *ichu* grass. Other relatives and friends also helped in the construction by means of *ayni,* the reciprocal work relationship that is an Andean strategy, essential to the survival of families and the community.[4]

As is true for most young families in Chillihuani, Julia and Lidio have only a small herd of fifteen llamas and alpacas to which each partner contributed; thus, they do not have much animal dung, which, when dried, can be used as fuel to cook meals in the earthen stove. Their house is small and preserves body heat and heat generated from the fire while meals are cooking. Although in winter temperatures can fall at night to −15 degrees Celsius, people cannot afford to heat their houses in the largely treeless heights of their village. But the young couple made sure that their small one-room house would be large enough to accommodate a third person, a tiny one who is soon to arrive.

Julia had helped her mother raise two younger siblings and is well aware of the pleasures and hardships that come with raising children at such high altitude. On several occasions Julia has witnessed births and the happiness associated with a new arrival. But she has also seen stillbirths and the death of both mother and child after a long, painful labor far away from any help. Factors such as malnutrition, extreme climatic conditions, problems with high-altitude pressure, and great distances between the homes of families, who could be asked to help should problems occur, put both a mother and her newborn at considerable risk.

The first years of a child's life are also very difficult given the existing environmental stress factors. Many children die before they reach school age. Centenarian Segundina Qolqe affirmed that in the past even more mothers and their newborns died in childbirth or soon thereafter. Yet Julia is confident that given her own knowledge and her mother's longtime experience as a midwife, everything will turn out all right. Julia's mother has frequently been called to help young women during childbirth if the pregnant woman's own mother could not be present. Mothers most commonly assist their daughters in childbirth. Sometimes a husband assists. In the absence of adults, children over twelve years of age are normally able to assist in uncomplicated births.

Throughout her pregnancy Julia continued her routine work, including housework, taking animals to pasture, and helping her husband on the potato fields. She left the more strenuous chores, such as carrying heavy loads, to her husband and the other male members of her extended family. As is true for pregnant women in her village, she continued to eat normally, adding no extra food.[5] For the first three months of pregnancy, Julia sometimes felt slightly nauseous; otherwise she, like other women of the village, experienced little discomfort.

There are certain beliefs that influence the behavior of pregnant women. In Chillihuani and other regions of the high Andes it is a common belief that the thoughts a mother has during pregnancy enter the mind of the baby in her womb. Therefore, Julia avoided thinking of unpleasant or troubling events that could negatively affect the health of her baby.[6] People in high-altitude regions generally believe that pregnant women should neither spin nor weave, for fear that the baby will get entangled in the umbilical cord, causing complications during the birth process. To keep away the *uraña wayra,* the malevolent wind that causes misfortune, disease, and death, women twist threads of black and white wool toward their left side, an activity called *lloq'esqa* in Quechua, and wear the resulting strings around their wrists and ankles and sometimes around their waists. This notion of the power of strings and associated beliefs are also expressed in other parts of the Andes and were present in Inca times (Rowe 1963:314). Anthropologist Gerardo Reichel-Dolmatoff noted during his research among the Kogi of Colombia that "many religious contacts between the individual and the supernatural powers are conceived of in terms of a union that is established by a connecting thread. Also, all diseases are 'like a thread' which entwines the sick person, and a strong cotton thread tied around the wrists or the ankles hinders the entrance of disease to the body. On the other hand, many sacred songs are thought of in terms of 'threads' which connect the singer with the deity to which he addresses his song. One must untie these threads in order to avoid evil influences, or one must tie oneself firmly to those forces which are benevolent" (1985:299). Some Chillihuani villagers assert that pregnant women should not carry meat, since this would cause complications and even death. Not all Chillihuani families share this particular belief.

Giving Birth

It is the middle of June, the coldest time of the Andean winter. Julia is on her way home from the high pastures, where she took her animals to graze. On the long descent she starts to feel pains in her lower abdomen. She knows the meaning and makes a detour to her mother's hut to announce that she may soon be giving birth. Her mother, Doña Qoa, smiles in anticipation of a happy event. She fetches a special carrying cloth (*q'epirina* or *q'epina*) that is always packed in the event that she is called to assist a birth. It contains several pieces of woven cloth, a string of wool to tie the umbilical cord, fleece to put on the umbilical cord to absorb the blood, and incense and herbal teas, mainly nettle tea (*Ortiga*) to speed up the birth process and cleanse the body. The herb *Mamani alqa* (*Ouricia chamaedrifolia Benth*) is also believed to facilitate labor and help expel the placenta. When both plants are available, they are mixed to make tea. But these herbs are also effective on their own. As is common practice, Doña Qoa's bag contains neither scissors nor a knife, but instead a sharp piece of tile (*teja; barro roto de cerámica,* Sp.) to cut the umbilical cord. Chillihuani herders assert that the navel becomes stronger when the umbilical cord is cut with a piece of broken earthen ceramic. If it is cut with a knife or scissors, it is believed that the child will wear out his or her clothes very fast.[7]

With the bag of utensils in her hand, Julia's mother follows her daughter to her small one-room adobe hut. She closes the door to keep the cold wind out and conserve the warmth and humidity that will emanate from the fire she is about to light and the boiling water she will prepare.[8] Soon the burning incense provides a pleasant smell throughout the hut and prevents the spirits of the malevolent winds (*uraña wayra* and *soq'a wayra*) from entering.[9] Winds can, indeed, be dangerous to one's health in the high Andes, not only as metaphors but also because they bring along icy temperatures and ferocious gusts that can be so strong as to disable and even kill a person.

Julia's mother starts a fire in the earthen stove to boil water for humidity and prepare nettle tea, which speeds up the birth process. She also boils meat to make a broth so Julia will remain strong throughout her labor. While Julia's labor pains are still irregular, she fashions a small bouquet using three *coca* leaves and offers this *coca k'intu* to Pachamama, asking her, in return, to grant her a fast labor, an uncomplicated delivery, and a healthy baby.[10] As Julia's pains become more regular and increase in intensity, her mother gently massages her daughter's abdomen to relieve the pain. She proceeds to rub *qollpa*, a white mineral that she collected from a site close to a mountain lake and then ground into a fine powder, all over Julia's body to purify her and keep away the malevolent winds.[11] Rituals and activities of this kind, which are meant to work against evil spirits and in favor of benevolent spiritual forces, give psychological support in situations where people can only hope and pray. This is not only true in the high Andes but is also the case in other parts of the world, as noted by Yvonne Lefèber and Henk Voorhoeve. In their study on childbirth in different parts of the world, they noted that "communication with the ancestral and supernatural world seems to be an essential part of the expertise of the midwives. They claim to be aware of good and bad spirits and are supposed to be able to resist possible bad influence from evil spirits" (1998:8).

Lidio returns from his fields. The smell of incense tells him that Julia is in labor. As he enters the hut, he quickly closes the door behind him to keep the wind out. He sits down beside his wife, who kneels on an alpaca fur. Holding her hand, he smiles at her in anticipation of the birth of their first child. But he cannot hide his anxiety. What if something goes wrong?

Julia has been in labor for over six hours, and the pains become more intense. Trying to ease the pains, she alternates position frequently. She kneels, squats, stands up, and walks around the room, as is common among women in Chillihuani, who seldom, if ever, lay down during labor.[12] At intervals Julia's mother asks her daughter to stand erect in order for her to check the position of the baby. It seems to be all right, but to be sure, she takes a woven shawl, lays it around Julia's back and hips, and gently pulls back and forth in a rotating fashion, holding on to the ends of the shawl. This method, called blanketing (*sususka*), helps bring the baby into the right position for entering the birth canal. Then Julia squats again, trying to ease her pains.

Lidio leaves to fetch more water from the creek to keep the kettle boiling and the room humid. Julia must be warm at all times and must sweat to ease her pains and speed up the birthing process. Intermittently, Julia's mother gives her stinging nettle tea to drink and broth to keep her strong. She does not get solid foods. But the baby is not yet ready to come. Chillihuani healers and midwives assert that on the average births take between four and twelve hours, but can take several days.[13]

Julia's mother looks concerned. She knows that she could not help should a major problem arise. Although two of her children were born without problems, it took three days for her third child to be born. Her husband finally found a midwife in a distant village who had the reputation of being able to help with difficult births. She remembers that she felt at the brink of death when the midwife was finally able to deliver her baby after turning it into the right position through the method of blanketing. Although this practice is well known throughout the high Andes, few master it to the degree where a baby in an unusual position can assume the proper position to enter the birth canal.[14] Some midwives, in addition to blanketing, also use their hands to put the baby into the right position to enter the birth canal headfirst. (See also Werner 1986:257.) The herders of Chillihuani recount that formerly there were more midwives (*parteras,* Sp.) and *parteros* (Sp., male healers who know about childbirth) who had greater knowledge than is the case nowadays. This knowledge was transmitted throughout generations of healers. Some of the ancient knowledge about midwifery was within the public domain, while some practices were kept secret by the respective healers. Other practices seem to be lost altogether. Midwives with special knowledge who came to the village from afar were paid a small amount for their assistance (about 15 *soles,* or two to three U.S. dollars).

The high death rate among mothers and infants during the birth process in remote communities is of concern to the population at large and cannot be erased from the minds of Julia and her attendants. Should complications arise, they would not be able to reach the health station in the valley, over thirty kilometers away. The terrain is precipitous and it would be risky to take Julia, who is sweating in the small humid room, out into the night where the temperature is below the freezing point.

Hours pass. More water is boiled, more incense is burned, more teas are brewed. Everyone fashions *k'intus,* asking Pachamama and the great Apus, where the spirits of the ancestors live, to help in the birthing process and to let the baby be healthy. Lidio gently massages his wife's abdomen and back to ease her pains. Then he fetches a small bottle of sugarcane alcohol, destined to be offered to the deities in the upcoming fiesta. He gives some to his wife to bolster her strength and warm up her body.[15]

Julia continues to push hard. The breathing technique is not known in this herding society. Doña Qoa puts firm pressure to her daughter's back with the palm of her hand and moves downward along the vertebral column. It has been fourteen hours since the labor pains started, and Julia becomes weaker, groaning with pain. She squats down over an alpaca fur, pushing with all the energy she has left. Finally the top of the baby's head appears. Several strong pains follow, and shortly thereafter Julia's mother holds a precious baby, who starts to cry immediately.[16]

While Lidio holds the baby, Julia's mother ties the umbilical cord in two places with strong woolen threads and cuts the cord between the tied knots with the sharp end of a tile, at a distance of three to four fingers (about three to four centimeters; some say it should be six centimeters). She places some fleece on the cord to absorb the blood.[17] She then wipes the baby with a clean cloth, puts *qollpa,* the white mineral powder, over its body as a protection against evil spirits, wraps it in a blanket, and lays it in Julia's arms. The baby will not be bathed until the umbilical cord has fallen off. With joy they look at the new member of the family. "*Warmi wawa paqarimun*" (It is a girl), Lidio whispers, looking at his tiny baby girl as his eyes fill with tears. He kisses his wife and the baby. Julia's mother massages her daughter's abdomen and back to make sure that the placenta will be expelled. It appears soon thereafter.[18] Lidio washes the placenta and burns it in the open fire using much firewood.[19]

The perineum did not tear as Julia was giving birth. This is normal among Chillihuani women, some of whom state that nothing can be done should tearing occur. Others assert that a piece of cloth must be placed on the tear and the next day the medicinal plants *mapa* (*Senecio rhyzomatosus Rushby* [S. T. Rivero Luque, personal communication]) and *uñuka* (scientific name not known) are to be applied.[20]

In case of continued hemorrhaging, a new mother receives a treatment called *walthasqa*. At this occasion her body is rubbed with a preparation of macerated herbs—*chiri chiri, romero, mapa,* and *mutuy* (*Cassia hookeriana Gill* [Brack Egg 1999:116]).[21]

The Chillihuani herders do not weigh their babies at birth, so I could not find out exactly how much newborns weigh, but the healers estimate that at birth a baby weighs between two and three kilograms and measures between thirty-eight and forty-five centimeters. In his research on Mount Kaata,

FIGURE 1.1. A young Chillihuani couple beams with joy as they introduce me to their firstborn baby girl.

Bolivia, Joseph Bastien noted that the average weight of newborn babies is only four pounds (1985:87).

The family is exhausted from the long labor but happy that the baby looks healthy and is a girl. In the high Andes, boys and girls are equally loved. In accordance with an ancient belief, however, a family will experience good luck and economic well-being if the firstborn is a girl (Figure 1.1). If the firstborn is a boy, the family will have to struggle to make a living.[22]

A similar idea is expressed in the valley in Cusipata during a race on August 15, the day of Cusipata's patron saint, Asunta. Two young men disguised as husband and wife run through the village to a designated site. The whole village cheers for the "wife" to win so the harvests will be good and food will be plentiful. This belief has its roots in the fact that women are the household economists. They organize all tasks within the house; they decide which produce can be used for consumption and which for seed, sale, or barter. Women are also in charge of small-scale market activities. They are believed to incorporate the power of fertility.

As long as the firstborn is a girl, the gender of the later siblings does not matter so much. Yet parents like to have both daughters and sons, to help with their respective tasks.

The herders of Chillihuani do not know about genetics. Instead, the birth of a boy means that the father is stronger, while the birth of a girl means that the mother is stronger. Chillihuani herders also believe that the moon is important with regard to conception and birth: boys tend to be conceived and born during full moon and girls during new moon. In the course of his research in Kaata, Bolivia, Joseph Bastien found that "the sex of the child is determined by whether the husband or wife 'wins' in intercourse" (1985:86).

Caring for the Newborn

Julia proceeds to nurse her baby. Since no baby formula is available in this village, and there is no money to buy it in a pharmacy in Cuzco, a baby depends exclusively on mother's milk. Mothers who do not have enough milk stimulate the flow with fennel (*hinojo*, Sp., *Foeniculum vulgare*). Other informants relate that a soup made from a woodpecker[23] is prepared for this purpose. In some regions at a distance from Chillihuani I was told that to stimulate the flow of mother's milk mothers drink *quinua* soup, made from the lungs of a sheep.[24] When a mother cannot produce milk, she may ask a nursing woman, or a woman whose baby has died, to nurse her baby until she can produce milk herself. Herbal tea made of anise (*Pimpinella anisum L.*) is given to a baby while it waits for mother's milk to be stimulated.

In 1998, upon my return to Chillihuani, a family came to visit me with their two-month-old baby. Contrary to all the other babies I had seen, little Alan was extremely thin. The mother, who was over forty years old, told me that her milk did not flow except for a few drops at a time and that the baby lived on herbal tea. In the case of this mother, fennel tea did not have any effect on making her milk flow. There was no other woman who could have nursed the skinny baby (Figure 1.2). Luckily, we found a pharmacy in Cuzco that sold baby formula, which Alan consumed until he was approximately six months old, when he started to consume broth with *chuño* (freeze-dried potatoes) and fresh potatoes that were prepared for him in the same way as for adults. When I saw Alan a year later, he looked strong and healthy. Thus far it seems that he has not suffered from a diet that consisted predominantly of herbal teas with a few drops of mother's milk for the first two months of his life. Now, at age five, Alan is alert, interested, and creative (Figure 1.3).[25]

While a woman continues to eat normally during pregnancy, her diet must be free from salt for a specific time after giving birth. Thus, for the next two weeks Julia will eat meals without salt. Some women restrict eating salt-free food to one week; others believe they must refrain from ingesting salt for three weeks. But all agree that for a short time, a mother who has given birth may

FIGURE 1.2. Two-month-old Alan with his parents and other family members, who are concerned about the baby's inability to gain weight.

under no circumstances consume salt, which is believed to hurt the womb (matrix and uterus).[26] The recommended food for a new mother is *chuño* soup with the boiled meat of a sheep, alpaca, or llama and ground cumin (*comino molido*, Sp.), to be eaten three times a day. After one week she can eat potatoes. She continues to drink nettle tea to cleanse her blood. Sometimes blood pressure falls considerably in women who have given birth. In this case, they consume soup made from the meat of a black male sheep and may sip some coffee or alcohol if available. In order to regain her strength, a new mother should stay in bed or at least in the house for eight days.

As is common in the Andes, Julia's baby starts to nurse right after birth and will continue until she is about two years of age. Some babies stop nursing at that age without problems, while for others this change is more difficult. Several mothers advised that in order to discourage children from nursing, chopped pepper (*roqoto, Capsicum pubescens*) or *hollin* (Sp.), the soot from a pot that has been placed over the open fire, can be put on the nipples. Children sleep either in the same bed with their mother, or on a fur placed on the adobe floor beside the mother, until they are at least four or five years old.

During her pregnancy, Julia prepared clothes for her baby. She carefully washed older woven skirts and cut them into pieces to serve as diapers (*akawara*). She also wove a few new diapers out of sheep wool. The herders as-

FIGURE 1.3. At age five, Alan is bright and full of energy.

FIGURE 1.4. Family and community members admire a baby wrapped in a swaddling cloth.

sert that sheep wool dries faster and remains warmer than alpaca wool when wet. Julia's baby will wear diapers until she is ready to urinate and defecate outdoors, normally between one and two years of age. Her diapers are held in place by a swaddling cloth (*waltha*) that consists of a long, narrow cloth of alpaca, llama, or sheep wool that is wrapped around her, with her arms stretched out along the sides of her body (Figure 1.4).

When she starts to crawl, her diapers will be held in place by a belt (*chumpi*). In order to become strong and energetic and develop straight limbs, a baby wears the *waltha* at night until she is about two years old. This swaddling cloth also keeps a baby from hurting herself with her arms, hands, or fingernails; keeps her warm; and helps her to sleep. If the child still refuses to sleep, the mother takes the larva of a small bush-dwelling worm, called *puñuy puñuy* (sleep sleep), and puts it by the child's head. Metal items are also placed close to the baby to protect her from bad spirits. Julia will carry her baby at two weeks of age in a woven sling (*q'epirina*) until she is old enough to walk.[27]

Unuchakuy — *An Ancient Rite of Baptism*

Julia and Lidio's baby girl is three days old and ready to receive a name in an ancient ritual called *unuchakuy,*[28] which can be celebrated any day after birth until the baby is one week old. This first ritual is not considered a legal baptism by religious and political leaders and institutions of mainstream Peruvian society. Yet for the people in the high Andes, *unuchakuy* is an important Andean ceremony, believed to protect a child from mishaps until she is baptized by a priest.

Julia and Lidio have selected a godmother (*madrina*, Sp.) for *unuchakuy.* It is common practice that either the *madrina* or *padrino* (Sp., godfather) chooses a name for the child or accepts the name the parents suggest. The *madrina* now begins with *unuchakuy,* dipping her fingers into a bowl of water that has been blessed (*agua bendita,* Sp.) by saying three prayers. She traces a cross on the head of the child, naming her Alicia. All the family members offer *k'intus* to the deities, asking them to protect the child throughout her life.[29]

Simultaneously with the human *madrina,* one of the mountain peaks becomes protector of little Alicia. I was reminded at various occasions that parents do not select the mountain, but that "the mountain spirit finds the child." The child will not get to know who the mountain godparent is until a special event occurs, such as a severe illness. The parents, however, know the name of the mountain, which is revealed in a dream or by a shaman who reads *coca* leaves.

Regardless of a child's gender, a male or female mountain can become godparent. Male mountains are more common, though. In Chillihuani, people's mountain godparents are mostly from the immediate vicinity. Apu Ausangate, the most sacred mountain of southern Peru, is visible from the heights of Chillihuani.

Throughout Alicia's life, her parents will make offerings to her mountain godparent in return for the protection this deity offers her. On important occasions or during serious situations like an illness, an elaborate offering, with many ingredients such as *coca* leaves, alpaca fat, etc., is burned in honor of the mountain, asking him/her for help or advice. (For information about a complete offering, see Chapter 5). It is believed that a child who is not baptized in *unuchakuy* can be hurt by the malevolent winds that bring diseases and other problems.

Before Alicia is one month old, her name must be registered together with the date of her birth and the name and address of her parents in the vital statistics of the civil registry (*registro civil,* Sp.) in the district capital of Cusipata. Formerly, registration was not mandatory. Therefore, many adults and some youths and children who did not keep track of the year of their birth do not know how old they are. But they know exactly during which season they were born and in the course of which agricultural or herding activities.

When asked about the date of his or her birth, a person may respond, "I was born when my parents prepared *chuño.*" This activity of freeze-drying potatoes takes place during the cold and sunny season — the Andean winter — between the end of May and the beginning of July.

The birth of a child in Chillihuani is a sacred event. People believe that Pachamama, the Earth Mother, gives spiritual life to the child. At death she takes the child or adult back into her womb. Throughout a person's life, Pachamama watches over him or her together with the mountain godparent, providing food, drink, and protection.

The herders of Chillihuani view the origin of a child's spirit or soul in a variety of ways. Some say that the earth offers the spirit; others believe that the spirit can reside in a mountain peak or mountain lake, from where it enters the growing fetus. All agree that at death the spirit returns to some part of Pachamama, the great Earth Mother who incorporates all features of nature. Others specify that the body is received by Pachamama while the spirit soars to *hanan pacha,* the Andean heaven. At the death of an *altomesayoq* (a powerful shaman), however, his/her spirit is said to move straight to the house of the hail (*chikchi wasi*), in the highest and most sacred mountains.

Intriguing questions as to when and where the spirit enters a being were answered by the *curandero* Modesto Quispe. He asserted, "A child's spirit begins to grow from the moment of conception. It accumulates little by little in accordance with the growing fetus in the mother's womb. The spirit develops in synchrony with the body." Some villagers explain that "the spirit is life and it gives life." Others say, "The spirit is the gift of life that penetrates matter, such as the body."

When Things Go Wrong at Birth

Julia and Lidio are grateful for the healthy child that has been added to their family, and they thank Julia's mother and the Andean gods for their assistance. But not all families are as lucky as this one. Even today, death for mother and/or offspring is common during childbirth and shortly thereafter, and many children die before they are one year old.[30]

Casualties during the birth process have been stated as ranging between 10 and 50 percent. Centenarian Segundina Qolqe and other old people of Chillihuani confirm that in the past many mothers and/or their infants died in childbirth. Centenarian Roberto Yupanqui Qoa lost his wife as she gave birth to their fifth child.

Throughout the years of my research I have witnessed several tragedies related to childbirth, which were due to a variety of causes. In June of 1996, a mother died in the very high regions of Chillihuani after giving birth to her fifth child. When her husband arrived from the fields, he found both mother and child dead in their house. The cause of death was unknown to the family, and the husband had to carry his dead wife on his back sixteen kilometers (ten miles) downhill to the center of the village, where a nurse and an assistant from the valley had come on horseback to perform an autopsy. It turned out that the placenta had remained inside her body, causing her to bleed to death. As is often the case during times of hunger, this woman was too weak to expel the placenta.[31]

In February of 1999, during the rainy season, a woman living in the outer regions of Llaqto, far away from the center of Chillihuani and from other inhabited places, experienced problems during the birthing process. Her husband could not help her. Neither could he leave her alone to get a midwife or a healer because of the distance involved and the fact that torrential rains had washed away every trace of the narrow paths that run along the steep mountainsides. Only the next day was a healer informed about the woman's problems and her death in the early morning hours.[32]

The rather frequent deaths of mothers during childbirth are mostly due to one or more of the following reasons: the position of the fetus does not allow it to pass properly through the birth canal; retention of the placenta; excessive bleeding; and physical debility due to malnutrition and anemia. Sometimes a difficult birth can be predicted, but there is no money to go to a hospital and there is little trust on the part of the herders regarding the attention they receive in some of the state-run facilities.

In addition, bad harvests — and in some areas the total loss of crops caused by the El Niño and La Niña phenomena for three consecutive years, starting in 1997 — caused hunger, sickness, and disease among the population, adding to the already high death rates of mother and child in the course of the birth process.

Sick Infants

The first few years, and especially the first year, after birth can be very difficult for the children of the pastoralists. Major health problems in children relate to the respiratory and digestive systems and the urinary tract. Diarrhea, pneumonia, and tuberculosis take their toll. Some children die from childhood diseases such as measles (*rubeola,* Sp.), mumps (*parótida,* Sp.), whooping cough (*tos ferina,* Sp.), and scarlet fever (*escarlatina,* Sp.), although vaccinations are available for most of these diseases.

Children and adults who ascend to a high altitude from lower-lying regions often suffer from hypoxia, a condition resulting from a decrease in the oxygen supplied to or utilized by body tissues. Yet this ailment also expresses itself to various degrees in highland Indians. Flannery, Marcus, and Reynolds (1989:41) refer to Baker's (1968:30) studies on hypoxia in high regions in southern Peru, where it was found that "some aspects of native adaptation (to cold and hypoxia) take lifelong exposure to the environmental conditions and may be based on a genetic structure which varies from that of lowlanders." Although larger lung capacity and a higher rate of red blood cells help people cope with high-altitude pressure, young native children and especially newborns do have problems with hypoxia. During the years when I lived with the families of the healers Juan Mamani and Modesto Quispe in Chillihuani, several times I had difficulty breathing at night, although I normally feel very comfortable at high altitude. Every time this happened, several people came to the healer's house in the morning to report that their baby had died "from the cold." No other explanation was given. It could very well be that due to a drop in temperature from cold to very cold, the pressure also dropped, making breathing increasingly more difficult for the babies, for myself, and for the young animals—other than llamas and alpacas—that also died in the night. As noted previously, at altitudes between 4,000 and 5,000 meters above sea level, air pressure amounts to only around 50 percent of the pressure at sea level. (See also Hochachka et al. 1991 and Hochachka 1992 regarding hypoxia.)

As children grow, another health problem, referred to as *susto* (Sp.), *mancharisqa*, or *q'aqcha*, is added to the above ailments. The Chillihuani healers explained that *susto*, which consists of panic attacks, is a condition that affects most children in Chillihuani and other villages during some time of their childhood, usually when they are between eighteen months and eight years of age. The healers explained that *susto* can be caused in different ways. When a child gets bitten by a dog, for example, he may fall ill and the fear instilled can last for a long time. *Susto* can also be caused by the sight of a spider, especially the black widow (*viuda negra*, Sp.), whose bite can be fatal.[33] Some children also become extremely scared when they hear stories about the *kukuchi*, ghosts that are believed to appear at night, speaking to them in a high voice.

Children who suffer from *susto* normally get diarrhea and fever. One of the healers explained, "When children suffer from *susto*, we *curanderos* say that the soul or spirit of the child has left him, that the child lost courage and resigned himself. We blow *k'intus* for Pachamama and the Apus, asking them not to seize the child's spirit but to bring it home. We call out '*hamuy animo*' [come back spirit]. We also fumigate the house with the vapor of incense, sugar, and anise boiled over the fire. And we twist strands of wool toward the left to protect against bad spirits." It is believed that *susto* can only be cured through psychological means, such as the "calling of the spirit" (*waqyaykuska* or *llamada del espíritu,* Sp.).

Susto also comes with *qhaqya onqoy,* the thunder sickness, which is an ailment caused by lightning. Children and adults may experience severe shock and can become unconscious and waste away unless a *paqo* (psychological healer) can cure them. The tremendous fear of lightning is justified, since death caused by lightning bolts are quite frequent in the high Andes.

Despite the efforts of knowledgeable healers to save children, many have died before reaching school age. Given a number of grassroots projects that we have implemented throughout the years with the help of the healers and a trusted nurse at the Chillihuani health station, casualties have diminished, but they are still the cause of much sadness in this village.

The death of a child is greatly mourned. The belief that his or her spirit will join Pachamama, from where it will return in the form of a newborn, instills some hope, but does not take away the immediate pain. But children who survive in the barren heights of Chillihuani grow up in an atmosphere of compassion, tolerance, and respect. Their lives amid material poverty are filled with hidden riches that make it all worthwhile.

CHAPTER 2

Early Childhood

Learning to Care in a Culture of Respect

C hillihuani's children amazed me in many ways. From the first moment I arrived in their village, I was captivated by their respectful behavior, self-confident demeanor, and astonishing creativity. In July of 1990, when I met three-year-old Anali in her home located at almost 5,000 meters (16,400 feet) above sea level, she came to greet me in Quechua. Living so far from the mainstream of society, this was her first meeting with a foreigner, but she did not seem to mind that I looked, spoke, and acted differently from the people around her. While her parents were busy preparing a meal, she took over the role of the hostess. She filled two cups with water, kept one for herself, and offered one to me with the words *"Kuska ukyasun"* (Let's drink together). She cared for me in an elegant and quite determined way throughout my stay at her home (Figure 2.1).

As soon as the children become conscious of their environment, they are introduced to a culture of respect. Respect is not only given to other people and the deities, but is conveyed also to all forms of life — both animate and inanimate — as the Andean people see it. Pachamama, the Earth Mother, and the Apus, those sacred mountains, are loved, honored, and brought offerings in return for the favors these deities grant. All parts of nature — the earth, mountains, springs, rocks, and the entire cosmos — are believed to be imbued with life and demand respect. Children grow up knowing that without respect and compassion for life in all its forms, life cannot continue to exist.

The deep love for nature is expressed in many ways, often in the form of songs and poems, which are dedicated to even the most miniscule plants. This attitude of respect for life becomes part of every child. It fosters solidarity not only with family and friends, but also with other forms of life, thereby assuring that the fragile high-altitude environment is treated with kindness and can withstand the human intervention that is necessary to make a living.

The herders insist that animals — both wild and domesticated — deserve respect, love, and compassion in their own right. This attitude is further supported by the belief that animals belong to the deities, who watch over their

FIGURE 2.1. At age three, my godchild Anali has already learned to be a charming hostess who knows the etiquette of her society.

well-being and who become unhappy and sometimes angry if their animals are not treated well. Condors are the birds of the Apus, and they incorporate the spirits of these mountain gods. "Alpacas and llamas are our sisters and brothers," the herders say, and in some Andean societies these camelids are believed to be ancestral to humanity. But it is not only the great significance ascribed to animal spirits and their intimate connections with deities and humans that demands respect; the fact that people rely for their livelihood on their herds also fosters much consideration for their well-being. The close metaphoric relationship of animals, people, and the gods is also expressed in North American native societies and indigenous cultures elsewhere. In their deep appreciation for animals, these native people share their concerns with the world's great minds, such as Mahatma Gandhi, Leonardo da Vinci, Bernard Shaw, Pythagoras, Alexander von Humboldt, and many others. Albert Schweitzer stated, "A good human being considers life itself as sacred, whether it is the life of a plant, the life of an animal, or the life of a human" (Preuss 1997:29).

Whenever an animal is born, the herders rejoice. They thank Pachamama and the Apus with an offering of *coca k'intus,* asking, in return, that the newborn have a healthy and happy life. Children learn to care for animals and give them love and respect in everyday life. They help their families hold celebrations in honor of the animals and their protective deities. During the Pukllay festivities in February/March, alpacas and llamas are honored with *k'intus;* they are sprinkled with *chicha* and piles of flowers (see Chapter 5).[1]

Once in a while, the spirit of a domestic animal must be sent to the mountain gods. Such a sacrifice, which normally occurs in the course of a festivity, honors the gods and simultaneously allows people to add meat to their meager diet of potatoes and other tubers. Sadness always shows on the faces of the family members as they lay the llama or alpaca on its side, with its head facing east and resting on the lap of its owner, who offers *k'intus* to the mountain god. Placing a *k'intu* in the mouth of the animal, the owner whispers into its ear, "Chew this *coca* so you can rest comfortably." Family members take their hats off in respect for the animal and its journey to the great mountain god. As the blood gushes forth, a handful is offered to Apu Ausangate, the highest snow-covered mountain in the vicinity. He is asked to accept the spirit of the animal and return it in the form of a newborn. (For a detailed description, see Bolin 1998:53–54.)

Sometimes the herders of Chillihuani and other villages ask me how animals are honored and celebrated in my country on their special days of the year. They also ask what rituals we perform when the spirit of an animal is sent to the great mountain deity, who assures that it will be reborn in the corral at a future date. When I tell them that pets are usually loved by their owners and that we do have special days dedicated to animals, but they are seldom if ever remembered, and there are no festivities or rituals in their honor, people are puzzled. When they find out that farm animals are slaughtered without consideration for their spirits, they look at me in disbelief. An elderly lady, with tears rolling down her cheeks, asked me, "Don't you hold the head of your animal in your lap, don't you give the animal *k'intus* so it can rest comfortably, while its spirit soars to its maker"? My answer, that this is not how farm animals die where I come from, made her sad. Young boys who insisted that I tell them how the spirits of farm animals are really sent to their maker in my country were disenchanted when I indicated how they are slaughtered. "But this is not respectful," one of the boys said in disbelief. The others shook their heads in silence.

I have never told my highland friends about the cruel ways in which so many animals are raised under crowded, filthy, and inhumane conditions and without love, respect, and compassion in many "modern" societies. I could not possibly tell them about the horrible lives and cruel deaths of animals in factory farms. The herders would never understand how anyone, unless they were totally stripped of dignity, could engage in such cruel affairs or stand by and let it happen. They know that in valley towns animals are not treated with the same respect as in the high mountains. If I told them about the atrocities that take place in some slaughterhouses and labs in the "civilized" world, they would be unable to combine such behavior with the norms of a dignified society. I am sure that their respect for me would vanish as well.

For many years I did not see chickens in Chillihuani and assumed that this herding society knew little about the needs of these animals. But in 1994 I noticed that the Mamani family, who lives in the center of the village, had acquired four chickens. They roamed freely during the day, and at night they slept in a little henhouse filled with sand and a nicely carved roost. The children explained that chickens need to scratch and bathe in the sand and that they sleep much better at night with a roost to sit on. Incidences of this kind reveal why child raising is not fraught with problems in Chillihuani and why adolescents integrate easily into a culture of respect.

Enculturation and Socialization

In the high Andes, children are always in close contact with their mothers or other caregivers. Babies are tucked in a woven carrying cloth (*q'epirina*) that is folded into a triangle, with two of its ends attached around the caregiver's shoulder (Figure 2.2).[2] Infants are most often carried by females, but older male siblings and adult males also carry babies this way. From their high seats in the slings they can observe everything that happens in the house and outdoors. Since most public activities occur in the open, and private activities take place in a one-room house, these children have ample opportunity to observe the whole spectrum of events that take place in their society.[3] Thus, infants and young children observe their older siblings and adults and imitate them in every way. By the same token, since small children are never tucked away in daycare but are always with family members, older siblings and cousins have much time to observe infant care and can, therefore, take over themselves whenever need arises.

There is little difference in the way parents in Chillihuani treat their male and female offspring, and there is scant segregation of children's activities according to gender. During infancy, both boys and girls wear the same clothes, consisting of a woven shirt and a rectangular woven cloth (*phalika* or *kulis*) that is wrapped around the body and tied at the waist with a woven belt, called *chumpi*. At about six years of age, children start to wear the kind of clothes adults wear (Figure 2.3).[4]

FIGURE 2.2. Fiestas are for all people, whether they come on foot or wrapped in a *q'epirina.*

Children are well cared for by a variety of family members. They are seldom left alone during infancy and then only for short periods of time. Although child rearing may differ to some degree among families of the same village, a permissive way of upbringing is the rule, as long as the child does not get into dangerous situations. Overly cautious behavior on the part of parents and other caretakers is seldom seen. Families normally let their children develop at the pace they set for themselves. They can always engage in new activities, which allow their curiosity to run free.

Those children who survive the hazards of extreme weather conditions and periods of severe food shortages grow up to be quite energetic and are prone to mischief. The herders know that this energy must be channeled in the right direction with kindness and understanding to avoid trouble later on. In efforts to do so, not many words are used. The elders say that it is better to set a good example for children to follow than to do a lot of talking.

Chillihuani herders do not spoil their children. Yet they love and cherish them, and when very young, children are often at the center of attention. All family members attend to children with patience, and so do neighbors and friends, who admire and cuddle them whether they are their own or those

FIGURE 2.3. Anali (left) and Tomás (center) wear the *phalika*. Six-year-old Luzwilma (right) already wears adult clothes.

of other families. Small children move from arm to arm. Women, men, and older children are delighted as infants pull their hair, play with their clothes, and jump on their laps without tiring (Figure 2.4).

Their exuberance is tolerated and admired even when the playing is a little rough. A particular fondness for children has also been reported by investigators from other regions of the high Andes (Bastien 1985, Flores Ochoa 1979, Stein 1961). William Stein, in his research in Hualcán in the highlands of Ancash, notes that "a great deal of affection is lavished on the infant. People like to play with babies" (1961:157).

Throughout the years of my research, I rarely saw a child misbehave and when this was the case, the problem was settled within a short time without physical punishment. I have never seen anyone spank a child, although the herders told me that this happens sometimes when a child continues to misbehave after all channels to divert his attention to other activities have been exhausted. I witnessed only a light slap a couple of times when a child played too roughly with his younger siblings. Overall, a serious look or tone of voice by the caregiver is all that is required to make the child behave. Some parents assert that it is enough to explain why unruly behavior cannot be tolerated and insist that children, in the same way as everyone else, must show respect. When four-year-old Víctor pestered his little sisters, his parents finally spoke to him in a serious tone of voice. Crying, Víctor looked for help and sympathy among the other family members, but no one proceeded to hug or comfort him. The adults were always consistent in showing little Víctor that what he had done was wrong. Only after he apologized did he receive a hug and smile, usually first from his grandparents. The fact that Víctor cried was all right. In Andean society, both boys and girls are allowed to weep and cry. The phrase "boys don't cry" does not exist.

When little Marcos was five years old, he practiced making a fire with the use of two stones, as he had seen his parents and older siblings do. But now, instead of remaining outdoors, he sat in the doorway of a small shed used for storage. When he finally sparked a flame, it caught the dry grass spread on the floor and within a short time the roof and some objects in the shed were burning. Family and neighbors rushed to the site, helping to put out the fire with buckets of water. The little boy was scared and ashamed of what he had done. After the fire was extinguished, Marcos's father talked to him, remind-

FIGURE 2.4. Víctor pulls his Mom's braids to the delight of both.

ing him in a serious tone of voice that lighting a fire is dangerous in any place where it cannot be contained. Otherwise there was no punishment.

Child-rearing strategies seem to be equally permissive in other parts of the high Andes, such as Paratia (department of Puno, Peru), where Jorge Flores Ochoa did his research. He observed that "children are not physically punished with spankings; instead, obedience and discipline are demanded by raising one's voice." He also noted that "grandchildren maintain an easy camaraderie with their grandparents, who may be extremely permissive and indulgent" (1979:61).

There are times, though, when a serious look or tone of voice is not successful in keeping a young child from misbehaving. When this occurs, a parent will take recourse in evoking outside agents, such as dangerous animals — foxes, bulls, biting dogs — or supernatural phenomena. Among the latter are the feared *kukuchi,* which are ghosts or the souls of the dead who appear during full moon and can harm people — especially disobedient children, whom they may also carry far away. Yet these menaces are seldom used.

Children, and some adults, also fear remote and uninhabited places that are often close to a precipice. These places, referred to as *pacha tira,* are believed to bring harm to people who fall or slip and often die without any hope of being cured. Such warnings may serve to keep children from straying to remote, unknown, and precipitous places. (See also O. Núñez del Prado 1973:36–37 for beliefs in *pacha tira.*)

Overall, the children of high-altitude herders behave well not only at home, but also within the village at large and in school. As is true elsewhere, however, young children in Chillihuani have a tendency to show off, although this kind of behavior is discouraged as they get older and is never seen in adults. Children show off in different ways as they try to get people's attention.

In the Yupanqui household, four-year-old Luis was allowed to carry his one-year-old sister Lorenza around the house. Lorenza screamed with delight whenever he played rough with her. Playing with his sister was also an occasion for Luis to get attention, as he showed her how to play music using a pot and ladle or catch the colorful hats he threw into the air. Proudly he listened to the laughs of the adults caused by his actions.

Although children in Chillihuani get along well, feelings of jealousy tend to mingle with their urges to get attention. In the high sector of Llaqto, Luzwilma and Anali, at ages eleven and ten, showed me how they spin and weave. As I admired the girls' skills, the three younger boys in the family stood by. Within no time, Tomás (eight) climbed on the roof and ran down the wall like an acrobat (Figure 2.5). Hipólito (six) did what he does best, namely imitate

FIGURE 2.5. Tomás shows off as the family's top acrobat.

FIGURE 2.6. Víctor beams with pride after receiving enough cookies to give one to each family member.

the dance of the *ukukus,* metaphoric creatures resembling bears or alpacas. Marcos (four), who also wanted my attention, ran to the kitchen to show me the precious carrots his Dad had bartered in the village.

Despite certain squabbles and some jealousy among siblings, they do care for one another and for the family at large. Thus, whenever I gave a few cookies to little Víctor, he proceeded to count them. When he discovered that there were not enough cookies for each member of the family, he politely explained to me who in his family would be without a cookie. The fact that food or anything else of value must be distributed correctly is a strong trait among Andean people. This trait is also reflected in rituals where each deity and every spirit is acknowledged and given respect, as well as food and drink. In order to maintain respect and compassion for all, nobody can be forgotten; an oversight could bring about misfortune. (See Bolin 1998.) Little Víctor is too young to comprehend the overall Andean ideology, but he is old enough to understand that no one should be left out (Figure 2.6).

Such consideration for others is also practiced at the level of the community. Widows, orphans, and old people without immediate family never live alone but are always included into the family of a more distant relative. Although in times of hunger food cannot be distributed freely to all people, village authorities and healers are concerned about the poorest people in the village, who must get some food in order to survive (Figure 2.7).

Becoming Part of the Adult World

Well-known Peruvian scholar Rodrigo Montoya writes, "Among the Quechua people of the Andes there is nothing that can be called a happy childhood" (1995:81). This observation does not hold true for Chillihuani. His statement that "among the Quechua of the Andes, the notion of childhood does not exist as an autonomous phase" (1995:78) does, however, apply to Chillihuani in every way. Children's culture in remote Quechua communities is not separate from that of adults. Children feel proud as they learn adult tasks little by little, as they sing the same songs and dance the same dances as do adults, and as they grow up in a culture that respects children in the same way as it respects adults.

The children of the herders become self-sufficient at a young age for several reasons. They are curious, caregivers are permissive, and children's help is much needed. The fact that the whole family congregates in a small one-room house as soon as it gets too dark to work outdoors also prepares young children to carry out adult activities at an early age and to understand adult concerns.[5]

Little Luis Yupanqui was allowed to climb a steep staircase without a railing when he was only eighteen months old. He usually did this on all fours, and he never fell, not even when it was wet and slippery. Someone in the family always observed him, but did not intervene. Given a caring but not overly protected upbringing in a rugged environment, children soon become surefooted. They learn to understand every aspect of their physical environment and the dangers it presents during all seasons. They seldom are injured by accidents in the mountainous terrain.

When Luis was two years old, he ate by himself and got his own food and drink. One day, as we all sat in a circle eating a meal, he noticed that his grandpa did not eat with a spoon but instead used his fingers to pick the potatoes from his soup, as is common in most households in Chillihuani. Luis got up, took a spoon from a pot by the fire, wiped it, and without saying a word stuck it into his grandpa's bowl. The family was amused.[6]

FIGURE 2.7. An orphan girl proudly displays the flutes she carries for her adoptive father during a fiesta.

Living together in close quarters, as herding families do (the average house is three by five meters), children soon learn about all kinds of adult concerns. When Víctor was four years old, I lived with the Mamani family, who had annexed a small room to their little house where I could sleep. One night, I had much writing to do and therefore, contrary to my usual habits, retired to my room before the family went to sleep. Early in the morning, Víctor knocked at my rattling wooden door and then scooted in with the coloring book and color pencils that I had brought him under his arm. As he colored, he talked with me about my *qosa* (husband) and my *wawakuna* (children), wondering what we could do so they too could come to live with me and his family and I would not be lonely. He asked many questions, including how long it would take my family to come by airplane and to climb up to the Mamani house. His concern was not only about me, but also about my family, who had to be without me for so long. Three weeks before I had to leave Chillihuani, I told Víctor that I would soon be home, at which time he was satisfied that there was no need to relocate my family. He was happy when I told him that eventually my family would accompany me again to Peru. I imagine that Víctor's family expressed concern about me being lonely and so far from my own family, and I am sure that he informed his family about our conversations during the long evenings they spent together in their little adobe home. Andean people are always concerned about whether someone could be lonely, since loneliness is considered a very painful state.

Apart from getting closely acquainted with family and community matters, children also learn about the lives of their ancestors three to five generations removed and about historical events in the region. I have known a few people whose knowledge reached back to pre-Columbian times. Centenarians Roberto Yupanqui Qoa and Doña Segundina Qolqe told me about the wisdom the grandparents of their grandparents had transmitted to them. When Roberto was a young boy, sometimes his grandparents shook him if he fell asleep as they told him about their ancestors, the Incas. "Stay awake and listen," they implored and commanded. "You must know about our ancestors. You must tell your children and their children our story. It may never die" (Bolin 1998:201). Still today, as families congregate around the fire in the evenings while the meal is cooking, the children like to listen to stories from long ago.

Since there are no specific children's stories, songs, music, or dances, the youngsters also participate in the adult world of the arts. Stories and songs about animals and flowers and love songs are the favorites of all ages. Four-year-old Marcos amused his family and the visitors who came to celebrate

FIGURE 2.8. Andrés Felipe's young son learns to play musical instruments through observation, as did his own talented father.

Pukllay (carnival) with them. He sang the love songs people sing during this fiesta and added his own words whenever he could not remember the actual lyrics. At around three years of age children begin to sing and invent songs. When five-year-old Alan went with his father on a bus ride that lasted for several days, he was squeezed into a corner of the vehicle for hours on end. He never complained but instead passed the time marveling at a landscape and things he had never seen. He sang many songs, inventing much of the lyrics from his impressions of the trip, fitting them to known Andean melodies. Sometimes he invented both the lyrics and the melodies he sang.

Children learn to play musical instruments by observing members of their family and the community. Among these instruments are different kinds of flutes, the whistle, trumpet, drum, bass drum, mandolin, guitar, and *charango* (a small guitar played by Indians). Andrés Felipe Quispe taught himself to play the flute when he was seven years old. By the time he was in his early twenties, he knew how to play five instruments and he composes many songs (Figure 2.8). Most people know how to make their own flutes and drums. Other instruments are usually bartered during fiestas in the valley in exchange for the herders' produce.

Some children excel at singing and playing instruments, with girls taking the lead as singers and boys playing the instruments. Other children are ex-

ceptional orators, dancers, and equestrians. Yet regardless of their achievements, they never brag about their talents. They are neither competitive nor
harsh in judging others. On the contrary, both girls and boys are very sensitive and often quite emotional. Sensitive, elegant, and respectful demeanor is
a cherished trait in both sexes within the behavioral repertoire of the herders.
Boys are allowed to cry and express sensitivity in the same way as girls. The
village nurse often commented on the great sensitivity of boys, adolescents,
and adult men, a trait that does not exist to the same extent in the valley,
where the macho attitude is more prevalent.[7]

Apart from being gentle and respectful, children are helpful, alert, and
courageous. One day during the Pukllay fiesta, dusk had fallen when I returned with twelve-year-old Luzwilma and eleven-year-old Anali from the
highest sector of Llajto. As we crossed a narrow bridge over the roaring Chillihuani River, the girls noticed that the bridge was not in good shape due to
torrential rains. Before I knew what was happening, they quickly proceeded
to put some of my equipment on top of their carrying bags, and Anali insisted that I hold her hand as I jumped from the bridge to the slippery, muddy
ground. The children's fast reaction reminded me of the time when I went
with their father, their Aunt Ignacia, and other family members and friends to
the sacred lake Waqraqocha, tucked between steep mountain peaks. To escape
a thundering whirlwind that had arisen within minutes out of a calm atmosphere, we had to race downhill on precipitous inclines. Instead of watching
their own steps, Modesto and Ignacia held my hands to assure that I would
not slip and tumble down the precipice in a landscape I did not know (see
Bolin 1998, Chapter 13). On this and other occasions, I noticed that children
are alert at an early age in the same way as adults; they recognize danger and
assist whoever needs help.

Children's Rights and Responsibilities

Whenever I ask the herders about their childhood and youth, they always
answer, "It was very good." Older people smile as they recount the good old
times when the pastures were greener, the potatoes grew bigger, and there was
more energy during the fiestas. Work was always plentiful and from a young
age children participated in the chores around the house, on the fields, and in
the pastures. Now, as in the past, these youngsters feel that the responsibilities
they carry are fair and they appreciate the rights they are given at work and in
the course of initiation rites, such as *unuchakuy,* the Andean baptism. After
unuchakuy, children are at the center of two more celebrations that honor

their rights and responsibilities: the Catholic baptism and the First Haircut. These celebrations place young children in a religious context within a network of ritual kin and allow them to start collecting property of their own.

BAPTISM THE CATHOLIC WAY

Traditional Andean beliefs are strong in the heights of Chillihuani. Therefore, in the past *unuchakuy* was not always followed by a Catholic baptism. Yet the herders know that baptism by a priest is essential, since it allows their children to be in good standing by authorities in the valley and anyone else outside the community. Thus, within recent decades most families have baptized their children, thereby obeying the rules of the mainstream society. In the valley, people told me that children who are not baptized "will never see the face of Jesus. Instead they will encounter misfortune in life, their souls will not be rescued, and they will end up in hell." Some people explained that the souls of children who are not baptized are in limbo, i.e., they find no place to rest.

The practice of baptism does bring certain benefits to a child and his/her family through the widening of a network of spiritual kin. Baptism adds more godparents to the spiritual relatives of a family; there are significant rights and responsibilities between godparent (*padrino* and *madrina*, Sp.) and godchild (*ahijado* and *ahijada*, Sp.).

The selection of godparents is made with several objectives in mind. A godparent, ideally, should be high up in the socioeconomic hierarchy. He or she must have an impeccable reputation and should be a model to be followed by the child. Both godparents and godchildren have rights and responsibilities. A godchild is supposed to help the godparent in the house, on the pastures and fields, or when the godparent is sick. In return, godparents help their godchildren when they are sick, need advice, or need material items such as clothes and school supplies. Ideally, godparents look out for the welfare of a godchild and their advice is honored and followed even more readily than that of a parent. A godmother or godfather who exerts influence can defend a child when there are problems. But most significant are the trust and love between godparent and godchild. "We want our child to become like you," parents often say when they ask a person to become a godparent. Although this is generally true for Chillihuani, I have seen godchildren who had to work very hard to satisfy their godparents in the valley.

Catholic baptisms are generally performed during religious fiestas. In Chillihuani, baptisms take place during the festivities of the Fiesta de Santiago (July 25 and 26), at which time the priest undertakes a hike from the valley to this mountain village.[8] He starts by holding mass in the small church for those couples who have decided to add a Catholic wedding (*casarakuy*) to their Andean marriage (*rimanakuy*). He continues by giving his blessings to the Fiesta de Santiago and then proceeds to baptize the children.[9]

The healer Juan Mamani and his wife Luisa were happy when I consented to be *madrina* (godmother) to their daughter Teresa's six-month-old daughter Delia. Several days before the fiesta, Don Julián, an esteemed village elder, came to the healer's house where I lived to ask me to be *madrina* to his one-year-old granddaughter Melisna. Given my long acquaintance with Don Julián and his family, I accepted, although I must start declining this honor in order to be able to attend well to the many godchildren I already have.

On the day of the scheduled baptism, we climb to the high promontory Capillapampa, also referred to as Churumarka, where the families of the children to be baptized assemble in front of the church together with the *madrinas* and *padrinos* selected by their parents or grandparents.[10] The priest asks the godparents to state their names, the name of the child to be baptized, and its date of birth. He enters the information in his book and collects a fee of ten *soles* (about U.S. $3.50 in 1998) for each child he baptizes. Then the godparents, with the children in their arms or standing by their sides, form a straight line opposite the priest. In a serious tone of voice the priest speaks to the godparents, reminding them to help in the moral formation of their godchildren, to strengthen them in their religious beliefs, and to help them whenever need arises. Then he reads from the bible. The priest now calls the name of each child, saying solemnly, "I baptize you in the name of the Father, the Son, and the Holy Ghost." Holy water mixed with salt is placed on the tongue and forehead of each child. The priest told me later that this is done to wash away the original sin and denote the child a Christian.[11] The priest proceeds to pray and again reads from the bible, and the ceremony ends.

I can barely hold on to the two little girls, one in each arm, who seem to get heavier by the minute. At a later date the baptized children will receive a certificate of baptism that has social and economic value. It allows them to prove their name, date of birth, and provenance—important if they intend to deal with authorities in the valley.[12]

The parents of Delia and Melisna and all the other family members hug me in a loose embrace as they smile, calling me *comadre* (co-mother). The children call me *madrina* (godmother). Then we walk to their homes, where a festive meal of potatoes, *chuños*, *ch'arki* (dried alpaca meat), *qochayuyu* (algae from the mountain lakes), and vegetables bargained for in the valley awaits us. In return, I offer gifts to each of my godchildren. I am now united in ritual kinship with the two families (Figure 2.9).

FIGURE 2.9. Two of my godchildren are wrapped in their carrying cloths right after baptism.

CHUKCHA RUTUKUY—A CHILD'S FIRST HAIRCUT

A child's First Haircut[13] is a ritual that dates back to Inca times, when it was central to an elaborate celebration. Among the Incas, the hair-cutting ceremony was accompanied by the name-giving ritual that was held after a child was weaned:

> Relatives and friends assembled for the feast, followed by dancing and drinking, after which the child's oldest uncle cut its hair and nails, which were preserved with great care, and gave it a name. Then the uncle and other relatives gave it presents: silver, garments, wool, etc. They prayed to the Sun that the child's life be fortunate and that he live to inherit from his father. The name given at the hair cutting was retained only until the persons reached maturity.[14]

The ceremony of a child's First Haircut is still practiced among the high-altitude herding societies and by families in other rural regions.[15] Regarding specific ritual activities, there are differences between regions, villages, and even neighboring settlements. In Chillihuani the First Haircut is a significant event in a child's life and is normally celebrated when the child is between one and six years old. It is one within a series of events where children are honored, kinship ties are established, and children's rights to property are confirmed. It proceeds as follows.

The parents of five-year-old Anali, who live in the heights of Chillihuani, asked me to be *madrina* of her First Haircut. On July 25, during the Fiesta de Santiago, right after the thundering horse race close to the permanent snow on Oqe Q'asa Pata, we walk with members and friends of the Quispe family to their homestead. All of the family members, wearing their best clothes, assemble in the bright sunshine on the stone patio in front of their house. At close to 5,000 meters (16,400 feet) above sea level there is not a sound to be heard except for the soft murmur of springs and rivulets and an occasional cry from the birds that circle through the air close to the snowy peaks.

Anali's father, Don Modesto, places woven blankets and ponchos on the stone bench by the *mesarumi* (table or altar of stone). He asks us to take a seat. Anali's mother and female relatives have been busy all morning preparing the festive meal that is now ready to be served. Anali's mother, aunts, and grandmothers fill the plates with potatoes, *chuño, moraya, oqa, ulluku,* and *ch'arki* (dried meat), as well as maize, cabbage, and carrots bartered in the valley. Modesto and other male relatives take the plates from the women with both hands and offer one plate to each of the guests in an elegant gesture that signifies "I give this to you with all my heart." Everyone present thanks Pachamama and the hosts for the delicious meal. A second helping is offered, and then the male relatives take the plates back to the kitchen.

Don Modesto returns with *coca* leaves and *chicha.* In a gesture called *phukuy,* we blow over the *k'intus,* inviting the Apus, the sacred mountain lakes, and other spirits of nature to celebrate with us. We sprinkle drops of *chicha* on the ground for Pachamama and toss some of the drink between thumb and forefingers to the mountain peaks. Then we drink to the welfare of Anali, wishing her a healthy, happy, and successful life.

The central hair-cutting ceremony now begins. Anali's aunt places an empty plate and a pair of scissors, to which she attaches a white ribbon, on the *mesarumi.* White ribbons are for girls; red ones are for boys. As *madrina,* I start by fashioning a *k'intu* using three perfect *coca* leaves. I blow on it in honor of Pachamama and the Apus and ask these deities to protect the child. Then I place the *k'intu* on the plate and cut the first lock from Anali's thick and shiny black hair, putting it on the plate together with a gift in the form of money to be used to increase her herd and keep it healthy. I hand the scissors to her father, mother, aunts, uncles, and visitors. Each person cuts off a lock and places it into the plate together with a gift or the promise of a gift and then returns the scissors to me. My *compadre* Antolín, who came from the valley, was elected to be secretary. He notes the gifts given and/or promised on a sheet of paper. Among other things, Anali is promised clothes and an alpaca.

A second round of hair cutting follows. Gifts and promises of gifts continue to accumulate on the table and on Antolín's sheet. The plate is full of hair. Antolín wraps Anali's cut hair into a small bunch and ties it together with a red string. The color of the string has no significance. When all promises are fulfilled—that is, when Anali has received all her gifts—her hair will be buried in a sacred place in the womb of Pachamama.

The kind and amount of gifts a child receives depends on what a family and the ritual kin can afford. Love for a child and his/her behavior also figure in gift giving. Anali is a charming child who takes her responsibilities in and around the house and with the animals very seriously. She smiles as she is honored in such a lavish way and does not seem to mind that her hair is cut in an uneven fashion by so many different people.

With the ritual kinship established, I have another godchild. Anali embraces me and calls me *madrina*, and the adults of the extended family call me *comadre* as they thank me with a loose embrace. During the ceremony, Anali's parents were not at the center of activities but participated at the same level as everyone else. The herders say that this must be so in order to avoid confusion. It is believed that the spirits of the invited deities must concern themselves exclusively with the new ritual kin relationship that is in the making between a godchild and his or her *madrina*.

We continue to exchange *k'intus* among the adults and thank the deities for their blessings. We chew the leaves and drink *chicha,* confirming the ritual kinship that was created.[16]

The private ceremonies of baptism and First Haircut lay the foundations for a child's rights to extended kin and to property and define obligations vis-à-vis the ritual kin. Children continue to receive property from their parents and other family members during official celebrations such as Pukllay (see Chapter 5). Given Andean ethics that attach much pride to work, work is a right and at the same time a responsibility. Thus, with the right of owning a herd comes the responsibility of taking care of the animals.

A Typical Day with a Chillihuani Family

Within the last seventeen years I have spent much time in Chillihuani and have gained considerable insight into the workings of this society. Yet I still find it amazing how people can work year after year under the most grueling conditions. Those who are lucky enough to remain healthy can even reach a ripe old age.

Since 1988 I have lived almost every year with the Mamani family and know what a typical day in their household looks like. As I stayed with other families, I realized that the specific composition of a household, including the number, age, and sex of its members, as well as their state of health, determines to some extent how work is accomplished and how interactions take place. Although Chillihuani is an egalitarian society without pronounced socioeconomic differences, some families carry out their work in a more meticulous way or have access to a greater pool of knowledge than do others. As noted earlier, the division of labor between males and females is quite flexible. When male and female members of various ages are present in a family, males work in the fields, transport produce from the fields to the storage areas, look after horses, help to make *chuño,* bring firewood and water to the house, and do some spinning and weaving. Women keep the home running, start the fire, cook, help fetch water, take care of the children, do some of the herding, help to make *chuño,* spin, and weave. Boys and girls help whenever need arises. They are mainly responsible for taking the family herd to pasture.

To observe a typical day of a Chillihuani family, we are visiting the Mamani Illatinco household in the middle of June, the cold Andean winter, an important season during which freeze-dried potatoes, the staple of the herders' diet, are prepared. The household consists of the healer Juan Mamani, his wife Luisa Illatinco, three daughters — Teresa, Alicia, and Libia Mamani Illatinco (the oldest daughter, Irme, lives in the valley) — Teresa's husband, and their three children, Víctor, Luisita, and Delia.[17]

At 6 a.m. everyone stirs in the little adobe hut that is still cold from the night's freezing temperatures. Teresa starts a fire to prepare potato soup for breakfast. Little Víctor observes her every move. An intelligent, precocious child, he is eager to learn about every activity in which his parents and grandparents engage. Six-month-old Delia sits on the floor playing with scraps of vegetation, destined for the guinea pigs to eat. Beside her lies three-year-old Luisita, disabled after being born in a Cuzco hospital. She swings her arms in the air, unable to coordinate them, making noises as though she is eager to say something. But the words do not form.

Soon the healer Juan Mamani and his wife, Luisa, return from their sleeping areas with big smiles on their faces that hide the pains endured during the cold night. Luisa shivers; she passed the night on a bed of *ichu* grass in an open lean-to at below-freezing temperatures. Although she feels the biting cold, she hopes that there will be frost for at least two more weeks so the potatoes that are spread out on the *ichu* grass can freeze during the nights and dry in the hot sun of the day.[18] For the last few weeks, the effects of El Niño have caused much snow to fall, followed by unseasonable torrential rains that washed much of the potato crop into the river and caused many of the already harvested potatoes to rot. If a considerable amount of freeze-dried potatoes are not stored for years to come, survival is at stake. So for several weeks Luisa must, in the company of one of her dogs, watch the potatoes to keep animals from stealing the small amount that has not yet been ruined by the rains.

Healer Juan Mamani has been sleeping in a small round adobe hut left open in the front, from which he can view the corral with the alpacas, llamas, and sheep. His dogs help to watch for disturbances in the corral. This year has not been a good one for the animals either, since one-third of the herds died due to adverse weather conditions that caused accidents and brought hunger and disease.[19] Although the healer and his wife are always tired after a hard day's work, they only allow themselves to doze off lightly at night. They cannot fall into a deep sleep, since their animals and the potatoes are too precious to be stolen by foxes, pumas, and perhaps someone from beyond the village. They must remain alert every night to avoid disaster.

Yet the uncomfortable, icy-cold night is forgotten as Juan and Luisa enter the house, happy to greet their children and grandchildren who have been washed, dressed, and combed by Teresa. Teresa's husband has given breakfast to Luisita and Delia and washed the children's clothes in the water he carried from a spring.[20] Alicia ladles the hot potato soup into bowls, which the healer and Teresa's husband serve to each person, holding the bowls in both hands to denote respect. Everyone eats the soup quietly, thanking Pachamama for this cherished food.

At about 8 a.m. the sun appears from behind the mountain peaks in the east, warming the air and melting the ice crystals on the grass. Ice crystals are a good sign that frost has furthered the preservation process of the potatoes. The liquid will soon be squeezed from the frozen potatoes, to be evaporated by the hot rays of the sun.

Before returning to her potato fields, Doña Luisa attends to those animals of the family herd that have problems. She washes the eyes of the sheep that are plagued with a common eye disease, referred to as *ñawi unquy* or *ñawi ñawsay,* a Quechua concept meaning "take away the sight of the eye." The problem is caused by small mites and is quite serious, since the eyesight of untreated animals can become so bad that they fall from precipices or from the narrow bridges into the river. Without treatment, the animals can become blind and also infect other animals in the herd. Luisa uses spring water to wash her animals' eyes and then applies the herb *q'eso q'eso* (snail shell of the eyes) that has been immersed in water for some time.[21]

After breakfast, Alicia takes the animals to pasture. Llamas and alpacas can be left on their own for some time, but sheep require attention throughout the day. Libia leaves for the family fields in the distance, trying to gather more potatoes as well as the tubers *oqa* (*Oxalis tuberosa*) and *ulluku* (*Ullucus tuberosus*). Given the great distances at which these particular fields are located, she will not come back until the early evening.

Grandma Luisa returns to her site, where she separates the dried *chuños* ready to be stored from the rest of the potatoes, which require further freeze-drying. From a hook on the wall Juan Mamani takes a rope to climb onto the steep rocks on the other side of the river, where he will cut the *qayara* plants (*Puya*) that grow from their cracks. The green parts of this plant are eaten by the guinea pigs; the roots are dried and used for making a fire in the earthen stove. Yet today, as has happened so often in the past, Juan must change his plans when a young man arrives from the south of the village, at a distance of more than ten kilometers. He announces that his wife has had a terrible stomachache for two days and none of the herbal teas he has prepared for her have helped. The healer grabs his bag, which is always packed, takes leave from his family, and the two men hurry off toward the mountains in the south.[22]

Teresa's husband leaves the house to help his mother-in-law sort potatoes while Teresa tends to her children and starts preparing the midday meal. (For specific children's activities, see Chapter 3.) Throughout the day members of the extended family, neighbors, and friends stop by for short visits. The young children's great-grandmother, the only living great-grandparent, visits to help with the children, meals, and the mending of clothes. As is true for many of Chillihuani's old people, she is a pleasant and positive woman with a great sense of humor. She no longer does heavy work, but she is esteemed for her company, advice, and the work she can still accomplish.

It is about two o'clock in the afternoon, and the meal is ready for the family members who work close by. Alicia and Libia have taken potatoes and some *ch'arki* (dried meat) along for their lunches. Following the meal, the family members resume their work. When times are not as busy as during planting, harvesting, and the freeze-drying of potatoes, men, women, and children fix their clothes, spin, weave, knit hats, make ropes, and fabricate other much-needed items. (See Chapters 3 and 4.)

As dusk falls, Libia returns from the fields with a sack of potatoes, some *oqa,* and some *ulluku* loaded on her donkey's back. Shortly thereafter, Alicia appears on the mountainside with the herd. Grandma Luisa and her son-in-law join the family before dark in their small house, where the children receive them with enthusiasm. Grandpa Juan is still with his patient behind the towering mountain range to the south. While Juan is absent, Teresa's husband offers a bowl of his wife's soup to each person. Before he himself eats, he feeds his disabled daughter Luisita. Then the adults fashion *k'intus,* and everyone thanks Pachamama for the food.

Evenings are a time of fun, laughter, and storytelling. The girls sing, and the boys and men sometimes play their instruments. Children are at the center of attention before they retire to their sleeping corners. They are played with, joked with, and tickled. They are never neglected, regardless of how tired parents and grandparents may be. Since loneliness is considered the saddest of states, everyone makes sure that no one lacks attention. Schoolteacher Marcial Willka stressed that at home and, if at all possible, in school, children are listened to and have the right to speak out for themselves.

As the fire dies down in the stove, Doña Luisa exchanges her place in the house for an icy-cold spot in her lean-to close to the freezing *chuños.* In the absence of Juan, the healer, his son-in-law watches the herd in the corral from one of the small adobe huts surrounding it. Libia helps to observe the herd from a hut on the opposite side of the corral. Teresa and her sister Alicia clean up the place and spend the night with the children.

In the early morning hours, Juan Mamani returns home. He had remained with his patient until the medicine he had given her had taken effect. But he must return in a couple of days to check on her progress. Many times during my stays in Chillihuani, I saw Juan Mamani leave on the spur of the moment when he was needed. He never shied away from the most disastrous weather conditions, and he stopped any work he was doing in order to attend to patients within a large part of the village. Teresa follows in the footsteps of her father, ready to help the sick.

Patients who are able to walk arrive at the healer's house by day and night. They always get free food, accommodation, and treatment. Juan Mamani and the other three healers' efforts are done with love; there is never any charge. Very ill people are taken to the Yachaq group in Cuzco for free diagnosis and treatment, and severe cases are brought to the hospital Lorena. The Yachaq group pays for these expenses whenever possible, using donations from friends, students, and family.

As is true for other residents, the Mamani/Illatinco family is poor in material terms. Especially when weather conditions are adverse, there is little if any surplus of agricultural produce. Many animals have died in recent years, and their wool can be sold at only a low price. Yet these people show resilience, compassion, and generosity beyond comparison. The patience with which they care for their disabled child is equally astonishing.[23]

Disabled Children

We have seen that a person must be strong of body and mind in order to survive in the marginal environment of Chillihuani. To be disabled, or to care for a disabled person, makes life even more difficult. Yet the care given to disabled children is extraordinary.

The children who survive in Chillihuani are much appreciated by their families and the community for the help and support they provide. But these are not the only reasons why children are deeply loved. This becomes evident as young people leave the countryside to find work in the city, where they often are barely able to provide for themselves, let alone help support their parents. In fact, these young people frequently depend on the potatoes, *ch'arki,* wool, and other goods they receive from their parents. Regardless of the lack of contributions from these young people, they are loved and always welcomed when they return home.

The same attitude prevails regarding the few disabled children who live in Chillihuani. Little Lucio, the great-grandson of one of my centenarian friends, was five years old and deaf when I met him in his family's adobe compound below the sacred mountain lake Waqraqocha. Outgoing and exceptionally charming, he was treated with love and consideration by his family. He was proud to help his great-grandpa spread potatoes on the ground in preparation for the freeze-drying process and was complimented for collecting dung used for fuel in the earthen stove. Given his disability, he sometimes was disoriented, but he still was welcome to participate in hide-and-seek games with his siblings and cousins. Only in his adolescent years, when he went with a family member to work in an urban area, did he experience discrimination, not only because he was a mountain Indian, but also because he was deaf. His young life came to a sad end when he was run over by a car in the streets of Quillabamba.

Tragic events also surrounded the birth of Maria Luisita, Teresa's daughter and the granddaughter of the healer Juan Mamani and his wife, Luisa. Luisita was born in the city of Cuzco, where her father spent some time working in construction. Teresa remembers the nightmarish time when she and her child almost died in the hospital. Luisita, who experienced asphyxia during birth, will never be able to walk, talk, sit up by herself, or eat on her own. Little Luisita has a beautiful smile, but she can only communicate by uttering cries and joyful giggles. It is not easy to make ends meet, let alone care for a disabled child. But the family cooperates well in all subsistence activities, giving special attention to Luisita. Although there is no hope that the condition of this little girl will improve to any degree, all family members continue to care for

FIGURE 2.10. Beautiful Luisita in her father's arms and leaning on her grandpa, who prepares a ritual.

her in the same loving way. Holding her in his arms, her father feeds her every night. With utter patience he spoons soup into the mouth of his daughter, who is not able to eat solids. He tickles her tiny feet close to the warming fire, making her laugh and giggle. Only after she is done eating does he eat himself. All family members take turns massaging the child and exercising her limbs to avoid stiffness and stimulate muscle growth. It would be difficult to find a more dedicated father anywhere, or a kinder and braver family. Sometimes, however, I see Teresa cry when she looks at her disabled child (Figure 2.10).

Luisita's body gets sore from lying on the makeshift bed, and she must be moved from time to time. Whenever the sun warms the cold winter air, Teresa places her on a blanket outdoors in a sunny spot sheltered from the wind, so she can warm her thin limbs. But when the wind blows the dust throughout the earthen patio, she must be brought indoors. The family wonders whether little Luisita will be destined to pass the rest of her life in a bed in this dark one-room adobe house. Now, she is light enough to be moved from one place to another within and outside the house, and she can be taken for a walk wrapped in a sling. But what will happen when she is too heavy to be carried around? Often her parents look at her with tenderness, but their facial expressions cannot hide their sorrow about their child's condition, her future, and the future of the whole family, since herding and high-altitude horticulture barely allow the family to subsist. Yet I never heard any of the family members complain about the additional work involved in caring for little Luisita in an already tight work schedule.[24]

When Death Comes Too Soon

The death of a child, whether disabled or in the prime of health, is the most tragic event that can arise suddenly and unexpectedly in the high Andes. Young children die frequently from problems of the respiratory and digestive tracts and from time to time in accidents, mainly during the rainy season when landslides are frequent and the waterlogged earth gives way beneath their feet. Sometimes strong winds cause children to fall or be swept against a rocky wall.

Children may die in the midst of winter, "from the cold" or from other causes that cannot be detected. This was the case with eight-year-old Ramón, a healthy, strong, and handsome boy, the son of my friend Ignacia. When I arrived in Chillihuani, he was already dead after having suffered from a severe stomachache for some time. Because the family had no money and little trust in the care given in hospitals, they could only hope for a recovery. But the young boy died, and the reason for his death has never been verified.

In a state of total despair, the family prepares an all-night vigil in appreciation of and respect for this boy. Ramón is washed, and his godparents clothe him in new garments—pants, jacket, a hat made from white sheep wool, and sandals made from the leather of a llama. The godparents also assist the family with the expenses that incur in the course of the funeral.[25]

In the late evening, the extended family, friends, and neighbors arrive at the family home. They put candles along both sides of the bench where the boy's body lies. The visitors talk about the life of the child and cry. From time to time they offer *coca* leaves and sugarcane alcohol to one another. Most of the people remain with the family until the next day, giving them comfort and support. At noon they walk to the cemetery high up on Capillapampa. Brothers, cousins, and other young men, dressed in black capes (*ayap'acha*), carry the body of the boy, wrapped in a blanket, on a device resembling a wooden ladder. As they arrive in the cemetery they dig a grave and place the body into it.[26]

The mourners stand around the grave and each one sprinkles a handful of loose earth over the body until the hole is filled. Then a young man in a black cape sticks a wooden cross with Ramón's name and the date of his death into the earth. The herders believe that the body of the dead boy is received by

Pachamama, while his spirit soars to *hanan pacha,* the heaven in the world of the Quechua. No priest is present in the village; the dead are sent on their journeys by family and friends.

The people attending the funeral now return to the house of the deceased, where they eat a meal, chew *coca* leaves, and take sips of sugarcane alcohol to dampen their grief. They continue to speak about Ramón's life, and they cry throughout the night.

The next day Ramón's sister and brother wash his clothes and store them in a bag. A member of the extended family or one of the most needy children in the village may get to wear them. Ramón's parents sweep the house clean and sprinkle holy water against the walls. They place incense, sugar, and anise on a hot surface close to the fire. The odor that escapes will deter evil spirits from entering the house. Some people say that the spirit of the deceased wants to take others with him to the grave. The *alma* (Sp., soul) of even a good person can cause problems for some time after his death. When a *coca k'intu* is offered, nothing bad will happen.

As is common throughout the region, eight days after Ramón died family members and friends, accompanied by a *rezador* (Sp.), a man who officially prays for the soul of the deceased, walk to the cemetery to say good-bye to the departing spirit.[27] They bring offerings of bread, fruits, sweets, and other products that were bartered in the valley, depositing them on the grave in the name of the dead boy. The *rezador* receives the products placed on the grave in a gesture of reciprocity. The people remain by Ramón's grave, drinking *chicha,* talking about the dead boy, and crying.

The spirit of a child is said to be pure and white, without sin. The spirit of an adult is considered according to the way he/she behaved during life. If a good person dies, the spirit is not dangerous, must not suffer, and does not cause pain to the living. But when someone dies who behaved badly in life, the spirit can cause pain for others and is condemned to walk on the scree of steep mountains (*susuwa*). Such a malevolent spirit is referred to as *soq'a*.[28]

After the visit to the grave, the extended family remains for the rest of the day and throughout the night in the house of the deceased, sweeping it and sprinkling holy water everywhere. People eat and drink and remain awake all night to comfort one another. I was told that the rituals contain ancient secrets: "They must be carried out correctly or the spirit continues to call and there may be other deaths."

No other ritual takes place for the deceased until Todos Santos—All Saints Days—when families go to the cemetery to clean the plots and bring favorite foods to the deceased so their spirits can rejoice. They pray for the souls of the dead and cry. The spirits of the dead are honored in this way for three years after death.[29,30]

Life in the high Andes is certainly not easy for anyone, and it is especially hard on the youngest members of society. Nevertheless, children assume good behavior, becoming well adjusted and helpful while enjoying whatever life can offer. They are grateful for anything they get. The key to such positive socialization is twofold. The fact that adults are models at home and within the community, and children have ample opportunity to observe their behavior, is paramount. Furthermore, this society's beliefs and behavior patterns reinforce respect and compassion for *all* life. Thus, children are not caught in a moral conflict deciding which aspects of life deserve respect and reciprocity and which do not. Children learn to respect life in *all* its forms.

CHAPTER 3

Children at Play and Work

In the high Andes, where people cling to the very margins of existence, children's play and work activities differ in many respects from those found in more affluent societies. Play and work are coherently integrated within the herders' overall philosophy. Work ethics are shaped by respect and by the ever-present necessity to make a living in a marginal environment. Far away from the modern conveniences of a city, play and work merge into one entity that includes pleasure, pride, and survival strategies.

In this chapter I will separate play and work where possible in order to conform to Western ways of understanding these activities. Given the focus of this book, the structure of Andean society, and the fact that children's ages are often unknown, I will not analyze play and work activities in accordance with children's age categories or against theoretical constructs.

Developing Creativity through Play

As I lived with a family of high-altitude herders in their one-room adobe hut, I realized that children's play there differs in many ways from play in Western societies. Herding children have virtually no store-bought toys. I must admit that at first I considered bringing toys on my next ascent so they would have something to play with. But within a short time I became fully aware that the children's playground inside and outside of their house was full of toys: toys in the form of tools that adults use, and toys that are found ready-made in nature or can be manufactured out of a great variety of naturally occurring substances. It became clear that play in the high Andes involves a learning process that is more creative and profound than it is in a society where prefabricated toys are readily available. Most importantly, play activities lead directly to an understanding of the tasks that must be mastered in adult life.

Within the home, children play with virtually everything they can find. From a young age they become acquainted with all those items that are of practical use and are needed for the family to subsist. Small children play with dishes, pots, cups, spoons, candles, blankets, bottles, and all kinds of edible things. They are allowed to touch and use anything that cannot hurt them or break easily.[1]

Food items also represent interesting playthings for children. Potatoes, for example, are always available in the house. They come in different shapes and colors, and children are allowed to play with them before they are peeled. They see shapes in the potatoes that resemble faces, figures, animals, or aspects of the landscape. The high-altitude tubers *oqa, ulluku,* and *maswa* similarly stir a child's imagination, and so do vegetables and fruits that are bartered in the valley. Existing shapes of food items can also be modified. Three-year-old Víctor eagerly accepted the cookie I gave him. He looked at it, then bit little parts from it until he believed it resembled a donkey. With his "donkey" squeezed between his thumb and index finger, he made it jump across the adobe floor, up the walls, along the earthen stove, and back to the middle of the room, where it met with the cats and guinea pigs. Then he finished eating it.

Outside the house, children's playgrounds extend as far as their eyes can see. They detect shapes in small- or medium-sized animate and inanimate objects and large features of the landscape. They may point to a rock that looks like a condor, a mountain lion, or a petrified human being. This ability goes back at least to the Incas, and probably to the pre-Inca past, when myths and legends referred to shapes of people or animals that could be detected in the natural environment and in the night sky (see Chapter 4).

But children are not satisfied to merely detect interesting shapes within the cosmos. They need to touch and manipulate the products of their imagination. So from a very young age they start to manufacture from the raw materials nature provides not only toys but miniature homesteads and irrigated fields within complex landscapes.

The landscape above the tree line in Chillihuani looks rather barren, yet it contains a great variety of materials, such as earth, stones, sticks, grass, leaves, branches, flowers, water, mud, etc. These materials can be used in many different ways in accordance with the imagination of a particular child.

One morning I observe Luzwilma (twelve), Anali (eleven), Tomás (eight), Hipólito (six), and Marcos (four) as they survey the landscape where they live, close to 5,000 meters (16,500 feet) above sea level. They have collected stones, sticks, grass, flowers, and traces of alpaca wool clinging to the vegetation. With their hands and skirts full of these precious materials, they settle down on the ground, ready to construct what they all will need when they marry and establish a homestead of their own (Figure 3.1).

FIGURE 3.1. Like their Inca ancestors, Chillihuani children work at becoming master builders.

Using small stones, the children build tiny houses. Each house needs a corral (*iphiña,* daily corral) close by and a path leading from the corral to the house and up to the meadows. Luzwilma also outlines a sacred corral (*muyu-kancha*) onto the ground, where the animals congregate three times a year during ceremonies held for the deities and the animals alike. She knows that this sacred corral needs a recess in a rocky wall (*q'oyana*), where the offerings are burnt.

The corrals are now filled with stones, which in some faint way resemble llamas, alpacas, and sheep. Outside the corrals, more small stones represent horses, donkeys, and dogs. Within the outlines of the house Anali has traced on the ground, she creates a stove by scratching its shape into the earth. With a handful of mud she fashions a slightly elevated area that serves as a bed for some of the family members. Smaller stones stand for cats and guinea pigs.

While Tomás puts a bit of earth, representing a load of dung for the fields, on his biggest stone llamas, Anali places some alpaca hair on one of her camelids, which will carry this shorn fleece to market. She also puts a tiny flower onto her stone alpaca's head: "My *chushllu* is now decorated for Macho Pagaray," she says with pride. Macho Pagaray is a festivity occurring on August 1, when the male alpacas and llamas, respectfully referred to as *chushllu* and *chullumpi,* are decorated with flowers or colored wool to honor their services of carrying loads to and from the fields. The children talk to their stone animals in the same way as they talk to the live animals they take to pasture.

Tomás now cooperates with Luzwilma. They designate a small elongated stone to be the herder; he walks to the pasture with his stone llamas and alpacas. The herd moves toward the high mountains, which are traced on the ground with small stones. The children place a jagged stone they call a condor on a large stone that represents one of the mountain peaks. Tomás cautions that the condor may snatch a young animal. He takes a blade of grass that serves as a *warak'a,* a sling to throw stones into the distance, and places it on the elongated "stone herder," who needs it to protect his herd.

Luzwilma notices that Anali has many interesting-looking stones that she would like to use. She takes two yellow leaves and one green one, which portray money of different value, and asks her sister to let her buy a couple of "animals."[2] Anali agrees and carefully puts the "money" into her *unkuña* (a small woven cloth used to carry important objects).[3] Luzwilma remembers that she forgot to give the herder lunch, so she quickly fashions it out of grass and tiny flowers as well as miniature rocks meant to be potatoes. Anali follows her sister's example.

I do not know how much further their imagination would have taken them had Tomás's mother not called him to fetch water from the spring. Anali and Luzwilma also ran off to their home, remembering the chores they had to complete before the next meal could be served.

Children's play at building complex "homesteads" out of stones and other natural materials carries over into adult life. Every year thousands of people make a pilgrimage to Qoyllur Rit'i,[4] in the Sinakara mountain range, which contains three large glaciers. On the slopes of the mountains, which are strewn with stones of all sizes, they fashion houses, corrals, and other items they would like to own. When they are done they present their wishes to the Virgin of Fátima (la Virgen de Fátima, see Flores Ochoa 1990), a deity residing in a large rock. If luck is on their side, she will grant their wishes. In Andean ideology, *enqaychu* (small stones of specific shapes resembling alpacas, llamas, sheep, horses, etc.) are believed to contain *enq'a* (life force) and are central to rituals, putting children's play within the context of Andean religious ideology and preparing them in both practical and spiritual ways for adult life (see Figure 3.2).

During the height of the rainy season, which may last from December through March, children are confined to their homes while the rains pour heavily from the sky. They must remain under an overhanging rock or some

FIGURE 3.2. With the *ch'unchus*—who represent Indians from jungle regions—in the foreground, people start to build their wishes in stone.

other protective device while they are on the meadows pasturing the animals. Rainstorms, however, create new conditions that can stir children's imaginations.

After a heavy rain had fallen, I observe nine-year-old Lorenza, eight-year-old Tomás, six-year-old Hipólito, and four-year-old Marcos play in the mud by a small creek created by the torrential rains. With sticks, stones, and their plain hands they divert water to create creeks and rivulets. They make little boats out of leaves and let them run down the newly created "rivers." Lorenza uses sticks and grass to fashion a bridge across the rivulet in the mud. Tiny sticks placed into the bridge represent people and their animals walking across the river. Tomás and Hipólito are busy patting down the earth between the rivulets to create "fields," where potatoes and other tubers can be planted. Across these fields they trace narrow horizontal lines, supposed to be irrigation canals that bring water to the land. Irrigation is used only in very restricted ways in this village, but it is used extensively in the valley and must have caught the attention of the children. Marcos watches how his brothers and neighbor "work" in a concentrated way. He brings them small stones and grass to use in their constructions. Only when little Marcos closes off a rivulet and causes a field to flood do his brothers suggest that he move away. He again tries to be helpful by bringing them raw materials, but he slips on the mud. The older children fear he will destroy their entire masterpiece and ask him to remain outside their working area. Crying, he runs home.

As I observe the children work in such a concentrated fashion, I remember the words of Luz Marina, who teaches in a high-altitude community in Acomayo. She asserted that children from rural areas make good engineers and architects. Watching their creative activities using soil, water, rocks, and other materials, I do not doubt her words.

One of the favorite materials youngsters in high-altitude regions use is small, sharp, quartz stones, called *qespe rumi,* which can be found close to snow-covered peaks. White, shiny, and hard enough to cut glass, children utilize them for make-believe play; the shiny stones serve as money to buy little stone alpacas, llamas, sheep, and produce. They also use them to build small houses, corrals, roads, whole villages, and entire settlements.[5] As children engage in make-believe play, they also pretend to be mothers, fathers, teachers, the priest, animals, or supernatural beings such as *ukukus.*[6]

Starting at about age five, boys and girls fashion toys such as dolls out of used clothes, grass, or straw. The dolls are usually wrapped in a swaddling cloth, much like babies, and thus do not require arms and legs. Girls play at being weavers by setting up tiny looms and stringing thread to a stick in the ground. Children also like to play with tops when they are lucky enough to find a flat spot. Some children and their parents know how to fashion tops by driving a nail or a sharp piece of metal into a wooden surface and wrapping it with string.

The only bought or bartered toys I saw Chillihuani youngsters play with were small ceramics from the marketplace in Cusipata. Traveling merchants from Puno, on the shores of Lake Titicaca, have been selling and bartering ceramics in Cusipata and in other regions along the Vilcanota Valley for many decades during the Fiesta of the Virgin Asunta.

Games Children Play

There are few games children play in the heights of the Andes, and these are mainly played in mixed groups (except for soccer, where boys and girls sometimes have their own teams). The most frequently played game is *paka paka pukllay* (hide and seek), which proceeds in much the same way as it does in any culture (Figure 3.3).

Another game, also portrayed in dances, is *takanakuy,* the pushing game, also called *k'uchi taka,* the agility game (*k'uchi* = agile; *taka* = push), where children playfully push against one another with their shoulders without

FIGURE 3.3. Girls get ready to play hide and seek.

using their hands. The stronger or more agile player succeeds in pushing his partner out of a circle or designated place.

Joking games—*chansanakuy*—are prominent especially during the Puk-llay fiesta, when joking and teasing is tolerated more readily in an attempt to create an atmosphere of fun and exuberance. The joking takes a variety of forms. Children pretend to be different people, or they joke about *casarun* (getting married), *chincasun* (going where no one finds us), and *saqey qari-kita* (leaving the husband).

Daring games, as they relate to activities such as climbing on rocks, walls, and roofs or jumping across creeks, are also practiced in quite energetic ways. All of these games continue throughout adolescence and sometimes into adulthood.

With the exception of soccer games, which were introduced into Quechua society from Europe, children's games and virtually all play activities are largely non-competitive. This attitude is reflected throughout the society. For example, the daring horse races that take place during the Fiesta de Santiago in July never have a declared winner (Figure 3.4; see also Bolin 1998, Chapter 10). The herders feel that it is not respectful to select a winner to the detriment of all others who participated in the game. Nor do the games played by boys and girls in Chillihuani contain elements of aggression. This stands in contradiction to certain other societies. Christine Robinson

Finnan's findings, that "boys' games are traditionally aggressive and competitive; girls' games are passive and accommodating" (1982:369), do not apply to Chillihuani.

Even more surprising than the scarcity of children's toys and games is the fact that there are no songs that pertain only to a child's world. As discussed in Chapter 2, from a young age children begin to sing the songs they hear adults sing during fiestas. They fill in with their own words whatever they do not understand or remember. When children are brought to bed or to their sleeping corner on the adobe floor, parents tickle, hug, and kiss them or play with them, but there are no specific songs, and no lullabies whatsoever. My observations on the absence of children's songs, poems, and stories in Chillihuani agree with Dr. Johnny Payne's findings in the high Andes (personal communication). The extensive studies of indigenous children in highland Peru by Rodrigo Montoya (1995), and his long-term research with his brothers Luis and Edwin (1987), which resulted in a collection of 1,150 songs of Quechua poetry,[7] did not reveal a single children's song. Montoya concluded that "there are no children's songs in the culture of the Quechua" (1995:68–69). Children learn from a young age about songs, myths, legends, poems, and stories destined for adults. (See also Chapter 2.)[8]

There are no specific dances for children either. As soon as they can walk,

FIGURE 3.4. Children learn early in life to give their best without "beating" the other participants.

they start to imitate the dancing steps of adults. They learn to dance by observing parents, siblings, or community members during fiestas. Six-year-olds know quite well how to dance the adult way, and soon they understand that dances have ritual significance, as they please the gods and appease them. The same is true for music. Children observe adults and soon can play simple tunes on a variety of instruments. Only when they start school do they learn songs, poems, and stories destined only for children, in addition to some dances from other South American countries.

Neither parents nor teachers could explain why there are no Quechua songs, poems, stories, or dances specifically for children in Chillihuani or other parts of the high Andes. As one observes the herders' way of life, however, and reads about the Inca past, it becomes quite clear why children immerse themselves into the culture of adults so early in life. Given a marginal environment, they must participate and even take over adult tasks in the house and on the fields and pastures. They must acquire knowledge and skills in areas such as agriculture, animal husbandry, traditional medicine, births and burials, fiestas, and *faenas*. There is no time that can be dedicated exclusively to a child's world as we know it. Without a well-functioning health and social system in place, children must rapidly move into the adult world, assuming adult rights and responsibilities, in case of death and disease in the family or the loss of crops.

Another issue, which has its roots in pre-conquest times, could also have contributed to the absence of a subculture dedicated to children. Since the Quechua language did not have a written component as we know it, before and even after the conquest of the Incas children had to learn the complex history, lifeways, and ideologies of their people by listening to stories and legends about their large empire. Roberto Yupanqui Qoa, an outstanding elder who died in Chillihuani in June of 1998, at the age of around 105, recounted, "When I was a child, I had to listen to the ancient teachings of our people. My grandparents told me about our ancestors every night. Often I was too tired to listen and wanted to sleep. But my *qoyacha* [grandmother] and *awkicha* [grandfather] insisted that I stay awake and listen, so I would know what has happened in the past, so I would know my ancestors. Sometimes my grandparents shook me hard if I fell asleep. 'Stay awake and listen,' they implored and commanded. 'You must know about our ancestors. You must tell your children and their children our story. It may never die'" (Bolin 1998:201). These people's desires to remember the lives of their ancestors and the history of the Inca empire through oral transmission left no time to learn stories, songs, or nursery rhymes that were only of interest to a child.

FIGURE 3.5. Everyone likes to listen to stories and legends from the past.

Chillihuani's youngsters do not feel sad about the absence of a children's subculture. In fact, they avidly listen to legends about ancestors, animals, and a myriad of folktales, and they amuse their listeners by adding their own lyrics to songs or mastering the dancing steps of adults (Figure 3.5). Healer Modesto Quispe asserts that "moving rapidly into adult society is beneficial to the children."[9]

Children at Work

As stated earlier, in the high Andes children's work and play can neither be strictly defined nor separated. The meanings of work and play differ when we consider the lives of highland pastoralists as opposed to people in urban societies. As was true in Inca times, work is still an expression of pride. The Inca greeting "*Ama llulla, ama suwa, ama qella*" (Don't lie, don't steal, don't be lazy) attests to the deep concerns of the Incas, which are still manifested by present-day populations. Juan Núñez del Prado captured the dichotomy of Indian and non-Indian ideologies very well, stating, "Hanaqpacha [the Andean heaven] is a place of agricultural activity in which even children work, and its paradisiacal condition lies in the fact that lands are abundant and fertile and harvests are not subject to losses or calamities. This concept contrasts with the occidental concept of paradise, which is presented as a place of eternal leisure" (1985:250).

FIGURE 3.6. These young men are happy to be photographed as they work the fields with their *chakitaklla,* a foot plow from Inca times.

The herders of Chillihuani value work. Thus, a *faena* — a work party where at least one member of every family participates — is considered as important as a fiesta. "You *must* come to our *faena*, it's a very special event," my herder friends often urged. The annual *faena* that is organized to clean the paths that run across the dispersed village is hard and exhausting work, but people approach it with much enthusiasm and a community spirit that is at its best. A deep sense of work ethic was also expressed by my centenarian friend Roberto Yupanqui Qoa. When I asked what he considered most important in his life, his immediate answer was "that I do good work every day" (Bolin 1998:121). Don Roberto could not imagine an existence without work. In accordance with Andean ideology he, too, believed that even the world above (*hanan pacha*) is a place with good harvests, healthy animals, and beautiful weavings, a place where hard work brings good results.

In Chillihuani, both men and women are proud to be able to work hard for their families and the community. Sometimes, when I asked whether I could photograph a group of people while they rested during a communal work party, they agreed, but they quickly grabbed their *chakitaklla* (foot plows) and ploughed the earth, so the picture would be of their work and not their leisure (Figure 3.6).[10]

Children grow up within this atmosphere of proud work ethics. At an early age they start to help their parents and are complimented for work well done, even if it is not perfect.[11]

When children are about three years old, they are allowed to do all kinds of little jobs in and around the house. Most activities are learned by observing siblings and adults. Four-year-old Víctor assists the Mamani household, running errands and helping take care of his two younger sisters. He brings his mother diapers, goes outside to shake small blankets, and holds the bottle for his sisters so they can drink. When about six or seven years old, he will take the animals to pasture, work on the potato fields, help to prepare meals, and select perfect *coca* leaves for offerings during fiestas. Soon thereafter he will assist with communal work parties and with all fiestas.

I have seen children at approximately eight years of age help their parents shear the herd animals, clean and wash the wool, and put it on rocks to dry.[12] There is no strong division of labor for boys and girls when they are young. In families where a boy is older or there are only boys, they learn to do both men's and women's work. The same is true for households where a girl is the oldest or where all the children are girls.

Asunta and Juan Braulio, who live in the highest regions of the village, have three boys, ages eight, six, and four (in 1999). Tomás (eight) and Hipólito (six), when they are not in school, take the animals to pasture, round up the horses, and help on the fields. Since this family has no daughter, the little boys also assist their mother in the kitchen and bring firewood and dried dung to cook meals. It was amazing to see how six-year-old Hipólito watched the steaming soup on the earthen stove. When it was done, he pulled his sleeves over his hands, leaned underneath the overhanging chimney, grabbed the heavy pot with the boiling soup, took it off the fire, and put it against the kitchen wall. Then he looked at me with a proud grin (Figure 3.7).

In families with both boys and girls, girls usually learn to cook and wash, becoming quite good at it by the age of 11 or 12. Caring for younger siblings is also usually done by an older sister, but in her absence boys can fulfill this task very well.

Given the dispersed nature of the settlements and the hardships of the herding way of life, young Andean children are required to manifest considerable abilities. Starting at the age of about seven, they walk alone to the valley —a distance of between sixteen and thirty-one kilometers—to buy urgently needed items. They may also engage in barter with people they know in the valley, if the family is lucky enough to have surplus items, such as potatoes, *oqa*, *ulluku*, *maswa*, *chuño*, *moraya*, *ch'arki*, ropes, wool, the veins of animals (used as strings for harps and guitars), animal fat, *llullucha* and *qochayuyu*

FIGURE 3.7. In the absence of a sister, Tomás, Hipólito, and Marcos are eager to learn to run a household.

(algae from the lakes), blankets (*costales,* Sp.), or weavings. They exchange some of these items for corn, spices, sugar, salt, tea, and other necessities.

Some children who live in the outer regions of the village must walk up to sixteen kilometers to the school, which is located in the central part of Chillihuani. They pick up firewood and dried dung on their way home. Most impressive, however, is to see small children engage in the herding of the family's domestic animals.

HERDING THE FLOCKS

The herding of alpacas, llamas, and sheep is one of the main responsibilities a child must take over starting at around five years of age. After young herders have accompanied a sibling or adult member of the family for some time, they know which pastures belong to the family and where the best grass grows during a particular season. For the first couple of years, young children take animals to pastures close by. At the age of seven or eight, they are allowed to lead their animals to higher regions, either alone or with a sibling (Figure 3.8).

The belief that herding is an easy task is erroneous. Young children must have a good understanding of the behavior of their animals, the terrain they are passing through, the regions where their family has rights to pasture, the climate and seasons, animal diseases and birthing, predators, and more. At seven or eight years of age, youngsters usually know how to use the *warak'a* (sling from Inca times) to throw stones into the distance in an effort to bring back straying animals. The stone is put on the hole in the middle of the sling, which is held at both ends. The herder then swings the sling in a circle over his head and hurls the stone into the distance by letting the shorter side of the sling slip from his grip.[13]

FIGURE 3.8. As night falls, Teresa and Libia return from the meadows with the family herd.

When approximately seven years old, children have gained considerable knowledge about all aspects of herding. This is required, since in times of trouble they are too far away from home to call for help and must handle difficult situations on their own. They must not only have knowledge of many aspects of high-altitude life, but must also be brave. I have seen children leave for the high pastures during thunderstorms, when the rains made the earth waterlogged and prone to landslides and lightning flashed through black clouds followed by deafening thunder. When the children return in the evening they are often cold and soaking wet. Yet they usually arrive with smiling faces and are received with love and appreciation for work well done and with a delicious hot soup.

Especially dangerous are weather conditions that bring lightning, hail, and snow. It is common belief that lightning is caused by the striking force of the thunder god (Qhaqya or Illapa), who kills people and animals and destroys homesteads. Children are scared of Qhaqya, being well aware of the danger this deity brings. A tragic event occurred in March 2002, when at ages ten and fifteen both daughters of the previous community president were killed by lightning as they took the family herd to the high pastures. The family was devastated by the terrible loss. Despite considerable inconveniences, they moved to a lower part of the village, where lightning is less likely to strike.[14]

In the high Andes hail always comes with lightning. Sometimes the hailstones are as large as chicken eggs, and their force can be devastating to people and their crops. Snow can also be dangerous, as it can lead to snow blindness. Chillihuani herders frequently relate that bright snow can blind them and cause extreme pain that can last up to 24 hours. They try not to leave their houses when snow and sun cause blinding conditions. Children and adults who must go outdoors protect themselves by putting the black soot from cooking pots around their eyes. Or, they use black wool to fashion makeshift sunglass frames that they tie at the back of the head. It is interesting to note that the herders of the high mountains of Nepal use the same methods to protect their eyes from the glaring snow. Andean herders might also put on a hat with a wide brim and hold their hands across their eyes during these extreme weather conditions, which are especially dangerous for children on the distant pastures.

Apart from lightning, hail, and blinding snow, children must also cope with torrential rains causing landslides that can bury people, herd animals, and crops under piles of rubble. One evening as we gather in the family home, I ask twelve-year-old Teresa Mamani to tell us about her experiences as a herder, about the good and also the difficult times she has when she takes the family flocks to the high mountains. She smiles shyly and starts talking in a whisper. "I like to take my animals to pasture. My mother always gives me a lunch that consists mainly of *chuños,* and sometimes of boiled potatoes when they are in season. Or she barters toasted maize in the valley. After a fiesta she puts some *ch'arki* [dried meat] into my bag. But usually we just have *chuños.* I always give some of them to my dogs because they are my companions, and we drink water from the springs."[15] She talks with increased enthusiasm as she continues, "Sometimes I meet friends on the pastures and we exchange food. We have fun talking and running through the meadows—sometimes we almost forget to watch our flocks."

Then her face takes a serious expression. "When it rains and the fog hangs low, it is difficult to herd. I feel cold and uncomfortable. During rains, sheep often move away from the main herd and congregate in small groups to find protection behind rocks and hills. When my herd splits into several groups to find shelter, it is sometimes difficult to get them together again, and as they disperse in the fog, it is easy for thieves who come from far away to steal them. Foxes also come to steal my animals, regardless of whether there is fog or sunshine." Teresa whispers again, "Sometimes the foxes approach so quietly that not even my dogs hear them. They quickly snatch a young animal and are out of sight. When my dogs hear the fox, they chase him away."

Losing animals is a tragedy for the herders, not only because of their economic value, but also because the herders are attached to their animals, whose names, tempers, and genealogy they know so well. In 1996, a puma entered the corral of a family who lives not far from the Mamani household. In two consecutive nights this animal killed several of the larger llamas. Juan Mamani and centenarian Roberto Yupanqui Qoa recounted that pumas used to come often to the region, but now attacks are rare because few live close by. I ask Teresa whether she ever had an encounter with a puma while pasturing her animals. She says no, but remembers a terrifying event that occurred when she was about six years old. "When I was herding my llamas and alpacas, a condor approached. He was enormous and hovered right over me. He came so close that I felt the air he moved with his wings. I screamed as loud as I could. A woman who walked up the path with her daughter came running toward me. She also screamed, swinging her arms in the air. The huge bird hesitated and then left." Teresa's mother nods her head, saying, "This woman has saved my daughter's life; I am so grateful to her." The healer asserts that condors rarely attack young children, but that they are eager to get young llamas, alpacas, and sheep.

I can understand Teresa's fear of condors. One year in April, right at the end of the raining season, I went up to the high pasture with the herders. Three condors came flying over us in a group, landing at a short distance below us. Their wingspans were enormous, about 3 meters wide, and their behavior left no doubt that they were eager for prey. After a short while they took off, flying west toward a region where one of the herders who was with us had his flock grazing. He was worried about his young animals, but was relieved to see all of them enter the corral later that evening—not one was missing. Adult llamas and alpacas usually crowd around their young to protect them when condors come in sight. Nevertheless, a considerable number of young camelids and sheep do fall prey to condors, especially between December and May, when they are still quite small. Condors are known to be scavengers of large animals who have died, but they also kill small animals whenever they can.[16]

Despite some frightening events and many hardships, Teresa likes herding. "I like my animals and the high mountains; I meet friends on the pastures, we sing and tell jokes, and sometimes we fall in love," she adds with a smile.

TENDING THE FIELDS

Children's herding activities are a major contribution to a family's subsistence. Their help tending the fields is also necessary and is likewise much appreciated by their families. When Andean people work the earth, they are not only engaged in efforts to subsist, but the close contact with Pachamama makes this a sacred activity as well.

All land belongs to the community. It is divided into parcels for cultivation and for pasture, to be used by families for an indefinite length of time. Each family has use-rights to three or four parcels of land. Fields are located at different altitudes and in different regions to avoid total crop loss due to adverse weather conditions. Fields are left fallow for five or six years after having been worked for one or two years. Families return to the same plots after the fallow years. Pastureland is used permanently; there are no fallow periods. Like the fields, pastureland is handed down within families from one generation to the next.

Chillihuani also has communal fields, which are worked by community members; usually one person per household joins the work party. The harvest is divided equally between the families who work the land. Communal pastureland can be used by any family. Usually herders pasture their animals on the meadows closest to their homesteads.

Children inherit a portion of their parents' fields and pastures at marriage; the rest is divided among the offspring in equal parts when both parents have died. The youngest son or daughter normally resides with the parents as long as they live. In return for the help and care given to the parents, he/she receives the house with all the implements and, in addition, his/her share of the land and animals.

While there is no difference in the way boys and girls perform their herding activities, work on the fields can differ according to gender. To prepare the earth for seeding in July and August, boys, beginning at the age of about eight years, start to work with the *chakitaklla,* a foot plow used since Inca times. This activity is called *yapuy,* or *barbecho* (Sp.), the plowing of the soil. Boys and girls and sometimes women put the spaded clods of earth in place. After children help put animal dung from the corral into bags, older boys and men place them onto their male llamas and alpacas, who carry them to the fields where, starting in August, potatoes and other Andean tubers are planted.[17] Men and boys break the clods of earth and mix them with the dung of llamas, alpacas, or sheep. Women and girls place the seeds into the earth and cover them with soil. It is commonly believed that only females may put the seed into the ground, because they have a special relationship with Pachamama that assures that the plants will grow. If men attempt to put seed into the ground, the plants may not grow. This belief reaches back to Inca times (Figures 3.9 and 3.10).

As the potatoes and other tubers grow with the rains that begin in September or October, the whole family helps to weed and hoe the fields. This is done once for potatoes and twice for other tubers, within two months of sowing.[18] Small children of either sex collect the potatoes that were dug up by older siblings or adults and put them into carrying bags. Strong adolescents load them onto male llamas and alpacas, which carry them to the family home.

As long as parents and grandparents are alive, children's help with daily chores is considerable but not excessive. In families where grandparents and one or both parents have died, children's work can be exhausting. When Ignacia Choqqe Quispe, the president of the Women's Committee, died leaving three children behind, her fifteen-year-old daughter took over the role of a mother. She was able to organize all the household affairs for the family of four. Given the rather high mortality rate of mothers during childbirth, and also of other adults in the marginal environment of the high Andes, adolescents often become responsible for household affairs, the herding of animals, and work in the fields. They are capable of performing the necessary tasks, which they have observed and carried out from a young age.

As children help in the house, on the fields, and in the pastures, they experience the entire cycle of the seasons. They also learn to organize social and religious events (see Chapter 5). Exposure to such a wide range of activities

FIGURE 3.9. Agricultural activities during Inca times. Drawn by chronicler Felipe Guamán Poma de Ayala ([1615] 1980:1053).

FIGURE 3.10. Today, as in Inca times, men till the soil while women put the seeds in the ground and cover them up.

provides them with the skills that are so important in their struggle to survive. Although the work is hard at times, children are proud to be able to help. They are given praise for work well done, and their spirits are high as they are surrounded by a whole community of hard-working people.[19]

Yet play and work activities prepare the Chillihuani children not only for adult life within their community, but also for scholastic achievements in various areas, especially mathematics.

CHAPTER 4

The Many Faces of Learning

When school principal Aníbal Durán and the teachers I met in Cusipata told me that the children of Chillihuani who continue schooling in the valley are always at the top of the class, I was eager to find out why. The teachers observed that a competitive attitude is not pronounced among these herders, which makes their children's academic achievements even more surprising. Before I had ever climbed to their village, I knew that the people in this herding society had something special going for them, since survival in a marginal region requires considerable physical and mental capacities. But I never expected to encounter such a variety of talents. The extreme simplicity of life in material terms can be deceptive until one discovers what is hidden beneath the simple surface.

As I began to live among the Chillihuani herders, I soon found out that their abilities include very good organizational skills. Whether dealing with a fiesta, a *faena,* a variety of tasks that require reciprocal assistance (*ayni* and *minka*), or any other local event that calls for organization, these people work in impressive ways. Yet the Chillihuani herders not only cooperate well as they carry out familiar activities, they are equally capable of handling new tasks, such as grassroots projects.

Prior to 1988 the people of Chillihuani had never received any support from outside their community. Shortly before I left Peru, they wondered whether they could get help with the completion of a small health station they had started to build in their mountain wilderness. I discussed with the village elders some guidelines for writing proposals for non-governmental organizations. Within two days the village authorities handed me a rather well-written proposal; it had been typed on an old typewriter that was stored in their small community hall. After we received funding, the community again showed superb organizational skills as they built and equipped the health station and other projects in subsequent years (Figure 4.1).

Since 1992, when I founded the organization Yachaq Runa, which deals with Andean medicine, nutrition, and ecology, it has been intriguing to witness the facility with which five Chillihuani healers have learned new concepts

FIGURE 4.1. As the community organizes itself to build a health station, children participate enthusiastically.

and conveyed their own knowledge to the Yachaq group. These people know how to translate theory into well-organized action (Bolin 1992, 1994a).

Knowledge and skills of this type are not limited to people who have had a few years of schooling; they also show up in herders who have never attended school. In fact, some of the most creative, alert, and organized people I met and worked with were illiterate and monolingual Quechua speakers. Since children are always in the presence of parents or other community members, they have ample opportunities to watch them work, organize, and celebrate. In order to discover more about children's overall disposition to learning, especially their easy grasp of mathematics, I observed what everyday life within families teaches them and explored the role that is played by the school.

Laying the Foundations for Creative and Holistic Thinking

Since I have lived with the Chillihuani herders in their small adobe huts, I have been able to observe adaptive child-rearing practices and the interesting ways in which children learn within their families and the community at large. Youngsters grow up observing and experiencing life as a natural process both in their homes and out of doors. For family members who live in a one-room house, things cannot happen behind closed doors. Everything is out in the open, from birth to death.

Children witness the life cycle of plants and animals and the changes that occur throughout the seasons. As they help to prepare the land and put the seed into the ground, they closely observe what happens as rain and sunshine contribute to the growing process. They see how animals are born and witness every aspect of their behavior as they take them to pasture. They observe the interactions between animals, plants, and humans. They learn to recognize what happens when people neglect their fields, pastures, and animals, or when the powers of nature refuse to cooperate in the growing process and instead send strong winds, hail, or drought to devastate crops, kill animals, and bring times of hunger and despair. Rituals held at the level of the family, the neighborhood, and the community convey to children a holistic view of life and teach them compassion.

Yet despite a great variety of activities and experiences, youngsters are not bombarded with too much information. New learning experiences are built on previous ones, are connected in meaningful ways, and are further solidified as they are put into practice. As children take their animals to pasture or head for the fields in the distance, they have time to digest any new information.

Thus, the lives of these highland herders, which look simple from the outside, abound with important real-life learning that is connected in integral and logical ways to the overall ideology of the society. This is not always the case in the "modern" world, and is an aspect often missing from school curricula and at university. In her insightful studies about the ways children learn in North America, Jane Healy deplores that "the last thing today's children need is more bits of learning without the underlying experiential frameworks to hang them onto" (1990:329). Stanford's Dr. Eliot Eisner points out that in previous times "many sources in children's lives outside of school provided continuity and meaning. This is no longer the case for many students where schools may provide their only opportunity for a 'connected experience'" (cited in Healy 1990:312–313). A child's learning experience within a village, including work, the arts, crafts, song, and dance, has been considered more valuable by a variety of scholars than the knowledge derived from school. Internationally known Peruvian anthropologist Oscar Núñez del Prado helped the traditional community of Qeros establish a school (1983a, 1983b, 1983c, and personal communication). Shortly after the school was up and running, though, he realized that this had been a mistake, because the children were no longer able to dedicate time to important traditional teachings and significant cultural practices, such as the art of weaving. But given a fast-changing climate with extreme weather conditions that endanger crops and animals and make survival in high regions increasingly more precarious, many children need the school experience in order to find work in towns and cities.

Schooling in Chillihuani

In 1938, the villagers of Chillihuani built a small school out of adobe blocks in the village plaza and equipped it with simple adobe furniture. Healer and village judge Modesto Quispe, now in his early sixties, recounts, "When we were children, we sat on low adobe benches behind small adobe desks. Each of us used a soft stone with which we wrote on our stone slate. The blackboard was also made of slate, and the kinds of chalks the teachers used were made of hard black earth, called *carboncillo* (Sp.), and of red earth, called *taku rumi*. The chalk was softer than the blackboard." The other elders nod their heads in agreement.

Gregorio explains, "When the school building was completed, the school board granted the village a teacher by the name of Jorge Bautista Palisa Amaya. He was a very good teacher, and so were a few others that followed, especially Luis Honorio Paredes and Emma Yawar Cuadros. They were strict, but fair and they worked very hard. Some of the other teachers were not liked so much, primarily because they punished us children for making errors. At first only boys went to school. Little by little girls started to attend classes as well. They were not treated as harshly as the boys were."[1]

Children start school when they are about seven or eight years old. They need time to adjust to grade one, given a set of difficult circumstances, such as the long walk to school. The elders estimated that the children who live sixteen kilometers from the school need to walk between two and a half and four hours. Especially during the rainy season, with its torrential rains, hailstorms, lightning, and unstable, waterlogged terrain, the children have a hard time making it to school and back. Language difficulties are also pronounced for some of these monolingual Quechua speakers who until recent years were expected to speak Spanish starting in grade one. Yet despite these and other obstacles, children and adults expressed pride when they told me on my first visit, "*kanmi yachay wasi Chillihuanipi*" (Chillihuani has a school).

Between 1988 (when I first visited the herders) and 2004 about three hundred children of school age lived in Chillihuani, but only slightly more than half were and still are able to attend classes. Apart from great distances and

severe weather conditions, there are several other reasons for the weak attendance. In families where parents are sick or have died, children are needed at
home, on the fields, and in the pastures. Although in grades one to three there
are as many girls as boys in school, girls tend to drop out faster than boys
before reaching grade six because their help is most needed by their families. Overall, women are not so eager to learn how to read and write. They
cling more to their traditions, since writing and other such crafts were introduced by the conquerors, who often used them to the disadvantage of the
Indians.[2] Furthermore, until 2000 the school buildings were too small to accommodate all children and many had to sit on the crowded floor or stand
up, leaning against the wall. In the year 2000, contrary to all expectations,
Chillihuani received a new schoolhouse with four rooms, built by INFES (Instituto Nacional de Infraestructura Educativa y de Salud).

Because no roads lead to Chillihuani, teachers find the hike to and from
this village quite cumbersome. The icy-cold nights and the absence of a heating system, electric light, stores, and other conveniences make it difficult to
live there during the week. Yet teachers agree that it is much more pleasant
to teach in this village under the clouds than in valley towns and cities, because the children of the llama and alpaca herders are much more eager to
learn and more respectful toward teachers and each other than are children
in the cities. Teacher Marcial, who has taught in different places, explains, "In
this herding village children know what's right and wrong. They are polite
and attentive. They have not yet attained a distorted worldview by watching
television, as is true for many youngsters in the cities. In city schools they
are less eager to learn, they get distracted more easily, they are more aggressive, and by far not as respectful as the children of the Chillihuani herders."
Another teacher said, "Children here are very loving. They greet the teachers with affection and always acknowledge them, while pupils in city schools
often ignore teachers when they meet them outside the classroom." Teacher
Yanet, who taught for many years in Chillihuani, reports, "Here, the children
are more innocent, more respectful, and more caring than elsewhere. They
have little to eat and sometimes are very hungry. Still, they share the few potatoes they bring to school with other pupils and with the teachers."

Teachers generally agree that problems with youngsters in town and city
schools are largely due to child-rearing practices that differ considerably from
those in the high mountains. They also deplore the fact that in city schools
there is too much emphasis on competition. Throughout the years, the teachers I talked to agree with Marcial that children's behavior in this herding village stands in stark contrast to the experiences they had in the valley schools.

Most Chillihuani children are happy in school and eager to learn. Although parents agree that overall, girls develop at a faster pace than do boys, teachers say that girls and boys do equally well in school. Some youngsters, however, have problems with concentration due to bad nutrition and hunger, which affect many of them some of the time and some all of the time. Teachers also relate that children whose parents have died, are sick, or are too poor to afford school supplies are sad and therefore cannot pay attention in class.

Overall, despite these obstacles, the Chillihuani pupils have an easier time in school than many indigenous children I have encountered elsewhere. In some parts of the Andes, school has been traumatic for the children of the high mountains. They must get up before dawn and hurry to the valley without breakfast in order to be in school on time. Tired, hungry, speaking only the Quechua language, and lacking the necessary school supplies, these youngsters must compete with classmates in the valley who speak Spanish and feel at home in the mestizo culture.[3] Some teachers do not consider the obstacles the indigenous pupils must overcome and blame them for being lazy and having neither interest in nor aptitude for learning. Misconceptions of this kind have created a stereotype of the native populations of Peru and other Andean countries that is incorrect and has caused much suffering to the indigenous people. Peruvian investigators Patricia Oliart and Patricia Ames (1998) observed that indigenous children are treated badly in mestizo schools. They are made to hurry into and out of the bus and are mistreated by teachers, looked down upon, and ridiculed for the mistakes they make. These observations are echoed by other investigators, such as Maria Heise, who writes, "Children endure the school years like an inevitable suffering, a time when they learn little. But something remains of those years, namely the conviction to be worth less, to be inferior for being native" (1989:177). Rodrigo Montoya, who undertook long-term research among Peru's native children, found that "school receives indigenous children with a severe and traumatizing aggression" (1995:84). He further notes that the education given in public schools is "dominated by a civilizing purpose that despises or ignores the subordinate cultures and intends to homogenize the country at any price" (1995:103).[4]

In Chillihuani, children experience economic, health, and environmental difficulties, but they are not exposed to the kind of abuse stated by Montoya and others. In the homogeneous and rather egalitarian society of Chillihuani, all people enjoy similar living conditions and stand together in solidarity. Other than a priest who comes once a year and a nurse who works in the health station, the only outsiders who regularly climb to Chillihuani are teachers. The pupils benefit from this situation, in which mestizo teachers come to a village of Quechua Indians. As stated above, the situation can be severe for Indian children who must attend school in a mestizo society that is foreign to them. Although some of the teachers who have taught in Chilli-huani have been somewhat arrogant, others did a good, even excellent, job. Yanet and Marcial, for example, who taught the herding children for several years, recognize and appreciate the high moral and social values of the society.

A New School Curriculum

In 1994–1995 a new curriculum and method of teaching was introduced to Peru; it reached Chillihuani in 1996. In grade one, topics are now taught in Quechua, the children's first language. In grade two, when the children have become used to the school system and to their teachers, the Spanish language is added gradually. Pupils no longer fail in the lower grades. Only in a higher grade might they have to repeat a class. The grading system now consists of only three grades and does not include a failing grade. A means very good, B means good, C means needs improvement. Now children attend school from 9 a.m. to 2:30 p.m. There is no school on Saturdays and Sundays, and some-times teachers start school on Tuesdays and use Mondays to climb up to the village and Fridays to descend to the valley.

The new curriculum, which has been used in grades one to four, is referred to as an articulation program (*programa de articulación,* Sp.). It is based on a holistic approach, as it relates the various subject areas to one another. Most importantly, the new program is based on fostering self-esteem, cooperation, decision making, creativity, and responsibility. These capacities are already well developed in the Chillihuani children. As they descend to the valley, how-ever, where they are looked down upon for their traditional lifestyle and are often treated with little respect, they feel uncomfortable and their self-esteem suffers.

The new curriculum no longer emphasizes teaching alone but focuses on the children's need to explore and discover what is important to them. They can, to some extent, choose the topics they want to study and the issues they want to address within each topic. In art, for example, they can choose the type of handicraft they want to make. They decide for themselves what ma-terials they want to use and they must find, prepare, and assemble the materi-als themselves. They also learn to make their own costumes. Teacher Marcial sums up the new method as follows: "We no longer teach in the traditional way, now we mainly guide the children in their own projects." Yanet, the director of the school, explains, "The philosophy of teaching has changed considerably. In Religious Studies [Educación Religiosa, Sp.], for example, pupils used to memorize stories about Jesus and the Bible. Now we take a more philosophical approach. We confirm that Jesus is good and reflect on how we can be good people and how we should recognize values and adhere to them."

The new educational system is based on participation and cooperation. The teachers say that this has several advantages. Children learn while being mentally and physically engaged in an activity. This way they remember much better what they have learned and do not get as tired as they did spending most of their school hours sitting behind a desk.[5] They are now encouraged to interact with one another by discussing subject areas among themselves. They are complimented for their creativity, which gives them pride in their achievements.

The new holistic approach to education suits the children well. It is much more in accordance with their upbringing. Children now receive the same respect as individuals in school that they receive at home. In the same way that youngsters must decide what to do when they take their animals to pasture far from home, they now make decisions in school regarding the topic they want to study within a general theme or the grade they think should be assigned to the work done by other students. Schoolchildren help one another by giving constructive criticism without belittling their classmates' work. Throughout my observations, children have been taking these new tasks very seriously, and their judgment about the work of other children has been fair and well accepted.

It can be clearly observed that the new teaching method, with its focus on guidance, stimulates children's imagination and participation in class. Whereas previously, pupils were rather timid in school, the new methods of instruction address the kind of self-confidence they display at home. In school, children now work at the individual level, in small groups, and as a whole class. This is also in agreement with their culture, where they must act independently from an early age while also recognizing their family and community obligations.[6]

The fact that the new educational system focuses on ecology is another reason why it relates well to the world of the herder children. As is true in their daily lives at home, they now closely observe ecological processes and the agents that shape them in school as well.[7]

Thus, overall the new curriculum and teaching strategies make the transition from home to school easier. There are, however, some contradictions, and only time will tell how this curriculum will prove itself in the long run.

Pupils are now permitted to talk in class, and the whole class is allowed to scream with joy and clap with approval when something interesting or pleasant is happening. Within their families and the traditional community, children also are curious and participate readily in activities, but they are soft-spoken and do not raise their voices above those of adults.

Not all Chillihuani families appreciate the new school curriculum as much as the pupils do, since it takes longer now to learn to read and write. Boys and girls are needed to work in the house, on the fields, and in the pastures, and illiterate parents want them to learn the basics as fast as possible so they can read documents that must be signed.[8] Some parents feel that in the new system, children spend too much time in what they consider play activities instead of getting down to work. Teachers agree that it takes longer now to learn the basics, since much time is dedicated to interactions and to self-discovery, self-confidence, and pride. Although proud and self-confident at home, boys and girls have always been shy within an unfamiliar environment; the new system may prepare them better for a life outside the village.

A few years after teacher Yanet started to work in Chillihuani, she took her pupils to competitions in the district and province. It is interesting to note that despite the fact that a competitive attitude is not appreciated and, in fact, not tolerated in Chillihuani, the children have done very well. Several years in a row they have won singing, dancing, and running competitions in the valley towns. One grade-five student won second prize in a math competition within the large province of Quispicanchis, where more than 70,000 people live in 12 districts on an area of 7,138 square kilometers (Banco de Credito del Peru 1984). But even before the new educational program was implemented, Chillihuani students who continued their education in Cusipata after grade six were consistently at the top of their classes. Alicia, the third daughter of the healer Juan Mamani and his wife Luisa, continued her schooling in Cuzco, where she earned second place in her grade after only one year in the city. How can children who grow up in extreme material poverty, without books and other reading materials, within a society of largely illiterate, monolingual Quechua speakers, excel in towns and cities? This remained a puzzle for everyone outside this herding village.

Mathematics—The Favorite Topic of Chillihuani Children

On my initial visit to Chillihuani I found that children had virtually no books in their homes, so on my second trip I brought books to my host family Mamani. The girls were thrilled and eagerly read until the light of the candle had died down and it was way beyond their bedtime. The next day they continued to read during every free minute they could spare, and I assumed that reading was their favorite subject area. To be sure that I had guessed right, I asked the girls about their preferred topic. Instantaneously they exclaimed: "*Matemáticas!*" (Sp.). They added that they like other subject areas as well, but that mathematics is by far the one that is the most interesting and also the most fun. The children of other families agreed. Later, when I brought paper, crayons, and colored pencils to school and the pupils started to draw enthusiastically, I asked the class about their favorite topic, expecting it to be the arts (Figure 4.2).

But the whole class exclaimed "*Matemáticas!*" The same thing happened again in the other three classrooms, and it also seems to be the case in other high-altitude regions of the Andes. Former teacher and school principal Ana Caviedes told me that during her career in different villages, the best students of mathematics were always found among the highland Quechua Indians. The son of a befriended family in Yanahuara recounted that his classmate Santos Churata, who came from the herding village of Wakawasi, high above the Sacred Valley of the Incas, had always been the top math student in his class in the valley. Children from high-altitude regions who have the chance to continue schooling in the valley and at university become very good mathematicians and engineers, according to civil engineer Jaime and several teachers. Some also excel in the computing sciences. A good number of high-school teachers and university professors who teach mathematics and statistics in the city of Cuzco come from remote villages in the countryside.

Teachers in the United States, on the other hand, deplore that "mathematics causes parents more anxiety than any other school subject. It is the only area of the curriculum with an identifiable 'phobia' attached to it" (Healy 1987:263). According to NAEP (National Assessment of Educational Progress) findings, math scores are "particularly dismal when students are required to sustain attention for problems requiring more than one step" (Healy 1990: 20). Furthermore, statistics show that boys do considerably better in math than girls.[9]

Given the intriguing situation in Chillihuani, which is diametrically opposed to that of the United States, I was eager to discover why these young herders love math above all other topics, why they do so well, and why there are no gender differences in the way they learn math. Throughout my research I have looked at a range of stimuli that could be responsible for instilling such a preference for mathematics in youngsters, leading to achievements that are recognized at the district and provincial levels. I also discussed this subject

FIGURE 4.2. Schoolchildren are fond of drawing, but math remains the favorite topic.

area with the teachers who come from towns and cities in the valley. They, too, are surprised by these children's knowledge of and love for math, attributing it to a strong curiosity on the part of the pupils and to their school's own teaching methods, which include mathematical games.

When I asked the new school principal in the valley village of Cusipata, who teaches those Chillihuani children who can afford to continue schooling beyond grade six, about the issue, he suggested that children who live in a cold climate are better at sitting still and concentrating than, for example, children in Peru's hot jungle region, where he had formerly taught. He believes that in order to keep warm, pupils huddle and concentrate.

Unfortunately, all teachers who have worked in Chillihuani grew up and were educated outside the high mountain regions. They are not aware of the learning processes to which young herders are exposed within their families and the community. To discover those aspects of upbringing that predispose children to such a good understanding of math, one must live with the families and observe their daily activities at close range. I am grateful to the Chillihuani herders who accepted me into their families and discussed this fascinating subject area with me.

Little children, starting at about age two, often amuse themselves by counting everything they can see in the house, and they also count the stars in the night sky. They say that playing with numbers is fun, and by the time they go to school many youngsters can count to one thousand or more and most can add and subtract and even multiply and divide. As one observes children's daily routine, it becomes evident that herding activities, which they start to take over between the ages of five and seven, prepare them for mathematical thinking as well. Children must know how many and which of the animals they take to pasture belong to their parents, a grandparent, or an aunt or uncle, and which ones are part of their own herd or that of a sibling. Not only must they "count" their alpacas, llamas, and sheep when they leave for the pasture and return home at night, but they also must account for them when they congregate in small groups in different parts of a meadow. They must know how many white, brown, black, or checkered animals they have; how many males, females, and young; and approximately how old these animals are. Animals in a herd cannot be counted one by one, because it is believed that this would separate the animals and bring bad luck.

Thus, children not only use their knowledge of numbers, but they also learn to recognize each animal by the color and pattern of its fur and by other features, which are reflected in the animal's name. As they look at their herd (the average family herd consists of about thirty-five animals), they see not only that an animal is missing, but they also know which animal it is. The healer Modesto explains, "When the children count their alpacas and llamas, they say their animals' names: here comes Yana [the black one], Yuraq [the white one], Chumpi [the coffee-colored one], Wik'uña [the one that has colors like the vicuña], Suri [the one with the long silky fleece], Muru [the animal that has small markings distributed all over its fleece], Yanauya [the one with the black face], Alqa [the animal with a combination of mainly light colors]," etc. Whenever these names are not descriptive enough, the gender, age, or size of an animal; the precise distribution of its markings; the quality of its fleece; and also whether it is a llama, an alpaca, or a *wari* (a hybrid between a llama and an alpaca) can be added.[10] As children discover at a glance whether all their animals are present, where and in how many subgroups they congregate, and should an animal be missing, which animal it is, they acquire a good sense of spatial relationships. This sense is further enhanced as they explore the outdoors while climbing on rocks, crawling into caves, and running through meadows. A young herder's ability to judge direction and distance increases when, at age seven or eight, he/she begins to use the *warak'a,* the sling by which a stone is hurled into the distance to bring back straying animals. Youngsters must constantly monitor how far their animals can wander from the central part of the herd before retrieval is necessary, either with the help of their dogs or with a stone that must fly beyond the straying animal without hurting it.

The ability to perceive spatial relationships, which has been considered "one of the best predictors of math ability" (Healy 1987:265), is further enhanced by a fascination on the part of the Quechua people for detecting metaphors in the configurations of the landscape and within the cosmos at large. This practice goes back to Inca and probably pre-Inca times and is anchored in legends and myths. The Inca myth of origin tells that the first of the four founding brothers turned into a lagoon, the second into *ichu* grass, and the third into stone, while the fourth became the founder of Andamarca (Cáceres 1986:115). At a young age, children develop an aptitude to unveil shapes and figures hidden in the landscape and the night sky. Every outstanding landmark assumes significance and a personality in its own right, which is sometimes rooted in mythology. At other times the young herders spontaneously recognize meaningful forms on their own. Often children, and also adults, point to landmarks, such as the rocky peak Condorenqaychuyoq, believed to be a condor that was turned to stone. Mistiwarkuna (the suspended mestizo) is the name of a tall rocky outcrop in Chillihuani that resembles a man with one of his legs missing. The story goes that a mestizo came to cultivate oranges and *coca* leaves at this site, but the Apus did not allow him to do so and turned him into stone. At the entrance to the sacred mountain lake Waqraqocha, a natural rock that looks like a sitting person stooped over represents a watchman, who was also turned to stone (Bolin 1998, Chapter 13). Rolling hills with bizarre shapes can be reckoned as resting or sleeping people or animals. Clouds of various configurations also represent a vast range of metaphors. The former Inca capital of Cuzco was constructed in the shape of a puma. The Quechua people believe that the earth lives, as do landmarks such as rocks, springs, lakes, and meadows, all of which partake in the life force that permeates the universe.

But it is not only the earth that provides opportunities to discover metaphors; the night sky is equally revealing to the Andean people. As was true for the Incas, the Quechua people of today still believe that for everything that exists on earth, there is a counterpart in the sky. Constellations such as the Pleiades (*qoto; cabrillas,* Sp.), or the big black llama with a young suckling in the Milky Way, have metaphoric significance as symbols of fertility. When one looks at the Pleiades before June 24, and they are large and clear, the crop to be planted in the first days of August will be good. When the stars in the Pleiades appear dim and small, the crop planted in September will be the better one. The constellation of the big black llama is perceived as a provider of rain, and Quechua mythology holds it responsible for the fertilization and nourishment of the universe (Randall 1987:75). Chillihuani herders see the morning star in the form of a condor; another clump of stars is considered to be a partridge with a cross in the middle of its body. Small children, who like to count the bright stars in the clear mountain air, already know about the constellations and what they mean with regard to people's subsistence and well-being.

The moon was considered the deified mother of the Qoya, the queen of the Inca empire. It is still closely observed, mainly as an indicator of agricultural activities. When the moon is yellow, it will rain; when it is white, rain will stay away.[11] In Chillihuani people put seeds into the earth during the full moon, believing that this will result in a good harvest.

The Incas believed that the sun is the father of the Inca rulers. The Chillihuani herders still greet the rising sun with great respect in the morning with the words, "*Ay Taytay Inti, ñoqa valikuyki sumaq p'unchayta kawsanaykupaq pacha paqarimanta chisiyanankama*" (Oh my Father Sun, I implore you to make this a good day from dawn to dusk for everyone; Bolin 1998:167).

The sun is also used to tell time. The herders explain that "children learn to tell time by the position of the sun and the shadow of a house, a wall, a stone, or their own bodies. In order to get a more precise reading, they plant a stick straight into the earth and use the shadow from the stick to tell the time of the day. When there is little shade from the stick or none at all, it is 12 noon. When the shade falls to the left side of the stick, it is about 9 a.m.; when it falls to the right, it is about 3 p.m." This way of reckoning time exemplifies how space and time are viewed as one unit, called Pacha in the Quechua language. The herders say that during the Andean summer it is difficult to tell time by means of the shadow because of cloudy skies, fog, and frequent rains. Telling time is easiest during the clear and sunny winter months, but more difficult in the spring and fall due to differences in sunrise, sunset, and the total duration of the solar day. Time can also be told by looking at the mountain peaks where the sun is standing, and by means of the stars that appear at different times of the night.[12]

Old people in Chillihuani who have never owned a watch seem to have a built-in clock that tells them what time it is, even when the sun hides behind the clouds. They also assert that they know what time it is at night. People usually go to sleep at 7 p.m. Then they wake up between 10 and 11 p.m., again at midnight, and again at 3 a.m., when it is time to get up in order to leave at 4 to work on remote fields. Some elders who own a watch confide that they wake up at these precise times between their dreams.

Time periods within the year are also perceived and measured using Andean perceptions of time. Thus, when people are asked about their date of birth, they are not always sure, but they do know exactly during what season they were born and what activities were going on at that time. These people are more familiar with the calendar of fiestas than with a calendar divided into months. (See also Müller and Müller 1984:164; Fischer 2002:178.)

The multitude of experiences discussed above allows children not only to comprehend relationships of space and time, but also to further their understanding of metaphors and thus of abstract reasoning. Most importantly, by personifying natural landmarks, children learn to respect and care for the many living and breathing manifestations of nature.

Mathematical and creative thinking is stimulated in other ways as well, as Chillihuani children play, work, and celebrate. As discussed in Chapter 3, creativity is required to turn natural materials — earth, water, stones, branches, wool, etc. — into toys and playlands. As Jane Healy suggests, "Making mud pies, believe it or not, is a readiness activity for algebra, the science of describing relationships of quantity" (1987:266). When children walk to the valley to buy items for their parents, they learn about the value of money in terms of goods. As they engage in barter, they learn to calculate the value of the goods they give versus the value of the goods they receive.

Work and play during fiestas celebrated within the family, neighborhood, or community offer youngsters a range of mathematical challenges. They learn to estimate the amount of food items required to prepare meals for a specific number of people. With some practice, they no longer count the potatoes and other food items, but know at a glance what amount is needed for the number of people expected to attend. The amount of *chicha* to be prepared must also be determined before corn is bartered in the valley. Precise calculations are necessary, since during fiestas no one may go hungry or thirsty and generosity is paramount. Yet by the same token, nothing should be wasted, given the scarcity of food. Household economics are mainly in the hands of women, who must learn to decide from an early age how much of a year's crop can be consumed by the family, how much can be used for barter or sale, and how much must be kept for seed potatoes (Núñez del Prado Bejar 1975; Bolin 1990a).

Similarly, a fiesta's rituals demand knowledge of the numbers and amounts of the required ingredients. In the ritual context, children simultaneously become acquainted with the symbolic significance of numbers and amounts. They learn, for example, that three *coca* leaves are needed to make the *k'intu* that is always at hand to honor the deities. The most significant Apus must receive at least 12 leaves during an offering. Arranged in threes, this results in four *k'intus*. *Coca mukllu,* the seeds of the *coca* plant, bring luck when they are added to an offering in even numbers—two, four, six, eight, ten, up to twelve. The tiny *qañiwa* seeds (*Chenopodium pallidicaule*) are metaphors for the procreation of innumerable alpacas and llamas. Several other ingredients are measured or counted in accordance with the meaning inherent in the amount and number of the particular item before being added to an offering. (See Chapter 5 for the preparation of offerings.)

As an offering is brought to a deity, the wish that is requested in return must be relayed in total faith and with deep concentration. Thus, children are encouraged to use their powers of concentration from a young age, a practice that may aid in solving mathematical problems.

Numbers can also carry metaphoric significance within a ritual setting. For example, on July 28, officially Peru's Day of Independence, ancient rituals are carried out among male and female hierarchies in the central plaza of Chillihuani. The symbol of the pre-Columbian cross, which, among other things, stands for the four cardinal directions and the number four (four signifies completeness, Randall 1987:89), finds expression in many ways throughout this festivity. (See Bolin 1998:197–198.)

The diversity of the activities detailed above, in which children are observers and/or participants, fosters mathematical thinking. Since each ritual item represents a metaphor for something else, the actual number of items used has significance in cultural or religious terms, and the importance of a number comes alive in a spatial configuration, children learn about the power of symbols, in relation to numbers. In this way they become familiar with the deep roots of their culture and with concepts that are central to the comprehension of mathematics.

Weaving and Mathematics

Yet another activity basic to the Andean way of life further stimulates mathematical thinking. As I observed the Chillihuani weavers throughout the years of my research, I realized that perhaps more than any other activity the art of weaving, combined with spinning and warping, gives rise to higher mathematical capacities in children, especially with regard to geometry and trigonometry.

The weaving of textiles is an ancient craft in the Andes and has been one of the most important art forms for the last 5,000 years, predating the arrival of the Incas by millennia. Rebecca Stone-Miller discovered that "textiles acted as a foundation for the entire aesthetic system to a degree unparalleled in other cultures of the world" (1994:13).

Weavings were among the most precious gifts for Inca royalty. Inca priestesses, called Virgins of the Sun, learned the art of weaving from the *mamakunas,* older women who were experienced weavers.[13] Although in Inca times both men and women wove, women were considered most accomplished in this art form, which was simultaneously, through the patterns used, a form of communication. Because of this, women have been referred to as the historians of society, perpetuating symbols in intricate designs from one generation to the next. (See Silverblatt 1978.) Unfortunately, the conquest of Peru destroyed much of the knowledge about Inca culture, including many of its weavings. The meanings of many designs can no longer be interpreted. In traditional villages, people continue to weave complex patterns, and children learn from their mothers, grandmothers, and other knowledgeable women about this ancient craft and art form.

A series of tasks must be performed before weaving can occur. Animals are shorn during the rainy season, when the weather is warmest. Youngsters help shear the animals and wash the wool, which is either left in the color of the animals' fleece — white, black, gray, and different shades of brown — or dyed with a variety of naturally occurring colors or synthetic colors bought

FIGURE 4.3. Adolescent girls, like other villagers, like to spin wherever they go.

or bartered in the valley towns. Dyeing can be done before or after the fleece is spun into thread.[14]

Spinning occupies both sexes and all ages. At around six years of age, children receive a small wooden spindle (*k'anti; huso,* Sp.).[15] As soon as they get the hang of it, they consider spinning a pleasant pastime. People spin while talking to one another, walking, or taking a break from doing other chores (Figure 4.3).

One day, as I walked with the healer Juan Mamani to a far sector of the village to see a patient, he proudly explained, spinning as we walked, "We people of the high *puna* are never idle. Whenever we don't work, we spin. We only give up spinning when we are ready to die."

Children are not taught to spin or weave. Rather, they observe family members who have mastered these crafts and imitate them directly, or they try to find their own special way of spinning wool and weaving cloth (Figure 4.4).

When it comes to weaving, it is amazing to see the contrast between the extremely simple tools used in this art and the masterfully woven cloth that flows from the hands of the weavers. The tools consist of the loom, heddle, wooden poles, stakes, and the *tullu ruki,* made from the femur bones of camelids and used to press down the threads that are woven through the warp. Only men use vertical looms with pedals, but there are few in Chillihuani. Women use the backstrap loom, the body loom, and the four-stake ground

FIGURE 4.4. Regardless of age and sex, everyone watches intently as weavers do their work.

loom. In order to weave simple bands, children often just put a nail into the earth and attach the threads.

At an advanced stage of weaving, a good knowledge of warping is required. The same process of warping applies to every type of loom. It consists of "winding the threads in a figure eight manner around two stakes. This results in a cross of threads and the elaboration of two sheds; one called the heddle shed and the other the stick shed. A second pole is placed horizontally to the vertically aligned warp threads and loops are placed around each thread, thereby creating a four selvage fabric" (Silverman 1995:10–11). In order to do the warping correctly, children must know the pattern they want to weave and be familiar with the weaving process.[16]

Weaving is performed by working the heddle to alternately raise and lower the various colored sets of threads.[17] It takes many years for young girls to achieve mastery in this craft. A few boys also weave, but boys are mainly occupied making ropes and slings, which also require considerable manual dexterity and concentration (Figure 4.5).

Slings (*warak'a* or *sojana*) are made from the wool of alpacas and llamas. They are braided in such a way that a cradle forms in the center to hold the stone that will be hurled into the distance. (See Cahlander, Zorn, and Rowe 1980 for a detailed description of sling braiding.) Slings used in dances and ceremonies come with all kinds of ornaments such as pompons, tassels, and fringes. The sling of the Andean herder serves a variety of purposes. It is used to retrieve stray animals and to keep wild animals away. Herders make their slings roar by swinging them ferociously over their heads, frightening off foxes, condors, and other predators that can be killed with a stone from the sling. In a metaphorical sense, a sling swung in the direction of an oncoming storm is used to chase away the hail. Slings also serve in mock battles and dances (Bolin 1998). During Inca times the *warak'a* was one of the chief hunting weapons and was also an Inca insignia (Rowe 1963:217). (See Figure 4.6.)

Braiding slings and making ropes for a variety of purposes introduces boys to techniques that require visual acuity and dexterity as well as an understanding of spatial configurations. Boys and adult men also weave their black pants and belts, such as the festive *kantunka,* which has much colorful wool attached, plain ponchos, and blankets. They also knit complex designs into their colorful caps with earflaps (*ch'ullu*).

Women weave skirts (*polleras*); small jackets for women and men (*haguna*); shawls (*llikllas*); ponchos; small blankets (*unkuñas*); small bags to carry *coca* leaves and money (*ch'uspas*); bags that are larger than *ch'uspas* made from llama or alpaca wool (*wayaqa; talega,* Sp.); and blankets of all

FIGURE 4.5. Concentration shows on their faces as girls weave belts and boys braid slings. Adults, including the author, look on. Except for rubber sandals and girls' hats, all clothes are self-made.

FIGURE 4.6. Incas used slings (*warak'a*) on many occasions. Here they chase away sickness and disease (Guamán Poma de Ayala [1615] 1980:226).

FIGURE 4.7. All work is interrupted to observe one of the herders' cherished animals.

sizes.[18] People prefer to weave in the hot sun, which stretches the wool and results in a tighter cloth. Figure 4.7 shows some of the clothes they weave.

This is not an exhaustive account of weaving, but I want to provide some background for analyzing how weaving can predispose children to a good understanding of mathematical concepts, while also helping to develop great manual dexterity and good eye-hand coordination.[19]

Children learn to weave in stages.[20] When my godchildren Anali and Luzwilma were eight and nine years old, they had set up a loom just by putting a nail in the ground, and they proudly showed me how they had advanced in the weaving of narrow strips of cloth, called *senq'apa*. This task requires knowledge of simple patterns, good manual dexterity, and the ability to concentrate for longer periods of time. At this stage children still count the threads to make sure that the pattern will turn out correctly. At ages twelve and thirteen, Anali and Luzwilma have reached the *chumpi* stage, where they make belts.[21] The loom is set up in the same way as for the *senq'apa* stage, but wider, and at the *chumpi* stage the girls no longer count the threads one by one. They know how to arrange and pick the threads in such a way that they can perceive at a glance how many threads they must pick at any time to achieve the desired pattern. As children learn to separate sets of threads of various colors, they create a variety of geometric figures—squares, rectangles, triangles, diamonds, zigzag lines, etc. But they not only deal with figures that are contained in themselves; they also must learn to recognize which threads pertain to certain figures and which overlap these figures as they become part of a larger design. Children know the extent to which they can be innovative without putting a pattern out of its cultural context.

Throughout their youth, children observe adult weavers who have reached the *awana* stage, in which they produce *llikllas,* ponchos, carrying cloths, etc. Anali and Luzwilma are not yet at that stage, but they have learned much by observing their mother and aunts, who are accomplished weavers and proceed from both sides of the warp with astonishing speed and agility. These weavers do not use patterns to weave motifs into cloth. As is true for the *chumpi* stage, the patterns arise as a visual construct in the mind of a weaver is projected onto the warp. This visual construct seems to be tuned to the tasks of the fingers, which apparently know what to do without receiving instructions from the weaver. Thus, the Chillihuani weavers can explain the precise steps that must be taken to get the loom set up, but they cannot explain the complex steps of the weaving process. It seems that they follow a visual image that takes shape as their fingers do what is necessary to bring the image to the warp. Rebecca Stone-Miller discovered that weavers "used highly developed powers of visualization, making use of what is known as eidetic thinking (as opposed to verbal or written information), to maintain a visual image of the final product while weaving under confusing perceptual situations" (1994:20). For non-weavers, this is difficult to imagine. Yet the act of typing is quite similar, in that long-time practice can erase our conscious knowledge of the positions of the letters on the keyboard. Nevertheless, the fingers quickly find the keys. Only when the typists become aware of a mistake do they stop and look at the keyboard.[22]

In Chillihuani and other Andean communities, two weaving techniques are widely used. These are *iskaymanta* (*iskay* means two) and *kinsamanta* (*kinsa* means three). The *iskaymanta* weaving technique uses two contrasting colors to produce motifs that appear on only one side of the cloth. The *kinsamanta* technique, on the other hand, uses two contrasting colors plus white, producing motifs in reverse on both sides of the cloth. Gregoria, the wife of the healer Modesto Quispe, explained that other colors are also involved but they merely accompany the main colors.

As weavers work intricate motifs into cloth, they are concerned with symmetry in a variety of ways. Most Chillihuani weavings have a line crossing through the middle of the textile, referred to as *sonqo* (heart). When children become acquainted with the symmetry of their geometric motifs and that of the entire pattern that appears on the cloth, they are exposed to a complex exercise in geometry. In fact, mathematician Hermann Weyl asserts that "one can hardly overestimate the depth of geometric imagination and inventiveness reflected in these patterns. Their construction is far from being mathematically trivial. The art of ornament contains in implicit form the oldest piece of higher mathematics known to us" (1952:103; Figure 4.8).

Weaving activities in both *iskaymanta* and *kinsamanta* expose the weaver directly to numbers, sets of numbers, geometric configurations, symmetry, asymmetry, and perhaps, as Silverman (1995:44) and others have suggested, to the notion of space/time that was such an intricate part of Inca ideology and left traces among present-day Quechua Indians.[23] Weaving certainly fosters an understanding of spatial relationships.

The question of whether the motifs woven in cloth constitute a means of communication is debated. Yet as one passes time in the Andes, one recognizes that weaving has significance within the cultural and socioeconomic context of Andean society, where it not only remains an important craft and art form, but it also communicates ideas that people within the same village or region understand. Thus, people's familiarity with visual images and the ease with which they discuss their meanings support the idea that the motifs have been and still are a means of communication.[24]

Since "individual weavers can never be separated from the socio-cultural context in which they create" (Stone-Miller 1994:23), weaving also unites in solidarity the people who understand the ideological themes expressed in the motifs. From a young age children fashion them with pride and feel a strong connection with both the master weavers they observe and also with their Inca ancestors who devised the motifs—which, in their abstraction, may well have represented the key ideas and values of their society.

Here it is beneficial to speculate on whether certain elements of Inca culture that have survived in remote regions influence the Quechua people's mathematical logic and perception. We know that the Incas used arithmetic in many ways. They had the decimal system, and they devised solar and lunar calendars. They worked with an intriguing device called a *khipu* (also spelled *quipu*), and organized their cities according to the *ceque* system. *Khipus* are knotted string devices that consist of a thick cord to which thinner cords of various colors and sizes are attached. Each cord contains knots arranged at different distances and in varying clusters. The Incas used them to keep records, through a *khipukamayuq*, the "keeper of the *khipu*." "The *khipus* are said to have been used to record both quantitative data as well as information concerning genealogies, histories, and other types of narrative accounts" (Urton 1997:178). Marcia and Robert Ascher, in their book *Mathematics of the*

FIGURE 4.8. Virtually all Chillihuani weavings are Inca designs.

Incas: Code of the Quipu ([1981] 1997), recount that Cieza de León, a Spanish soldier who entered Peru only fifteen years after the conquest, attributed the highly organized system of the Inca rulers to the use of the *khipu*. He noted that the Incas used the *khipus* to take census and to record the output of gold mines, the composition of workforces, the amount and kinds of tribute, the contents of storehouses—down to the last sandal, everything was recorded on the *khipus*. Garcilaso de la Vega, the son of an Inca princess and a Spanish conquistador, also remembers from his youth that the Incas knew much about arithmetic ([1609] 1966, Volume 1:124). They were capable of counting every-thing—adding, subtracting, and multiplying—using knots on strings of dif-ferent colors. The Chillihuani herders say that their grandfathers still used *khipus* with strings of many colors—black, red, yellow, and green—to keep count of animals, agricultural products, and other things. Unfortunately, the elders of today were too young at the time to learn how to use them. They recall that these devices had to be burned, and none are left in the village.

But it is not only the *khipu* that puzzles investigators as to the mathematics used. The Inca *ceque* system is equally intriguing and also points to a system of numbers and organizational principles that differs from what is known in Western society. The *ceque* system is a system of imaginary lines (*ceques*) that radiate from the temple of the sun in Cuzco. Groups of sacred sites (*hua-cas,* also spelled *wakas*) were lined up on the *ceques,* whose maintenance and worship was assigned to certain groups of people (Zuidema 1964). In his in-tensive studies, Brian Bauer suggests that "the *ceque* system is perhaps the most complex ritual system to be recorded during the Early Conquest period of the Americas" (1998:9). Although the *ceque* system as it existed in pre-Columbian times is no longer in place, some villages still show certain basic divisions. Thus, Chillihuani is divided into four sectors (*suyus*),[25] as was the Inca city of Cuzco.

More research is required to better understand Andean logic as it is ex-pressed in weavings, *khipus,* the *ceque* system, mathematics, and general as-tronomical calculations, and to determine the extent to which these ways of thinking are still extant among people in remote regions of the Andes.

In conclusion, this chapter has been an attempt to define the activities and ideological trends in the lives of Chillihuani children that contribute to learn-ing and especially stimulate their understanding of mathematics. Society pro-vides a solid basis for learning, as youngsters are left to develop skills at their own pace without being pressured, since age is not a measure for achieve-ment. Children are also free from the pressure of competition, since the com-petitive attitude is seldom seen and never appreciated. On the other hand,

FIGURE 4.9. In Chillihuani, the girls are as eager to play soccer as the boys.

children are responsible and like a challenge. They give their personal best without setting themselves above others. They enjoy math and other subject areas without wondering whether they must beat their schoolmates in order not to feel inferior. Children do so well in math given the above and because their participation in all facets of life, especially their many complex activities, gives rise to a good understanding of mathematical concepts.

The reason why there are no gender differences in the comprehension of and love for math is not difficult to detect. Boys and girls are treated with the same respect, and there is virtually no gender distinction in the way they play and work (Figure 4.9). Given this situation, both genders develop similar mental capacities that translate into equal performance at math and other subject areas.

As children become initiated into rituals and ceremonies in the course of a fiesta (see Chapter 5), even more opportunities to develop abstract reasoning and organizational talents arise. Another window opens into a rich array of symbols and metaphors that makes children aware of their place in the cosmos.

Rituals and Ceremonies on Top of the World

Rituals and ceremonies are significant aspects of Andean culture. They are believed to be as important to the well-being of people, animals, and all of nature as are pastoral and agricultural activities. Rituals carry deep-seated values of Andean society that are not easily understood by outsiders. I agree with Victor Turner (1969:11), who said that in order to perceive the underlying meaning of rituals, "one must try to discover how the indigenous people themselves feel and think about their own rituals."[1]

Certain details in the performance of rituals differ between villages and even among families of the same village. The deeper meaning is, however, very much the same, and its central elements persist throughout the high Andes of southern Peru.

As soon as a child is conscious of his surroundings, he becomes acquainted with the rituals practiced within the family. It is not only during fiestas that they are performed. Because the Andean people do not separate the secular from the sacred, many everyday events, such as giving a plate of soup to a family member or providing a needy neighbor with a handful of potatoes, take the form of a ritual performed with elegance and devotion.

Children observe rituals at home and in the community from earliest childhood and thus gain a thorough understanding of their meanings and purposes as they grow up. This facilitates a smooth transition from observer to participant. Yet youngsters may only take a leading role in a ritual performance when they have reached a good understanding of its significance. Children's help, however, is much appreciated at any age, as they assist their families in activities such as preparing festive meals, collecting ingredients for an offering, and marking animals.

The people of Chillihuani perform rituals at the family and community level throughout the year and on specific days during major fiestas. With ceremonies and horse races, July 25 and 26 are dedicated to the Fiesta de Santiago. Santiago is the village saint who was introduced by the Spanish conquerors. But below the Christian icon of Santiago, the herders recall their powerful thunder god as they hear the roaring noise of horses' hooves echo along the highest racetracks in the world. (See Bolin 1998, Chapter 10.)

July 28 is another significant fiesta, officially Peru's Day of Independence. This event is also marked by ancient ideology, as male and female hierarchies reminiscent of Inca times engage in parallel rituals of respect in the four corners of the village plaza (Bolin 1998, Chapter 11).

More festive occasions occur in the month of August. The Andean people believe that throughout this month the earth opens and offerings are brought to Pachamama, the Apus, and other deities. Male llamas and alpacas are honored on August 1, and so are the deities that protect them. These festivities and some other minor fiestas have great significance for the people of Chillihuani.

Pukllay—An Ancient Way to Play and Celebrate

Of all the fiestas, the most cherished is the ancient Pukllay, celebrated during the raining season.[2] The herders assert that Pukllay was already important in Inca and pre-Inca times. During this fiesta, the deities are implored to grant fertility to alpacas and llamas, to the land, and to the young people. The ceremonies center on respect, solidarity, youth, health, fertility, and well-being for all. Children and adolescents are actively engaged throughout this festivity, which lasts eight days. During this time *enqa*, the vital energy and fertilizing power that pervades all life, must be replenished.

In February of 1999 I followed the invitation of the healer Modesto Quispe to spend the Pukllay festivities with him and his family close to the permanent snow. This was an excellent opportunity to observe his children's initiation into diverse ritual events.

In the haze of the morning, mounted on his white horse, Modesto arrives at the house of the healer Juan Mamani, close to the village center where I have stayed for some time and where I have celebrated Pukllay in the past. With my gear on the back of his horse, we start the long ascent to the *suyu* Llaqto, which at almost 5,000 meters above sea level is one of the highest inhabited regions on earth. Hoping that the slight drizzle will not give way to a torrential rain, we follow the horse on the narrow wet path that leads to Llaqto. The steep slopes are waterlogged; every so often we climb across piles of freshly accumulated earth and rocks caused by landslides (Figure 5.1).

As we walk along a path still free from debris, the horse stops abruptly and rises on its hind legs, emitting shrill sounds. Its eyes filled with terror, the frightened animal races off the path and gallops down the steep meadow toward the rushing Chillihuani River. I look around but cannot see anything that could have put the horse into such precipitate action. Modesto calmly explains that "horses know when waterlogged earth is ready to move. They recognize dangerously unstable terrain as they hear noises we cannot perceive."

FIGURE 5.1. One of the many landslides that obstruct the paths in Chillihuani.

We continue on our way. The horse has calmed down and joins us as we cross a narrow bridge made of branches and earth that spans the river. On the other side, the rain has washed away the path. We climb uphill through the rubble and rivulets that crisscross the steep terrain. In the afternoon we reach the house, where Salvador Illatinco Chino lives with his wife and their two sons. Salvador's brother Ricardo, who has been elected community president, his wife, and their youngest child Alan have come from their small adobe home, which clings to a precipitous hill in the sector Chullu, to meet us here. Since landslides are frequent in Chullu, we could not follow Ricardo's invitation to visit his family. Knowing better than anyone else which parts of the terrain are still relatively stable, they decided to meet us at their brother's house. "We are so happy that you came to the high sector Llaqto to celebrate Pukllay," they say with welcoming smiles, greeting us in a loose embrace.

The steaming-hot soup that is ready to be served is welcomed by everyone. Then we talk about the great fiesta. Nine-year-old Armando, an intelligent and precocious child, plays the Pukllay melody on his flute, following the footsteps of his talented older brother Filomeno (Figure 5.2).

All men play the flute during this fiesta, at home and also on the high places between the *suyus*. Young women and girls sing ancient songs and invent new lyrics to fit the Pukllay tune. Today Filomeno and his fiancé Nibis get ready to walk to a distant place where young people from the four *suyus* will meet to discuss the organization of the dances to be held throughout the village during this eight-day festivity. As they leave the house, lightning flashes through the sky, followed by deafening thunder and hail. The ferocious wind causes the doors to rattle. But the tormenting weather does not deter the young people from taking the long hike. Nor do they consider waiting until the storm has subsided. They must be at their designated meeting place on time.

After the rainstorm has passed, we must continue our ascent in order to reach the homesteads of Modesto's family in daylight. But we cannot advance fast on the slippery waterlogged ground, and it is almost dark when we cross the last bridge, made of branches, earth, and stones and spanning a turbulent stream. Such bridges are hazardous during the raining season. Several people and animals have already died in the roaring muddy rivers this year, and the raining season is still in full swing.

The landscape becomes more barren and majestic as we ascend. Large spectacular rocks look as though they were carved, projecting an almost surrealistic image. The mineral content of the streams, springs, and rivulets adds various shades of red, yellow, and brown to the rocky outcrops, the earth, and the water, contrasting sharply with the snow-covered peaks in the dis-

FIGURE 5.2. Nine-year-old Armando is an accomplished flute player.

tance. This landscape—colorful and bizarre—is alive and central to myths and legends of times long gone (Bolin 1998:163).

In the distance we see the house where Modesto lives with his wife Gregoria, her sister Jovita, and his children Luzwilma and Anali. Both Modesto's and Gregoria's mothers also live with this family. Shortly thereafter we arrive at the house of Modesto's son Juan Braulio and his wife Asunta. Their three children—Tomás (eight), Hipólito (six), and Marcos (four)—come to greet us. At age four Marcos still wears the *phalika,* a cloth wrapped around his waist and held in place by a woven belt. Since Inca times this kind of clothing has been worn by both girls and boys until about six years of age. Marcos is barefoot. His little hands are icy-cold, but the smile on his face hides any discomfort he may be experiencing. He and his brothers are thrilled that his grandpa brought a visitor. The family greets us warmly with a loose embrace and helps to unload the horse. Luzwilma (twelve) and my godchild Anali (eleven) appear in the distance with the family herd.

Everyone is excited about the Pukllay fiesta, which lasts for eight days. Preparations are in full swing despite this year's extreme weather conditions, which have destroyed much of the growing crops. Many alpacas and llamas have died as snow and hail covered the pastures for days. People fear that worse is yet to come when the last *chuños* stored from the previous years are eaten. But the fiesta *must* take place. Without the proper rituals of respect for the divine spirits of nature, the solidarity among people and the fertility of all living beings, including the earth, will diminish. In the absence of the Pukllay rituals, it is also believed that *enqa,* the life force that animates *pacha*—the universe of space and time—will not be properly renewed.

Preparations begin days and even weeks before Pukllay. All family members cooperate as they dye and spin the wool. Children are eager to improve their skills. Weaving activities are carried out in accordance with age and sex. (See Chapter 4.)

Several days before the fiesta, Luzwilma had accompanied her parents to the district capital of Cusipata to get some of the ingredients required for the delicious meal, called *t'inpu* in Quechua and *pochero* in Spanish. Like other children around twelve years of age, Luzwilma learns to barter in town. In former years, she and her parents carried items to the valley that they produced in their own village—potatoes, *chuño,* and other Andean tubers such as *oqa, ulluku,* and *maswa,* as well as medicinal herbs, alpaca fleece, and some *ch'arki* (dried meat). Given bad harvests in recent years, however, the family could only take medicinal herbs and alpaca fleece to exchange in the valley. The ingredients that do not grow and cannot be produced in Chillihuani but are needed for the cherished *t'inpu* meal are maize, yucca, sweet potatoes, carrots, onions, apples, cabbage, garlic, salt, and pepper. Some families take woven ponchos, woven carrying cloths, and *ch'uspas* (small bags to carry *coca* leaves, money, and other small items) to Cusipata in exchange for food items and to get an extra portion of maize to prepare *chicha* (maize beer).[3] Luzwilma and Anali have been observing *chicha* making for several years and know the procedure, but mother is still the head of this ceremony and the girls assist her.

Coca leaves and other ritual items must also be bartered or bought in the valley towns. They are needed to assure that the ceremonies proceed properly. Families who do not own a horse or donkey must carry the goods on their backs up and down the mountains as far as thirty-one kilometers from their homes. Children learn from a young age to pack items into their *q'eperinas* and carry them over long distances.

Early in the morning, a few days before the festivities start, Don Modesto walked with his daughters and two older grandsons to the four cardinal directions to collect water from several springs for the ceremony called Ch'allaska.[4] The herders agree that in order to assure effective rituals, the water must be gathered before the sun rises. Should the sun witness how the water is collected, misfortune would come upon the animals and their owners. I assume that in accordance with ancient beliefs, the water to be offered to the gods must be virgin and may not be exposed to the fertilizing powers of the sun's rays.

For more than a week the children have been busy collecting the sacred *phallcha* flowers (genus *Gentiana*) in the highest regions of the village close to the permanent snow. Without these flowers, which are symbols of fertility, the rituals for the animals cannot take place. *Phallcha* flowers bloom between December and February. They come in different colors — yellow, orange, various shades of red, white, and gray. They are considered to be female, promoting fertility. The herders believe that these flowers bloom specifically for the ritual of *phallchay* or *phallchakuy*, when their blossoms are sprinkled over the herds. The flowers remain fresh for up to three weeks if they are kept in a *lliklla* in a cool dry place.

Suyay Ch'isin — The First Night of Rituals

Much depends on rituals. They must be performed properly to be accepted by the gods, who can grant people's requests. Suyay Ch'isin is celebrated within the confines of each family, in the presence of all children. The role each child takes in the ritual performances is determined by age, experience, and understanding. Small children are observers, while older children assist their parents.

As night falls and supper is cleared away, Modesto Quispe brings small earthen jars filled with the water that was collected in the four cardinal directions from the family home. We wet our fingers in a gesture that denotes a ritual cleansing. Then Luzwilma removes the jars while her father and uncle play the sacred Pukllay *taki,* the pentatonic melody that announces a night of rituals, on their long flutes. The children hum along. This tune will accompany us to the very end of the fiesta.

The children watch in awe as their mother brings the *mama q'epe,* a bundle containing the most cherished ritual items wrapped in a finely knit ceremonial cloth, from its hiding place. Although young children witness virtually everything that happens within the household, they are not shown where the sacred bundle is kept until they have gained a full understanding of its value. Through the flickering light that emanates from a candle, they watch how their mother discloses *pukuchus* (pouches made of the skin of an alpaca fetus or any small camelid that died shortly after birth), which Gregoria fills with *coca* leaves. Gracefully and with utmost respect the *pukuchus* are circulated among the adult members, who fashion *k'intus.* Holding the *k'intus* toward the east, we blow over them in a gesture referred to as *phukuy*—asking the deities to keep the animals healthy and let them multiply. The girls are old enough to receive a small *pukuchu* and join in the honoring of the gods and spirits, but they will not chew leaves until they are about sixteen years old. The age at which children chew *coca* leaves during festivities varies.

Coca leaves are integral to all ritual offerings. The leaves were held sacred by the Incas for their medicinal and nutritional properties. They contain many important vitamins and minerals that enrich people's simple diet.[5] At the religious and social level, *coca* leaves are believed to act as an intermediary between people, animals, and their gods. They are the social cement. They create solidarity within society and tie it to the ancestors and to the cosmic powers in the universe. *Coca* leaves also function in economic transactions, serving as a standardized unit for barter, purchase, and sale. The herders stress that these leaves are always used to invite the spirits when political issues are at stake, in order to avoid negative thoughts and bad language. Unfortunately, it is becoming increasingly difficult for the indigenous people to buy or barter *coca* leaves, given the variety of misconceptions about this plant.[6] Historian and film producer Alan Ereira remarked in his 1991 film *From the Heart of the World* that the *coca* leaf and cocaine are as different as rye bread and rye whiskey.

Modesto's mother now opens an earthen container, referred to as an *urpu*. The first cup of *chicha*—*ñawin aqha* (the eye of the *chicha*)—is tossed toward the east for the deities that are honored this night. As the *chicha* flows into *keros* (vase-shaped containers) and *purus* (gourds from tropical regions used as drinking vessels in rituals), we pour some drops on the ground in honor of Pachamama, the great Earth Mother and principal deity of Andean religion. We sprinkle some of the precious liquid between thumb and forefinger into the air in honor of the mountain gods, the god of thunder, and other deities that protect and bring about fertility. Then the adults drink *chicha* and the children drink herbal tea.

Now the healer spreads out the ritual cloth that contains the sacred objects and serves as an altar. He places two *enqaychu* on the blanket facing east. *Enqaychu,* sometimes called *illa* or *khuya rumi,* are small, fine-grained stones, usually granite, that resemble alpacas, llamas, or sheep. They come in different shades, from white to grayish, brownish, and black. The shapes of these stones resemble, more or less closely, the animals they are supposed to represent. There is general agreement among herders that they contain the most life force (*enqa*) in the form of fertilizing power when left in their natural states, but they are sometimes modified to resemble more closely the image of a respective animal. Under no circumstances may *enqaychu* be bought or exchanged (Bolin 1998:37). They are the most sacred items of all the powerful objects used. Believed to incorporate the spirit of animals, they can communicate with the deities on the animals' behalf (Bolin 2004). *Enqaychu* contain *enqa*—life force and fertilizing power—which must be replenished during this ceremony in order for the animals to remain healthy and multiply. These sacred stones normally may not be seen by anyone outside the family.[7]

The candlelight reveals the concentration on the faces of the people. Through the *enqaychu,* people manifest their wishes to the deities while focusing deeply on their requests. The power of thought or mental power has been significant to the Andean people since pre-Columbian times. Already children know about the power of the mind and the importance of deep concentration.

In the high Andes, virtually every ritual activity takes place facing east. East is the direction where the sun rises, where light, warmth, and the sun's fertilizing power are reborn each day. The east is associated with birth, youth, health, and a fresh beginning. It also signifies luck and success.

Facing east, the *enqaychu* watch as the offering to the deities takes shape throughout the night. The healer begins by placing a sheet of paper on top of the *unkuña* that rests on the ritual cloth. He adds a handful of dark red carnation blossoms for Pachamama and the Apus and some white carnation blossoms for Illapa or Qhaqya, the thunder god. Throughout the night we fashion *k'intus* for these deities and spirits of nature, not one of whom may be forgotten. The children learn the names of Pachamama's daughters, which are specific places such as fields and meadows. They hear the names of every sacred mountain peak, lake, creek, and other landmark as far as the eye can see. Special sacred places beyond the horizon, such as Apu Salcantay and the large mountain lake Sibina, are also honored and appeased. All receive recognition with a *coca k'intu* and are asked in return to watch out for the animals and their owners. Many other ingredients are added to the offering — the seeds of *coca* plants in even numbers up to twelve, thin gold- and silver-colored paper (*qori libro* and *qolqe libro*), and threads of gold- and silver-colored yarn (*qori lazo* and *qolqe lazo*), all of which symbolize prosperity. Colored beans (*wayruru*) and *qañiwa* (*Chenopodium pallidicaule*), a cereal consisting of many tiny grains symbolizing countless alpacas and llamas, are placed on the offering. Garbanzos (*Cicer arietinum,* chickpeas), nutritious yellow fruits with bulky husks, are added, as well as incense, the smell of which enchants the deities, as does the taste of sweets. Body parts of llamas and alpacas and some pure fat from their chests (*untu*) enrich the offering. (See also Randall 1987:72–73.) The healer asserts that each part stands as a symbol for the entire animal.[8]

Modesto sprinkles alcohol onto the four corners of the *unkuña,* on which the offering rests, and folds it in such a way that two ears form to mark its head, which always points east. Small seashells filled with alcohol make the rounds. We offer libations and proceed to drink in honor of the deities, the animals, and all the people present. The children carefully watch the light that emanates from the candles, from time to time placing new candles close to the offering so their parents can see in the otherwise pitch-dark night.

The gift for the deities is ready. Modesto carries it into the dark, rainy night followed by Luzwilma and Anali, who are initiated into the sacred act of burning it in the *q'oyana* (or *markachana*), a small depression in the wall of the *muyukancha* (sacred corral). There he unwraps the *unkuña* and places the offering within the white paper into the fire. It is not easy to get it to burn in the open corral, but finally the flames devour it and the smoke rises into the air to feed the spirits that descend to consume it.

The girls are relieved when they witness later in the night that the ashes are white and smooth; this means that the deities have received the gift with pleasure. Dark ashes and rough debris, on the other hand, mean that it has been rejected and the year to come will be a difficult one. Whenever this occurs, another offering is brought in the hope of modifying the outcome. If it is accepted, the coming year is believed to be intermediate. The children beam with pride after their initiation into this sacred, prestigious ritual, which recognizes their important role in the economic and spiritual welfare of the family. They know that fertility rituals are of the utmost significance in terms of the fertility of the land, the flocks, and the people. All are interconnected, and the continuation of life itself is believed to depend on them. For this reason, the rituals are performed with great care in the hope that the herds will flourish or at least remain stable and the harvests of potatoes and other Andean tubers will be good, so people will not go hungry. Yet despite hard work and age-old precautions, weather conditions can destroy all the fruit of people's labor and even the hope for survival.[9]

The effects of the El Niño phenomenon that started in 1997 and lasted through 1998 did much damage to animals and crops. In many areas torrential rains washed the crops from their steep beds into the rivers. The few potatoes that were harvested rotted on the *ichu* grass where they had been placed for the freeze-drying process. The normally icy nights in the month of June were not cold enough in 1998 to freeze the potatoes, and the rains did not allow for the drying process to take place. Many alpacas, llamas, and sheep died from diseases or were carried away by landslides and the turbulent Chillihuani River. Then, between October 1998 and the end of January 1999, usually the height of the raining season, drought conditions caused the vegetation to dry up. After the end of January, torrential rains poured from the sky, turning to snow in higher regions. La Niña had arrived with great force, wiping out the harvests for the second year in a row as hailstorms spread a solid carpet of ice on top of the snow, suffocating the plants. One-third of the herds perished from lack of pasture, exposure, and disease (Bolin 1999). For this reason, most of the herders had not had meat in a long time. Now, in February 1999, they need some meat for the fiesta, and above all they believe that the great Apu Ausangate, protector of all animals, must receive the most significant offering—the spirit of a llama or alpaca.

On the second day of Pukllay, early in the morning, all of the family members assemble for a ceremony called *arpay,* where one of the older llamas is offered to the great Apu Ausangate. They take their hats off in honor of the animal and the Apu. Blowing *k'intus* toward the east, they implore the snow-covered mountain deity to return the spirit of this animal in the form of a newborn and to let the herd multiply. The animal dies quickly, with its head cradled in the lap of its owner. As the spirit of the llama reaches the Apu, it stops moving its limbs. (See Bolin 1998:53–56.)

The children stand by quietly with tears in their eyes. They hope that Apu Ausangate will reciprocate so this animal can be reborn; perhaps many more llamas will arise from this gift to the great mountain god who receives the first blood that gushes forth. The children help as every single part of the animal is used; nothing may be wasted.[10]

Now it is time to honor and appease Pachamama and the thunder god Illapa on the potato fields in the distance. In an effort to minimize the risks of crop destruction, families plant their potatoes in various small fields, at different altitudes with a variety of microclimates. From the healers' houses we must descend to get to places where planting is possible. The children know precisely where their fields are located and lead the way. The crop on the first field we reach has been suffocated by a thick cover of snow and ice. Frozen potato leaves lie lifeless on the ground. Everyone looks concerned and blows *k'intus* for the deities, whispering their requests for a better crop the next year.

My companions are sad, but there is still hope that the lower-lying fields have produced at least a half-decent crop. We walk for hours on the waterlogged ground. Finally, we arrive at two of the family fields. Early potatoes (*maway papa*) were planted here. Given normal conditions they could serve the family in mid-February during the Pukllay fiesta. But the fields are drenched in water; snow still clings to some places and hail has previously choked the plants.

We blow *k'intus* in honor of Pachamama's daughters — the fields we are standing on — and ask them to grant us at least some potatoes. Luzwilma and Anali follow the gestures of their father and dig into the ground. They pull out small, half-rotten tubers. But in the end they find some potatoes that can still be eaten. "This is enough for a meal," Anali says with a faint smile and a tinge of hope in her voice. The others remain silent. The healer knows that given last year's crop failure, which required that virtually all *chuño* and *moraya*[11] stored from earlier years had to be eaten, the destruction of another crop would mean intense hunger. For families who own few or no animals that can be eaten or exchanged for other goods in the valley, crop failure in two consecutive years can mean starvation unless other villagers can help. But now all families have only the bare minimum on which to survive, and some are already very hungry.

The children stare at the ground in desperation, suppressing tears. Their father tries to comfort them: "Let's take the potatoes home, so we can cook a meal." But behind his attempt to cheer the children is a deep concern. What will his family, this village, and other high-altitude villages do this year until the next harvest in 2000? What will happen if another crop is destroyed or if there is no crop at all anymore?[12] Worse, there will be no seed potatoes to plant in July and August.[13]

Modesto Quispe and his family have a fair number of alpacas and llamas, but many of the young animals and their mothers have died from starvation and disease during the last two years. No more harvests and the death of so many animals could mean the end of the herding way of life. But where are people to go? There is no unoccupied land for them in the valleys, and subsistence herders have no money to buy land. There are few jobs in the cities.

Crop failure and hunger lead to disease. Modesto and his son Juan Braulio are two of the five healers of Chillihuani. They and the other three healers in the village have been extremely busy trying to cure the many patients who have become sick due to poor nutrition and constant hunger. Now the herbal medicine they have collected throughout the year is used up. Some herbs can be found below the snow line and at lower altitudes, but the search for those is time-consuming and dangerous given the water-logged earth that is prone to landslides.

We arrive at the adobe house of the healer Juan Braulio. His wife, Asunta, Hipólito, and Marcos greet us at the door. Asunta looks at the small bag of potatoes we bring along. No words are exchanged. Everyone knows what is happening. Even small children know what it means when crops are destroyed and animals are dying. The realities of life cannot be hidden from their eyes.

But this is Pukllay, an ancient festivity in honor of the gods, who are asked to protect the herds, the fields, and the people. At this occasion everyone must be generous, eat and drink well, affirm solidarity among people, and express respect for all life. This was so in Inca times (Zuidema 1982:20, quoting Cobo), and it still holds true today. Joy and exuberance must be generated during Pukllay, because the year to come is believed to be a mirror image of this festivity. The positive energy generated throughout the fiesta must last until the next celebration, when the rituals will again replenish *enqa,* the all-sustaining life force and fertilizing power.

We join Asunta in the kitchen. She animates the children to sing the Pukllay tune. They make up the lyrics as they sing along. Everyone joins, inventing funny stories to match the tune while busily helping to peel the few potatoes they brought for the festive meal. Then Asunta talks about the next day's events, when the young animals will be marked; she tells us about Tusuna Q'asa Pata, the dances on the mountaintops where the young people meet. Pukllay is not a time for sadness; the fiesta must go on, the gods must be honored, and the people must unite.

Asunta has exchanged some goods with family and *compadres,* and I brought various ingredients from the valley, so there is enough for the *t'inpu,* the most delicious meal of the year. To the potatoes we excavated she adds alpaca meat, *chuño, moraya, oqa, ulluku,* and *maswa* from previous years, in addition to maize, rice, onions, carrots, cabbage, salt, and pepper from the valley. She could not afford the other ingredients normally used, such as yucca, sweet potatoes, green chili, and apples. Soon Asunta ladles the meal into plates and Juan Braulio offers one to each person. As we eat the delicious meal no one talks; everyone appreciates the food on this special celebration, hoping it will last throughout the eight days of the fiesta.

Asunta has set aside several bowls of the precious meal for members of the extended family, *compadres,* neighbors, and friends, some of who live many kilometers away. She asks the children to carry these tokens of love and friendship to the respective families, wishing them health, happiness, and prosperity for the year to come.

Children from other parts of the village bring food to the Quispe family. Some of these children are hungry; yet they share their food on this special day and bring their good wishes for the coming year. A few young visitors only have *chuño* soup, without other ingredients, to offer. They could not harvest early potatoes, and they have no other produce to barter in exchange for products from the valley. The situation is especially severe where adult family members are sick or have died. Other community members can help at times, but they too must struggle to survive. These are difficult times, when people's survival is at stake, but this does not deter them from being as generous as they can afford to be. The children are excited that they share food with others, and everyone hopes that this custom of generosity and reciprocity will never have to die.

Drenched from rain and sleet, Anali, Luzwilma, and the two older boys arrive back home just before dark. The fire in the earthen stove that is lit only to cook meals has died down. Icy gusts of wind blow through every crack of the adobe house. The light of the candle is fading as the children huddle under their alpaca furs to warm up and get a good sleep before next day's Ch'allaska, celebrated in honor of the llamas and alpacas and the deities that protect them. On this day, too, the children have important roles to play.

Ch'allaska in Honor of the Family Herds

The children are up early in the morning while the snow still covers the landscape. With their bare feet in rubber sandals, they are ready to assist in the preparations for Ch'allaska, a ceremony held in honor of the deities who protect the llamas and alpacas; they are implored to keep the animals healthy and let them multiply. The animals are also honored in their own right.

Don Modesto, the leader of today's ceremonies, brings the sacred bundle from its hiding place, opens it carefully, and removes a *pukuchu*. Four-year-old Marcos follows his grandpa to the rustic stone wall outside the house, where the venerated mountain peaks, among them the great Apu Ausangate, line the horizon to the east. Every day of the year, and most of all during festivities, this mountain receives offerings of respect from near and far.

With a curious look on his face, Marcos asks his grandpa if he can see the contents of the *pukuchu*. Don Modesto selects three perfect *coca* leaves from the bag and shows his grandson how to fashion a *k'intu*, with the green side of the leaves facing up. Then, with deep respect, Modesto holds the *k'intu* toward the east, pronouncing solemnly, "Apu Ausangate, please accept this offering and in return let this day be bright and bless this year with a healthy herd." Little Marcos listens attentively, imitating his grandfather's gestures (Figure 5.3). Then both stand in silence, listening to the wind that carries their wishes to the mountain god. Satisfied, Modesto returns to his house, his little grandson holding his hand, smiling happily.

Inside the house, the women prepare the ritual objects and other items for the Ch'allaska ceremony. Luzwilma and Anali have already taken the animals to the sacred corral where the celebration takes place. As the family walks toward the corral, the sun appears from behind thick clouds. Millions of raindrops clinging to the vegetation sparkle in its warming rays. As was true for the rituals of the previous night, the ceremony of Ch'allaska is also restricted to the family circle. I am considered part of the family, since I am godmother to Anali and thus spiritual kin to the whole extended family.

We arrive in the sacred corral and take a seat on a long stone bench with our backs against a stone wall, facing the *mesarumi* (altar of stone) and the east where the sun rises. Gregoria places the bundle with the ritual items on the *mesa*, while Jovita puts a container filled with *chicha* beside it. The mothers of Gregoria and Modesto and Juan Braulio's wife Asunta add the drinking vessels. The children bring the piles of *phallcha* flowers they have collected and place them on the ground east of the *mesa*. These flowers symbolize fertility and are believed to transmit this quality to the herd animals. Anali adds carnation blossoms, while Mama Asunta puts *coca* leaves into each of the *pukuchus*.

The ceremony starts. Don Modesto takes a seat behind the *mesarumi*. As *madrina* I am to sit between him and his son Juan Braulio. His three grand-

FIGURE 5.3. Four-year-old Marcos imitates his grandpa, who offers a *coca k'intu* to the mountain deities asking for a successful day.

FIGURE 5.4. The Ch'allaska ritual is performed in honor of the deities, who are requested to protect the herds.

sons stand close by. The grandmothers, mothers, and daughters sit in a straight line to the right of the *mesarumi*. The whole group faces east, toward the great Apu Ausangate (Figure 5.4).

Modesto opens the bundle with the sacred items and gives a *pukuchu* to each adult. Luzwilma, Anali, and Tomás are old enough to receive a small pouch. Filled with *coca* leaves, these *pukuchus* make the rounds many times in a gesture of reciprocity, solidarity, and respect. The little boys imitate our gestures as we fashion *k'intus* in honor of the deities, asking in return for a healthy herd.

The offering is prepared in the same way as in the previous night. The *enqaychu* sit in the middle of the *mesarumi* facing east. In the outdoors, though, they are unwrapped only for an instant while being sprayed with *chicha*. It would not be safe to expose them to the multitude of energies out in nature.

Women pour *chicha* into *keros* (cups) and *purus* (gourds). Every adult sprinkles some of the precious liquid on the four corners of the *mesarumi* and toward the mountains in the distance. Modesto pours several drops on the four corners of the folded gift for the deities to drink while the children carefully observe every move and learn to recognize the sacred spaces between the four corners, which confirm their supernatural power. (See also Sharon 1978:41–42.) As we lift our glasses, the children, who drink water, wait respectfully until the elders begin to drink. The intense and focused thoughts and wishes for good health, prosperity, and well-being for all people, animals, and the gods are believed to replenish *enqa,* the life force and fertilizing power of the *enqaychu.*

Don Modesto takes the folded *unkuña,* hands a small bottle with some kerosene to his eight-year-old grandson Tomás, and walks with him to the eastern corner of the corral to burn the offering in the *q'oyana* that is carved into a stone wall. Tomás hands his grandfather fine kindling and the bottle; Modesto pours some of the kerosene onto the kindling and lights it. As the fire starts to burn, he takes off the *unkuña* and places the offering, wrapped in paper, into the flames. Both leave the site in respect for the deities, who need to be undisturbed while they consume the smoke emanating from the precious gift. Everyone respectfully averts their eyes.[14] As the gods receive the honors, they are asked in return to provide plenty of food for the herds and to protect them from predators, the rushing rivers, lightning, and disease.

The Quechua people believe that the Earth Mother, mountains, lakes, springs, rocks, and other aspects of nature live and feel in very similar ways to humans. They need food and drink, love and consideration. During a ceremony, children learn to give to the deities the best they can offer in return for the care and protection of their cherished animals. In a full cycle of reciprocity, this symbolic giving and taking assures that a balance is maintained within the cosmos. In their efforts not to forget any part of the life-giving nature in their rituals, children gain from an early age a holistic view of their universe, in which all parts interconnect in an eternal cycle of giving and receiving.

The gods have been honored and their needs are satisfied. Now it is time to shower the animals with water, *chicha,* and *phallcha* flowers in appreciation of their help and companionship. During these rituals and in prayers alpacas and llamas are respectfully addressed as *chushllu* and *chullumpi.* Gregoria starts by holding a gourd in her right hand. She fills it with water that was collected from several springs in the four directions. White maize, finely ground, is added to the water in the hope that many alpacas will be white and have fine wool. Then Jovita fills the gourd in Gregoria's left hand with *chicha,* adding *qañiwa* seeds so the animals in the flocks will multiply to become as numerous as the many tiny seeds.[15] The grandmothers first take their turns, and then the mothers and children spray the animals with water and *chicha.*

Now the children take handfuls of the sacred *phallcha* flowers and throw them over the animals in a ritual called *phallchay,* or *phallchakuy.* In an animated tone of voice they call out, "My animals, please flourish and multiply just like the *phallcha* flowers right by the snow!"[16]

FIGURE 5.5. Children learn to mark young animals with red paint during Ch'allaska.

Young alpacas and llamas born since last year's Pukllay are now marked in the ritual *irpay* using *lloqhetaku*, red earth from Puno on Lake Titicaca, mixed with water and *chicha*. Marking is done to distinguish one's own animals from the herds of other families and also to indicate which animals belong to what family members. Markings with red ochre are said to also avert disasters such as disease and accidents (Figure 5.5).[17]

It is not easy to separate the young camelids from the herd, since the animals feel nervous in the sacred corral, where they assemble only three or four times a year for ceremonial purposes. This time of year is also mating season, when males must be kept apart from females and young in the corral. But now they are together for the duration of the ceremony, causing quite a commotion. Anali, Luzwilma, and Tomás, who have been herding for several years, help to retrieve the young animals and lead them to the *mesarumi*. All five children assist to keep the camelids in place. Mama Asunta explains to little Marcos how to hold a young alpaca by the tail so it remains still without being hurt. He learns fast. The other children have already gained expertise in handling their llamas and alpacas. While Asunta and the children hold onto the young animals' heads and tails, Juan Braulio takes a strand of alpaca wool, dips it into *lloqhetaku*, and marks the animals. Markings can be made either on the head, neck, back, or shoulders, or on two or three body parts in simple lines or lines that cross.

Now the firstborn offspring of two female alpacas are made to stand side by side—the female to the right, the male to the left. They are marked as one unit. While the children hold the animals in place, the boys' father paints three times around their necks, then across their backs and sides. These two young alpacas are considered newlyweds. A second "marriage" of two young camelids follows. The herders believe that the animals are proud to receive such honorable treatment.

As each marked animal is given a name, all of the family members take off their hats in respect for the animals, the deities that protect them, and the sacred corral. A young alpaca is dedicated to the children who take the herd to pasture—Luzwilma, Anali, and Tomás. One is dedicated to their *madrina*. I name my baby alpaca Yuraq Phuyu (White Cloud). "I will watch out for your little White Cloud when I take the flock to pasture," my godchild Anali tells me with a charming smile. Modesto adds, "It will not take long before you will have a herd of your own." The other family members debate, half-serious, half-joking, whether I will then leave the *hatun yachay wasi* (university) to move to *suyu* Llajto to care for my herd.[18]

The ceremony is over. Luzwilma, Anali, and Tomás open the gate and take their animals to pasture. Thick black clouds mix with the white cumulus in the sky. The thunder god makes his loud voice heard, and it starts to rain as we leave the corral. We were lucky that during the ceremony, which lasted almost four hours, it only sprinkled slightly from time to time. Now the rain pours from the sky and we hurry into the house while the three children take the animals to the high pasture.

Dancing amid Thunder and Lightning

Pukllay is a time when the dual forces of life manifest themselves in a variety of ways. We have seen that during the Suyay Ch'isin rituals, seriousness prevailed in an aura of suspense mixed with the hope that the offerings please the gods and encourage them to reciprocate. Equally serious was the sacrifice of a llama and its spirit journey to the great Apu Ausangate. The ceremony of Ch'allaska was also marked by both feelings of apprehension as well as happiness, as the animals were showered with water, *chicha,* and *phallcha* flowers.

Now, on the night of the third day of Pukllay, after the major offerings have been brought, exuberance overshadows everything else and the young people dance until Kacharpari, the good-bye ceremony on the eighth day of this fiesta. If Pukllay is a happy event, so will be the year to come.

Laughter is everywhere as children and adults dress for the dances. Some people paint their faces and hands with *llanp'u,* white powder obtained by grinding soft white stone. The herders say that *llanp'u* is like snow—it purifies everything and is also used to calm people who are stubborn or rebellious. Children and young people take advantage of the festive mood to tease and add mischievous ideas to their songs, enjoying the laughter they stimulate among their peers and adults.

In the Quispe family, four-year-old Marcos painted his cheeks with the red color from the cactus plant *ayranpu (Opuntia soehrensii Briton et Rose),* which grows at lower altitudes. He is ready to dance to the tunes played by older boys who have come to visit. Dancing is an intricate part of religious ceremonies and social events. Children join in dances soon after they have learned to walk and can keep their balance. Even while wrapped in a mother's shawl, a baby can feel the rhythmic movements of her dancing steps. Dancing is an offering of love and gratitude to the deities. "The more we dance, the happier Pachamama and the Apus will be, and the more animals and crops they will give us," children explained on various occasions (Figure 5.6).

On the fourth day of Pukllay, we are invited to the home of Salvador Illatinco Chino, his wife Justina, and their two sons, eighteen-year-old Filomeno and nine-year-old Armando. Filomeno's fiancé has helped to prepare the delicious *t'inpu* meal, which we eat in silence. Then we thank our hosts and exchange *coca* leaves, while talking about this great fiesta.

It is time to leave for Tusuna Q'asa Pata, Filomeno insists. His father assists him with his elaborate Pukllay P'acha (festive Pukllay clothes), while Justina helps Filomeno's fiancé adjust her clothes in order to look her best. On festive occasions parents always aid their children in dressing in their best attire. Even older children who know how to put on their own festive clothes are assisted by their parents. Usually fathers help their sons and mothers attend to their daughters. This ritual is also seen during weddings, when the godparents dress the newlywed couple. It is an ancient custom that symbolically indicates that children are guided and helped in their lives by parents and godparents (see Bolin 1998, Chapter 9). This gesture is also done out of respect for the person being assisted and indicates that the young people have important tasks to fulfill.[19]

Another thunderstorm is on its way. The wind increases in strength, causing the doors to swing open. Rain has been pouring down all day, erasing paths throughout the village; the ground is waterlogged and gives rise to landslides everywhere. We see the lightning flash through the sky and hear the voice of the mighty thunder god soon after. But this does not deter the three young people from undertaking a four-hour walk to one of the high moun-

FIGURE 5.6. Four-year-old Marcos has painted his face with *ayranpu*. He is in a festive mood and ready to dance.

tains between two sectors of the village, where today's dance takes place. With radiant smiles on their faces, they take their flutes, say good-bye, and hurry toward the distant mountain range.

Starting on the third day of Pukllay, a dance is scheduled each day for a different site between the four sectors of the village. On the fifth day the dance takes place on the high corridor of Oqe Q'asa Pata (the high gray gorge), at 5,000 meters above sea level, close to the homesteads of Modesto and family where I live. At this altitude rain often turns to snow, hailstorms are frequent, and this year they have obliterated all paths that lead to the high gray gorge. With Don Modesto's family, we descend a hill to get to the small bridge over a turbulent creek. Suddenly I slip and slide down the steep, wet meadow. Arriving at the bottom, I find myself as waterlogged as the mountainside itself, and my clothes feel very heavy. I must have presented an awkward picture as I took the fast way down to the bridge, since the children can hardly suppress a giggle. We all burst into laughter and I learn what people mean when they say that during the height of the rainy season clothes get wet fast but may not dry for a long time.

As we ascend to a high plateau, we see hundreds of people from the four sectors of the village dancing and playing the Pukllay melody on their flutes (Figure 5.7). We approach the *mesarumi* in the center of the dancing field where the village elders have assembled. They greet us with loose embraces, welcoming us to this sacred event. We make libations of *chicha* for Pachamama on the four corners of the stone altar and blow *k'intus* in honor of the Apus and the thunder god, asking for a safe celebration.

Lightning zigzags through the sky, followed by loud claps of thunder. Anali explains that the sling of the thunder god produces the lightning in the sky and also the thundering sounds we hear. At this altitude no one is safe from the deadly strikes of a lightning bolt, but on this day nobody seems to care. Hail falls from the sky and a torrential rain begins that will last over two hours. I put my rain cape over my cameras to keep them from drowning. As the rain continues, the water rises in the mud puddles where we stand. Yet people seem unaffected by the weather. They came to dance and play tunes on their flutes as an offering to Pachamama, the Apus, the high mountain lakes, and Illapa, whose thundering voice echoes across the mountains. Nobody would interrupt the rituals because of bad weather. Ritual is important to the spiritual and physical well-being of every person, of animals, and of the community at large.

Young adults as well as children are eager to prove to themselves that they can withstand the raging powers of the weather god. The idea of bringing a

FIGURE 5.7. Neither rain nor hail deters the adolescents and young adults from playing music and dancing in honor of the deities, thus circulating the vital energy that connects all life within the cosmos.

sacrifice to the deities and giving one's best under any circumstance is deeply engrained in the ideology of the Andean people.[20] The rain continues and so do the dances. People still arrive from near and far (Figure 5.8).

Some young people have brought a small tree from the valley. They place it in the center of the natural treeless arena and proceed to dance around it. This is a custom that has recently been introduced from the valley towns, where dancers use a hatchet to hit the tree as they dance. The couple that finally brings the tree down has the obligation to sponsor next year's dance. Here in the heights of Chillihuani, this practice is new. The *cargo* system has thus far not been part of the ancient fiesta of Pukllay.[21]

Finally the rain stops. Black clouds at the horizon give way to a blue sky partially covered with white cirrus clouds. A rainbow within an almost surrealistic beam of light arches through the sky in the west. Then night starts to fall, but the dancers continue to tread the earth, their honored Pachamama, while playing ancient pentatonic tunes on their flutes that echo through the mountain world.

We leave Oqe Q'asa Pata and descend in the dark. The simple bridge made of wood, stones, and adobe that we had crossed earlier is now waterlogged and starting to disintegrate. We hurry across it and up the steep hill to the family house. It is amazing how surefooted the children are in their simple rubber sandals. Mama Asunta had returned earlier to cook potato soup for all of us. While we eat, we warm our freezing bodies close to the fire. But it dies down before our clothes are dry. Dried animal dung is scarce and cannot be used to keep the fire going after the meal is cooked. There are no trees or bushes at this altitude and no money to buy any other fuel. But we are in luck. This is Pukllay, when the festivities continue and so do the dances to honor the gods and keep warm. We hear the sound of flutes in the distance, and soon a group of people enters to sing, dance, play their instruments, and bring their hosts good wishes for health, youth, happiness, and prosperity. Small children on their alpaca furs are moved close to the earthen stove, which is still warm. The youngest ones sleep through the music, singing, and tapping of feet on the earthen floor. Some young children watch while their older siblings join in the dancing, singing, and laughing that lasts into the early morning hours.

Some of the songs of Pukllay are legends believed to date from the time of the Incas and their pre-Inca ancestors. A song in honor of the sacred Apu Ausangate is followed by a song about the downfall of Tawantinsuyu, the Inca Empire. This song is sung with deep emotion. The sadness in the voices of the

FIGURE 5.8. Young children observe all rituals and activities, ready to take over when they reach adolescence.

people and gestures of despair indicate that they still suffer from the brutal conquest and destruction of a great empire. But most of the songs are happy, and many are invented to tease others.

In the days that follow, adolescents and young adults participate in all of the dances on the high places between the four *suyus*. They visit elders, family, neighbors, and friends in the night, bringing joy, exuberance, and laughter. As was true in Inca times, regardless of exhaustion from lack of sleep or little food these young people demonstrate their strength, their willingness to bring sacrifices for the deities, and their wish to foster solidarity throughout the village. They continue until Kacharpari, or farewell, on the eighth day of Pukllay. During the dances between the *suyus,* young people often fall in love and may find a partner for life (see Bolin 1998, Chapter 7).

The festivity of Pukllay, more than any other fiesta, reminds the people of Chillihuani of their roots and of their place in the cosmos. From a young age children are exposed to the calm yet intensely focused activities throughout the ritual performances. Adolescents begin to understand the spiritual and symbolic connotations of existence in a delicate, fragile environment that demands that respect and consideration be given to all links that make up the intricate web of life.

CHAPTER 6

Adolescence: A Time of Many Challenges

The sun has set and it is icy-cold as the wind blows from the snowy mountain peaks on this July 27, the middle of the Andean winter. But the adolescent girls and boys seem unaffected by the weather and the many hours they have spent traversing the precipitous landscape in search of branches, roots, and dry grass for the bonfire to be lit tonight, the eve of Peru's Independence Day. Their smiles reveal the excitement of this fiesta, which starts tonight and will last through tomorrow. In Peru's towns and cities, Independence Day celebrations on July 28 are marked by political speeches. Here in the heights of Chillihuani, rituals of respect between elders and adolescents or young adults are filled with metaphors from pre-Columbian times (see also Bolin 1998, Chapter 11).

As I share the young people's excitement for this significant event, we begin to talk about their roles in the fiesta. "We are responsible for the bonfire — it must burn throughout this night's celebrations," a young man states proudly. One of the girls adds, "We know where to find the high grass and twigs even after night has fallen." It is not easy to find vegetal material to burn, given its scarcity and the fact that the few trees and bushes that grow at this altitude may not be cut. But despite certain difficulties, these adolescents seem to enjoy both the freedom to be out in the night and the trust their elders place in them to carry out important tasks for tonight's and tomorrow's celebrations.

At the brink of dusk, children appear from all directions holding up paper lanterns they have made with different shapes and colors. They circle the lower plaza several times and then join the adults in the upper plaza, where all assemble around the bonfire. During this night and part of the next day, under the leadership of their teachers, the children will listen to speeches about historical events and will sing, dance, and recite poetry.

But on July 28, after the official program organized by the teachers, the villagers begin to celebrate in a fashion reminiscent of their Inca ancestors. Four groups of people assemble in the four corners of the plaza. Two of the groups consist of male elders, who line up facing the young men, while the other two groups are female elders, facing the young women. The adolescents and young adults tend to their elders with food, drink, and courtesies. These rituals carry much symbolic significance, as was true in Inca times, when parallel and equal hierarchies of men and women were at the base of a well-functioning empire. A good balance of power between male and female members of society as it existed in Inca times persists in Chillihuani and is reflected in the rituals of this fiesta.[1]

As adolescents and young adults participate in the rituals in which they give respect to their elders and, in return, receive respect, they learn much about the deep-seated metaphors of their society. Four hierarchies of male and female elders assemble in the four corners of the plaza. They sprinkle *chicha* on the four corners of the table and mark four points over a glass of *trago* (sugarcane alcohol). Using symbols from the past, they recall the times when Tawantinsuyu, the four quarters of the Inca Empire, were alive and well. (See Bolin 1998, Chapter 11.)

Throughout this and other fiestas — and in everyday life — children enjoy the adolescent stage of their lives. Whether they are preparing for a village fiesta, carrying out their daily chores, attending school, dancing throughout the night, or engaging in sacred rituals, they feel good about their participation and the help they provide for their families and the community. As is true for adolescents everywhere, young people of this herding society are eager to associate with other adolescents. They meet during fiestas at designated places within the four sectors of their widely dispersed village to sing and dance to *wayñus* (also spelled *huaynos*), love songs from Inca times, and other melodies. These Quechua songs express much sensitivity and a strong sense of longing. As the young people fall in love, they also become more conscious of the clothes they wear, and one can see them sit for hours weaving intricate and colorful designs into their festive attire (Figure 6.1; see also Bolin 1998, Chapter 7). But most young people fall in love when they take their animals to pasture in the high mountains, close to the sacred Apus, in the wilds of the *puna*.[2]

Feelings of love and romance are strong among the young herders. But contrary to the situation in most "modern" societies, where beauty and status are often the deciding factors for choosing a partner, the young herders believe that partners must be able to work well together. A mate also must be responsible, cheerful, and compassionate.

It is not easy to find a partner from within the four sectors of the village, since only cousins of the fourth degree, i.e., the offspring of great-great-grandparents, may marry. Young people marry on average between eighteen and thirty years of age, and it does not matter if the bride is several years younger or older than the groom.

Adolescence is also the time when young people indulge in joking and

FIGURE 6.1. Adolescents in their best clothes meet at the fiesta to sing, play music, and dance. Libia's niece, tucked in a *q'epirina,* sleeps through the dancing.

teasing (*chansanakuy*), which becomes an intriguing part of social life. As they joke with one another, they sometimes take on opposing roles, such as "man and woman," or joke in a stylized form using wit and eloquence. Although *chansanakuy* can continue for hours, the participants always maintain respect. This joking game is not known to escalate to insults or fights as has been reported from other parts of the Andes (Allen 1988:210–212).[3]

As they reflect on their own lives, elders remember their adolescent years as very exciting. They say that by that stage in their lives they had learned much about their culture, about subsistence, and about their place in the community. These observations agree with those of other investigators of Andean societies. Thus, William Stein, in his research in Hualcán, department of Ancash, states, "By the time of adolescence, children have learned almost all adult activities and skills through observation and participation according to their abilities" (1961:161). Adolescence is a stage in children's lives where rights and responsibilities merge, bringing about exciting challenges. One Chillihuani elder remembered adolescence with the words, "This was the time when we felt strong—both men and women felt strong—we did not feel the cold, hunger, or fatigue. Adolescence was even better in my youth than it is now. There was more vigor, more production, better food, and more enthusiasm for the culture."

It is significant to note that adolescents not only gain confidence by knowing how to do the required work, but they also take pride in the work itself. Since Inca times, work has defined people and given them prestige. An existence without work is inconceivable for the Andean people, who hope for fertile fields and healthy flocks even in *hanan pacha,* the Andean heaven. Work keeps young people occupied, presents a challenge, and instills a sense of self-esteem and responsibility. Thus, when adolescents take animals to pasture, they take responsibility for the family flock; when they participate in an organized group, they take responsibility for the community. Although work well done is appreciated by family and community, no one is overly praised to the detriment of others. A handshake or a glance of appraisal is enough to make children feel good about themselves.

Adolescent boys and girls in Chillihuani are healthy and full of energy as long as the harvests provide enough food for the community. Crops are grown without the use of pesticides or any other chemicals. There is little pollution in the air, and children get much physical exercise in their precipitous world. Given the adolescents' youthful energy, elders have known since time immemorial how to channel this energy into the right direction. Young people are challenged by and entertained with meaningful activities relating to subsistence, village organization, ritual activities, and the arts. Moral values are emphasized on many occasions, and respect is central to all interactions. There are no juvenile delinquents in this village, and there is no crime apart from a few minor thefts, mainly of small animals and food plants.

Thus, adolescents do not present a problem to their community. On the contrary, they are indispensable to its proper functioning. Given considerable concern about adolescents in villages and towns in mainstream society, and especially in the major cities of Peru and other parts of the world, I became interested not only in exploring how Chillihuani adolescents keep out of mischief, but also how these children feel about themselves throughout this stage in their lives.

Gender Complementarity and Cooperation

As was discussed in previous chapters, in Chillihuani boys and girls are treated much the same, sharing many activities and chores throughout childhood and adolescence. Only when much physical strength is warranted do males take on heavier jobs. Physical changes as they appear during adolescence do not affect children in a negative way. On the contrary, menstrual blood, for example, is seen as something positive. It is a sign of fertility; it is welcome and indicates that motherhood is on the horizon. Menstrual blood serves as a paramount offering to Pachamama, the loved and respected Earth Mother who accepts this precious gift and will reciprocate in due time.[4]

Puberty rites as they were celebrated in Inca times no longer exist in the high Andes. Among the Incas, these rites were celebrated for both boys and girls (J. Rowe 1963:283–284). At the age of about fourteen, Inca boys were initiated once a year in the ceremony of *waracikoy*, while a girl's maturity ceremony, called *quicuchicuy*, was held at her first menstruation (J. Rowe 1963:284). Although these ceremonies no longer exist, female fertility and procreative powers are still considered to be of utmost importance in the sustenance of life. The importance of the female element in the Andes is also stressed by Jesús Cavero Carrasco in his research on the social function of the *qarawi*, a pre-Hispanic kind of singing that survived the conquest. He notes that the *qarawi* is sung only by women, because they "symbolize life, fertility and happiness. They give children for agricultural activities, for weddings, to herd the flocks, to construct houses, to work the earth, etc. . . . Without women no activity is possible, there would be no procreation. Therefore Pachamama and the Apus are happier when women sing the *qarawi*" (1985:237).

Andean women are believed to have a special bond with Pachamama. They like to be close to this great deity and prefer to sit directly on the earth — whereas men sit on chairs and benches. For both sexes it is an honor to work with Pachamama while tending the fields and cooking the food plants she provides.

Outsiders often incorrectly assert that in Quechua society men dominate. Although adult men speak up more frequently in the public arena than do women, women have the same degree of decision-making power. In some areas — household economics, for example — it exceeds that of men. Well-known Peruvian anthropologist Jorge Flores Ochoa states that "the status of the woman is never unequal to that of man; their roles complement one another harmoniously" (1988:240). Thus, children grow up in a society where respect for both genders is equally expressed.

Men and women cooperate in a variety of ways. Within families they may work side by side or assign themselves specific tasks, but these tasks are not strictly reserved for any gender. It is also interesting to observe that adolescent boys are very supportive of elder women. This kind of cooperation across gender and generation lines was clearly displayed on one of my arrivals in Chillihuani. Several male elders came to the valley to meet me and the visitors I had brought. Upon arrival in Chillihuani, not knowing that the women had prepared a program of songs, dances, and speeches, the male elders right away started to entertain us. The women were displeased and demanded their share of the time. Several adolescent boys supported the women's request and cooperated with them throughout the performance.

The above incident, where disagreements arose between the sexes, was exceptional, since in Chillihuani there is little, if any, competition between women and men. The competitive element is equally limited among and between children and adolescents. Although adolescents with certain talents, such as weaving skills, or excellence in singing and dancing, are appreciated, praise is never given openly, and I have never heard any child or adult brag about his/her skills and achievements. Not even after the spectacular horse races during the Fiesta de Santiago is a winner declared. To honor one person to the detriment of other participants is considered disrespectful. With or without certain talents, all children are important to family and community and are allowed to participate in a wide range of activities as long as they show good behavior and are eager to work and help others. Physical beauty is not considered an important attribute either, and physical or mental disabilities are generally no reason for being shut out from community activities. Thus, Andrés, who had the ulcers of leishmaniasis[5] across half of his face, participated in public activities with other young people of the village. I have never heard anyone comment on his unsightly face or the possibility that this condition could be contagious. Telesfora is blind in one eye. Yet she is charming and self-confident and happily married to a young man of the village. Little Lydia broke her hip in a fall from a cliff. The family had no means to consult a physician at the time of the accident. Now her body is slightly distorted; she limps and cannot run as fast as the other children. Still, she is a well-liked playmate. We have seen earlier that Teresa's child Luisita has been disabled since her birth in a hospital in Cuzco. Now, at the age of five, she can neither walk, talk, nor eat by herself. But no one asks questions regarding her disabilities and everyone treats her with kindness and respect. Even participation in the prestigious *cargo* system, which requires knowledge in a variety of areas, has not been refused to a couple of young herders who are a little slower than others. They are still welcome to participate in the religious and political affairs of the community in accordance with their abilities. The herders are very sensitive not only with regard to their own feelings, but also the feelings of others. This sensitivity is strongly expressed in adolescents and has often been remarked upon by teachers and the village nurse.

Fights among adolescents are rare, as they are among villagers of any age. I have never witnessed a fight myself, except for a few short scuffles when people have raised their voices during debates of the village council or when a child disobeyed. Disharmony does not continue for long, as efforts to reconcile for the sake of family and community are quite successful.

An Adolescence Free from Stress?

Since a wide range of physical and mental conditions is accepted without prejudice, adolescents experience a low level of social stress. People's behavior is predictable, emotions do not run wild, and aggression is kept to a minimum.

Stress is, however, not altogether absent. In previous chapters it was shown that stress does affect the lives of children to various degrees, starting at birth. Death or sickness in the family, a bad harvest, or extreme poverty can cause much grief. School can be a stress factor as well, especially for children who live far away, and daily activities can be stressful, such as herding on the high pastures, where children may meet with thunderstorms, lightning, wild animals, and thieves who come from afar. Some children are afraid of malevolent spirits that may be present in strong winds or linger in the landscape.

Physical and emotional stress is also experienced during difficult economic times, when adults and adolescents alike must leave the village to find short- or long-term work in valley towns, cities, or jungle regions (mostly Quillabamba and Madre de Dios). Often these people fall ill or die due to disease, overwork, and malnutrition. Most devastating for the herders is the fact that outside their milieu, they are often not treated with respect.

Libia and Telesfora had this experience at age fifteen, when they worked on plantations close to a jungle town in order to make money and get to know different places. Their parents had tried to convince the girls that given a decent harvest, it was not necessary to work outside the village. Yet the girls insisted on leaving. After two months they returned exhausted and with serious insect bites all over their legs. It took the healer Juan Mamani several months to cure them. After this episode, both girls were happy to be back in their high mountain village, where they are loved and respected. While living away from the village, they did not receive the respect they have always taken for granted, and Libia admitted with a shy smile that it had been very difficult to be at the whim of an employer who did not care about their feelings, health, or well-being. Other adolescents and adults have also commented on the lack of respect they had to face outside their village. Unfortunately, many misinformed outsiders look down on highland Indians, believing that the simple living conditions in their villages are a reflection of their overall abilities.

Other Chillihuani residents forced to leave the village in search of work are always happy to return to their families and their community. In several other Andean villages, however, I was informed that young men and women who left the village to work elsewhere returned with a different mindset and a more aggressive attitude. Aggression has not been a problem in Chillihuani thus far, but I have observed that some of the adolescents who have worked outside their village smile with a grain of doubt as their parents engage in ancient rituals and ceremonies that differ from the more Christian rituals in valley towns. When I first met seventeen-year-old Irme, who was born in Chillihuani but lived with an uncle in the city for much of her youth, she felt ashamed about the extremely simple living conditions of the highland herders. Several years later, as she came to the village to attend a fiesta, she had changed her opinion and admitted that she no longer hides her origin, but proudly participates in ancient rituals.

It is important to note that the stress factors discussed above are experienced by people of all ages and are not reserved for the adolescent stage of life. Stress rooted specifically in adolescence is rare, except for a few instances such as the occasional rejection by a young boy or girl who has a different partner for life in mind, or an unplanned pregnancy. A degree of promiscuity is not frowned upon until marriage or a firm commitment has been made. Yet until recently it was not considered proper for a young girl to have a baby without being married. Within the last decade, this outlook has changed, and the few young girls who did get pregnant without a firm commitment now raise their offspring with pride, whereas formerly the grandparents would have taken care of the child.

Today, as in the past, youngsters in Chillihuani enjoy the rights and freedom that come with adolescence in addition to the increasing responsibilities vis-à-vis family and community. Although in this highly egalitarian society the socioeconomic situation is similar throughout the village, people exhibit different personality traits and perform tasks in slightly different ways. But in order to cope with environmental givens and the demands of society, certain personality traits are shared by virtually all individuals. Thus, people of all ages, but especially adolescents and young adults, are brave and resilient as they withstand the vagaries of the climate and the challenges of the fields, pastures, and fiestas, when nothing may deter them from doing their part. They are resourceful given the scarcity of food and other things necessary for survival. They are self-reliant, especially in situations where professional help is not available, such as during difficult births and severe illness. They are always respectful and lend a helping hand. A combination of these personality traits results in the indomitable character for which the people in the

FIGURE 6.2. Children and adolescents learn about the art of healing.

heights of the Andes are known. Despite their sensitive feelings, they seldom cry and hardly ever show signs of depression. Even when times of hunger make life miserable, they continue to sing during fiestas and may dance right into their graves.

Approaching Adult Life

Throughout infancy and adolescence, Chillihuani children learn about adult activities by observing their elders in the private and public arenas. By the time they reach adulthood, they have learned to make a living for themselves and their families. They know society's moral, religious, and cultural values and are eager to continue on a path to become appreciated members of the community. This also requires that they learn about common health problems and how to cure a variety of ailments. In the absence of a physician or the money to go to a hospital when severe illness strikes, they must do the best they can under the circumstances. Young boys and girls who are interested in becoming healers observe the senior healers of the village, who take them to visit patients and allow them to observe the preparation of herbal medicine (Figure 6.2).

Formerly, shamans, or *paqo,* also referred to as *altomesayoq* (the shaman with the high table) and *pampamesayoq* (the shaman with the low table), were famous for their knowledge. In recent years, fewer of these specialists are working in the village, and the tasks of healing fall largely on the shoulders of village healers (*hampiq; curanderos,* Sp.) or health promoters (*promotores de salud,* Sp.). These healers attend workshops in the valley on first aid and hygiene but still retain some shamanistic beliefs, especially with regard to psychological healing.[6] Although Chillihuani's health station has finally received a nurse, the widely dispersed nature of the homesteads requires that healers be present in different regions of the village and that all adolescents learn as much as they can to be able to cure themselves and their families.

Before reaching adulthood, adolescents have also achieved a good understanding of the workings of their community and how to participate in its proper functioning. According to law, young people reach adulthood at eighteen years of age. Already, around the age of sixteen, they can join organized groups that work at the community level. This kind of participation prepares them to eventually take over the affairs of the community and to learn about its ties with the district and province. Participation in these groups is without remuneration, but it fosters experience and additional esteem within the community. Foremost is the adherence to moral values that young people see displayed by their elders and also learn through the deeds of notable personages. Among the historical models they esteem is José de San Martin, the only one of the freedom fighters who gave valid recognition to the indigenous population, confirmed the legality of the *ayllus,* and acknowledged Quechua as an official language. Most admired are the noble Tupac Amaru II and his wife Micaela Bastides, who were of Inca descent. Tupac Amaru II, a widely respected merchant, was born in Tinta, in the Vilcanota Valley, not far from the district of Cusipata. In the early 1780s, together with his wife, he led an ill-fated revolution against the outrageous exploitation of the native people by colonial authorities. Contrary to their intentions, though, the uprising turned into the most severe rebellion of the colonial epoch (Sallnow 1991:285), in which both native people and the Spanish suffered devastating losses. On March 18, 1781, Tupac Amaru, his family, and other leaders were executed most cruelly in Hawkaypata, the large central plaza of Cuzco (see also Fisher 1966 and Bolin 1998:4). Tupac Amaru and Micaela Bastides live on as heroes in the minds of the people of the high Andes, and youngsters strive to be fair and honorable like them.

In an effort to meet other young people and learn about the workings of a group, adolescents start by joining the *qhaswa,* an organization named for an Inca folk dance that was created a few decades ago. Given the dispersed nature of the four sectors of Chillihuani, it is not easy for young people to encounter others, except during major fiestas. The *qhaswa* has successfully provided a setting for young men and women to meet once a week and exchange ideas, participate in recreational activities, play music, sing, and dance. The organization is similar in its structure to that of the village, with a president, vice president, secretary, treasurer, and members at large. Thus, as young people get to know one another, they simultaneously learn about the formal tasks involved in an organization.

The next stage that prepares youngsters to serve the community starts when they are fourteen years or older, at which time they begin to participate in an honorary, unpaid career called the *cargo* system. This career involves an apprenticeship in three stages:

1. A young man becomes a member of a group of eight *arariwas,* who have been elected in a village meeting for a one-year term. *Arariwas* are responsible for the crops within village boundaries. During the day they guard them from straying animals, and at night they sometimes burn offerings for Pachamama, the Apus, and the god of thunder, asking for plentiful harvests. Burning also keeps the frost from attacking the tender plants. Once a year the municipal representative walks with the eight *arariwas* through the potato fields of the village, calling the spirits of the plants and asking the deities to protect them.

2. Having completed the rather demanding task of *arariwa,* a young man seventeen years or older, together with three others, is elected by the villagers to become a *cobrador* (Sp.), a *cargo* he will also hold for one year. In this role he performs rituals of respect, serves food and drink to the village authorities, and assists them in every way while learning their tasks. He also collects dues and cleans the offices of the village council.

3. The following year, sometimes several years later, the third stage of a young man's apprenticeship starts when he is elected to work as a deputy (*agente policial,* Sp.) for one year. Deputies meet every Saturday and are largely responsible for maintaining law and order within the community. *Arariwas, cobradores,* and *agentes policiales* are all included in the Quechua term *chaskiqkuna.* All young men are elected to these groups one after the other in due time; no one is left out. When they have successfully completed their apprenticeship, they can be elected to the village council as secretary, treasurer, district attorney, or member at large; later they can assume the post of deputy governor, municipal representative, justice of the peace, vice president, or village president. All positions in the *cargo* system are unpaid (Figure 6.3).

FIGURE 6.3. Two of Chillihuani's adolescents begin their apprenticeships under the guidance of village elders.

Women also participate by advising their husbands, sons, or partners in all related matters and providing food and drink for the events. Given the scarcity of food, provisioning is highly regarded. Women's roles are parallel and complementary to those of men. Women are also elected to the Women's Committee, which is similarly structured with a president, vice president, secretary, treasurer, and members at large. The Women's Committee deals with issues pertaining mainly to child rearing, health, food, crafts, and animal breeding. (The Women's Committee has been inactive for several years due to the crop destruction that started in 1997.)

Another organization in which adolescents and young adults participate is that of parent representatives (*padres de familia,* Sp.). Both men and women discuss their roles as parents and participate with teachers in issues pertaining to the school. A group of eight parent representatives fill the appropriate roles of president, vice president, etc. In addition, four young assistants (*tenientes escolares,* Sp.) take care of the schoolhouse, cleaning it and observing the tasks of the parent representatives. They also serve them food and drink during festivities.

Rondas Campesinas: Strengthening Solidarity and Self-Defense

Adolescents who have participated in the village organizations above have gained considerable knowledge about their community. They have learned to organize, accomplish tasks in a respectful manner to the satisfaction of the village council and the villagers at large, and cooperate among themselves and with their elders. They have also been instrumental in helping curb crime within the village and beyond village boundaries. Yet until recently a few minor thefts of small animals and agricultural produce left outdoors had still occurred each year at the hands of villagers. Thieves from other regions are responsible for the theft of larger animals and produce. But since the Rondas Campesinas (Sp., autonomous communal organizations) — often referred to simply as Rondas — were established in Chillihuani in 1996, crimes have been virtually eliminated.

These new organizations have been successful in rural parts of the Andes not only in curbing crime, but also in instilling pride, a sense of responsibility, moral and cultural values, and respect within the population at large. Although these values have always been strongly expressed in Chillihuani, the Rondas did take root in this herding village as well.

I cannot discuss the entire mandate of the Rondas Campesinas in the context of this chapter, but I will highlight their central concerns, since they provide adolescents and young adults throughout rural regions with a considerable learning experience. The young people who participate make the district and province safer for everyone while also helping to solve a series of social and economic problems. Adolescents are thrilled at the prospect of joining this organization as they approach adulthood.

The idea of the Rondas Campesinas emerged in 1984–1985, in the department of Ayacucho, Peru. It was put into practice there in 1986, during the rule of president Alan Garcia, in an attempt to protect communities from terrorism. In 1995–1996, when terrorist activities had ended, this form of communal defense was established in communities across Peru.

These autonomous organizations abide by their own regulations and those of the communities in which they work.[7] They cooperate with the village councils and with other Rondas at community, district, and provincial levels. Men and women between eighteen and sixty years of age who have a good reputation, are appreciated by the community, and, in turn, respect and appreciate local customs, culture, and religion, are elected by the General Assembly of Villagers. People who are younger than eighteen can also be elected if they have established an independent household. Children, adolescents, people with disabilities, and people over sixty are considered collaborating members. They participate mainly by attending meetings. Older people are appreciated, as they bring their ideas and wisdom to the attention of the board.

The number of young *ronderos* required to make the rounds of inspection within and beyond village boundaries relates to the size of the village. Chillihuani, with its 1,600 inhabitants, has eight *ronderos* — one woman and one man in each of the four sectors of the village. Adults and adolescents, especially the young deputies (*agentes policiales*), are expected to assist the Rondas whenever need arises. People who refuse to help must pay a fine. All members work on a voluntary basis without pay.

Young *ronderos* take turns watching the community by day and night. This is necessary, since animal theft, for example, occurs most frequently at night. *Ronderos* use leather whips as weapons as they make their rounds of inspection; they communicate with other *ronderos* using whistles. They oblige people who come from outside the village boundaries to show a piece of identification. Since this law has been established, animal theft by thieves from other regions — long a serious problem — has greatly diminished. The Rondas Campesinas have the support of the whole community.[8]

These organizations, which have been established throughout rural regions, also promote the fair participation of women on the governing board and elsewhere and defend the rights of children, adolescents, and old people. They also plan to work on economically, ecologically, and culturally sustainable development in connection with state institutions. In Chillihuani, the workings of the village council and other groups have always been transparent, but villagers elsewhere declare that due to the efforts of the Rondas they are now informed about all problems in the community and the actions that are taken in an effort to bring justice.

The learning experience is considerable for adolescents and young adults as they defend the lands of the community while respecting the physical, moral, and cultural integrity of its inhabitants. They learn to peacefully solve conflicts within the community and maintain the democratic and cultural traditions of the villages. Although these goals had been in place in Chillihuani before the Rondas took effect, this organization has brought considerable benefits there as well. Village elders tell that small thefts within the village have decreased from an average of four per year to one or none at all. More serious thefts by outsiders have also decreased and in some areas are altogether absent. These new organizations strengthen other Chillihuani youth groups (*chaskiqkuna*), protecting traditional customs, cultural values, and village solidarity, which are being threatened by the infiltration of a number of religious sects.[9] Not only neighboring villages, but also the whole region has become safer, thus benefiting the Chillihuani herders as they descend to the valley. Furthermore, the herders, who have not always received respect given their simple living conditions and adherence to tradition, are now recognized for their excellent organizational talents, hard work, and high moral values, which are all in accordance with the mandate of the Rondas Campesinas. This renewed esteem was also reflected in the election of a Chillihuani herder in 2003 to president at the level of the large province of Quispicanchis.

The above discussion reveals that given a wide variety of activities and challenges, adolescence is indeed a cherished stage in the lives of the Chillihuani children. One may ask why this trend differs so much from what we see in many "modern" societies.

After only a short time in the community, I noticed that the herders have a good understanding of human nature. The elders irradiate a spark of wisdom of the kind I have seldom seen elsewhere. Although people's worldview abounds with metaphors and much symbolic thought, they know well how to combine the spiritual with the practical everyday life. They understand the needs of people at all stages in their lives and know that adolescents and young adults must continue to give and receive respect, as they have learned since infancy. They also recognize that adolescents have an extra dose of energy that must be channeled in the right direction through meaningful tasks and exciting adventures. Elders know that young people need to live a balanced life within a predictable society where they have work, fun, and freedom and feel appreciated by family and community alike. As adolescents grow up in an egalitarian society with common values where there are models to follow and no one dominates or subjugates, they learn to coexist peacefully, allowing everyone, regardless of talents or disabilities, to feel at ease. After only a short time in Chillihuani, I began to understand what the elders mean when they say, "Our children approach adolescence and adulthood with confidence, because they are prepared for life in every way."

CHAPTER 7

Building a Society of Respect

Long before I met the Chillihuani herders I anticipated that survival in a marginal environment would require special skills and moral values promoting cooperation among people and respect for all forms of life. Before I actually lived in the highly egalitarian society of Chillihuani, however, I could not imagine that a culture where the competitive attitude is minimized would produce people who excel in so many ways. Neither could I fathom that children who learn only through observation could easily grasp complex ideas and put them into practice. Perhaps most surprising was to witness children who grow up in extreme material poverty and yet maintain a positive attitude, are enthusiastic and creative, and develop an understanding of the human condition to a degree I have not encountered elsewhere.

When I discovered that life in Chillihuani was based on respect, I began to understand how people's respectful behavior translates into cooperation, compassion, and responsibility. These attributes, in turn, allow people to create an atmosphere that is fertile for learning, sharing, and developing self-esteem. It became clear why this society functioned so well despite grinding poverty and environmental stress.

In this chapter I will place the central issues discussed throughout this book in a wider comparative and geographical framework in order to present a clearer picture of the strategies that are required to build a society in which respect is the catalyst for responsible and dignified living.

More specifically, I will try to analyze what makes Chillihuani's child-rearing strategies so effective. Given marginal living conditions, one must ask how children can have a happy childhood and an exciting adolescence and how young adults can become esteemed members of the community eager to maintain a culture of respect.

First, one may wonder whether the Chillihuani herders are basically better people than those elsewhere, with higher moral values. In this context it is interesting to consider Colin Turnbull's findings among the Mbuti pygmies of Zaire, Africa. He states, "If there is little mendacity and virtually no crime, little attachment to material wealth and great attachment to moral values, it is not because they are 'good' or consider these qualities to be virtues, but rather because this is what they have to be in order to survive" (1983a:11).

The situation in Chillihuani agrees to some extent with that observed by Turnbull in Zaire. The Andean herders may not be inherently different from people elsewhere, but it is clear that their specific behavioral norms centering on respect are necessary to make society work and assure survival. These people know that in order to live in their marginal environment, they must take good care of the earth and water, making sure not to disturb the ecosystem and the life it contains, and they must care for one another within family and community. The long-standing belief that all matter is imbued with life force or vital energy and thus requires care, respect, and compassion is still at the roots of the herders' ideology, determining their thoughts and actions.

One wonders why so many societies cannot grasp that the key to successful and sustainable living rests on respectful behavior toward *all* life. Do only those who live close to nature know that its life-sustaining powers must be met with respect and sensitivity? Among the wise societies are the Kogi from the Sierra Madre of Colombia. These people live with utter, self-imposed simplicity that enables them to focus on the issues that really matter. The Kogi know about environmental destruction and its negative impact on the perpetuation of life. They worry about the behavior of the "little brothers" (outsiders) who do not listen to the advice of the "big brothers" (the Kogi). As is true for the people of Chillihuani, the Kogi believe that only by acting responsibly can one positively influence the powers of nature, which respond by aiding in the propagation of life on earth.[1] The worldview of any exceptional society, such as that of the Kogi, differs greatly from the global mainstream ideology, which is concerned with immediate benefits regardless of long-term consequences. Wise societies know that the values that bring about a sustainable way of living based on respect must be instilled in children at a young age.

What Makes for a Happy Childhood?

As we have seen, children in Chillihuani grow up in poverty. Yet as we take a closer look at this society we realize that there are values that offset the poverty-related disadvantages. Children are raised in a permissive manner. They are loved, cuddled, fed on demand, and allowed to explore anything that does not prove dangerous or fragile. I have never seen a small child being spanked, yelled at, or treated roughly in any way. Yet children do not turn out to be spoiled. They soon learn about the behavioral norms that are accepted by family and community and demonstrated by adults and older siblings. At a young age they are introduced to the unwritten law of reciprocity, the hallmark of Andean life. This requires that respect be given and received in an eternal cycle that maintains their lives in balance.

The harmonious and predictable environment in Chillihuani is conducive to learning and creating. We have seen that children are treated with respect and allowed to develop at their own pace, largely in accordance with their inclinations. In the absence of children's songs and stories, they invent their own or add to those they hear adults sing and tell. Without premanufactured toys, children search for raw materials inside the house and out of doors, creating their own diversions and building entire miniature homesteads and irrigation works out of mud, stones, sticks, and grass.

Living in close contact with the extended family and being surrounded by the community prepares a child for the future in more ways than one. Children are not tucked away in nursery school or placed in front of a television set; they are always with a parent or older sibling. First they get to know the world by viewing it from the carrying cloth on their mother's back and later by participating in adult activities. They see community interaction from all angles. Maturity sets in early given this exposure to the manifold spheres of life.

Although these circumstances help a child become well prepared for the adult world, one might ask what is especially happy about this kind of childhood. Yet as children play and work, pride and a feeling of accomplishment show in their faces. Not only are children proud because they can help their parents and the community, but work itself carries much prestige. Since there is no strict separation, work is not looked upon as drudgery while play is considered fun. Both play and work are significant, pleasurable occupations that further knowledge and self-esteem and simultaneously sustain the family.

Apart from the high Andes, there are other societies that differentiate little between work and play and equally enjoy both spheres of activities. This worldview affects society in very different ways than does a view that strictly separates these issues. Thus, in comparing her experiences in Samoa with those in North America, Margaret Mead argues that "our children make a false set of categories, work, play, and school; work for adults, play for children's pleasure, and schools as an inexplicable nuisance with some compensations. These false distinctions are likely to produce all sorts of strange attitudes, an apathetic treatment of school which bears no known relation to life, a false dichotomy between work and play, which may result either in a dread of work as implying irksome responsibility or in a later contempt for play as childish" (1967:228). Similarly, David Lancy, in his research of the Kpelle of Liberia, states, "In many cases the transition from play work to real work is nearly seamless" (1996:89). Neither do people in the Himalayan state of Ladakh and in other remote pockets of the world distinguish between work and play.

The fact that Chillihuani children help in the struggle to make a living is much appreciated by their families. Gender is no obstacle to the performance of tasks. Although boys and girls may have preferred activities, in the absence of a brother or sister, any gender can perform virtually all work that is to be done. Neither are children pushed to perform new tasks in accordance with age. Age has seldom been recorded in the past and is not a criterion for learning a skill. Children learn new tasks "when they are ready," as the Chillihuani herders define it. Pushing a child to do something for which he or she is not ready is considered disrespectful. This flexible attitude regarding a child's gender and age avoids the kind of stress that is so prominent in Western societies, where boys and girls are expected to acquire certain skills or perform specific activities at a prescribed age.

Since the Chillihuani children learn through observation and are not actually "taught" society's life skills, manners, or beliefs, they benefit greatly from a flexible schedule for acquiring knowledge. They can take all the time they need to observe and then proceed to accomplish any new task at their convenience. This method of learning not only relieves children of stress, but also prepares them to become astute observers.

Learning through observation in a non-competitive environment has also been considered important by other societies in the acquisition of knowledge. In his research among the Kpelle of Liberia, Lancy found that "children learn what they see around them. Societies depend on this inherent desire for children to copy their elders and on the wonderful ability of the young of our species to observe, imitate and self correct" (1996:200). John Gay and Michael Cole (1967) also found that Kpelle children learn as they observe and are not punished for making mistakes but are simply told to try again. It is interesting to note that Aristotle suggested that when children "have passed their fifth birthday, they should for the next two years learn simply by observation whatever they may be required to learn" (Leach 1994:146). Learning through observation is not only advantageous to children's development, but it also facilitates child raising considerably for parents and other caregivers.

Perhaps most important in reducing stress among children is the herders' concern with maintaining an egalitarian society where no one wants to put himself above his fellow villagers. Thus, cooperation is necessary and always

welcome, while a competitive attitude does not fit into the behavioral repertoire of the herders. This does not mean that people will not give their best at
work and play. But as they create miniature homesteads and exquisite weavings, cook delicious food, or participate in a spectacular horse race on the
Fiesta de Santiago, they do not attempt to defeat others, nor do they expect
or accept much public recognition. They give their best to please the people
and the deities who witness their performances. More specifically, there is
a difference between wanting to win to be better than others and using the
"challenge" of others to give one's best. The former is a negative, aggressive
approach to competition, and the latter is a positive, constructive, develop-
mental approach. The latter is a process in which success comes from learning
something, rather than from an all-or-nothing, win-or-lose, one-shot effort.
The satisfaction is not in winning but in seeing improvement in oneself over
time.

To view excessive competitiveness as undesirable is not unique to the high
Andes. Several well-known educators and investigators (Gatto 1992, Lancy
1996, Leach 1994, Mead 1967, Turnbull 1983b, and others) deplore the highly
competitive attitude in "modern" society, which leads to problems at many
levels. Colin Turnbull regrets that in North America "even the team spirit,
so loudly touted in school athletics, is merely a more efficient way through
limited cooperation to 'beat' a greater number of people more efficiently"
(quoted in Haviland 1997:410). Turnbull's observations among the Mbuti of
Zaire are in sharp contrast to those of North America: "Mbuti children could
be seen every day playing in the *bopi,* but not once did I see a game, not one
activity that smacked of any kind of competition, except perhaps that competition that is necessary for us all to feel from time to time, competition with
our own private and personal inadequacies" (Turnbull 1983b:44).

These examples indicate that in the absence of an overly competitive environment, *all* children can become self-confident and self-reliant within an
atmosphere where they are respected and appreciated. Although Chillihuani
children work alongside and in benefit of family and community, they have
much freedom to carry out their own activities. Thus, self-reliance is further
promoted as these children range freely within the four sectors of their community and beyond to all places that can be reached on foot. This stands in
contradiction to situations that present themselves to many children in North
America. Penelope Leach states, "The child who must always wait on the
convenience and whim of an adult to take him and pick him up and make
formal arrangements for him to get together with friends, is deprived of autonomy and of confident self-reliance" (1994:151). With the increase of crime

in mainstream society, children's freedom becomes increasingly restricted to the extent where they must be constantly monitored.

Chillihuani clearly shows that a philosophy of life that lacks an aggressive, highly competitive, and self-centered attitude allows for cooperation and compassion among villagers. This, in turn, gives rise to a learning environment — at home, in the community, and in school — where children can live and learn relatively free from stress and where they excel in most unexpected ways.

Learning the Skills for Life

When the school principal of Cusipata told me that the children of the Chillihuani herders who continue schooling in the valley are always at the top of the class, I was surprised. After I visited their village and discovered the children's love for mathematics, I was puzzled. Slowly I came to grips with these issues, which seemed contradictory at the beginning. As I continued my studies and consulted the literature of learning specialists and investigators in other societies that share some of Chillihuani's concerns, I have been able to shed more light on these intriguing issues.

It is known that the ideology and lifestyle of a society influences the way children think and act. We have seen that Chillihuani's children learn a great deal within their families and their well-organized community before they start school. Traditional learning continues side by side with the four to six years of schooling in which half of Chillihuani's children are able to participate. Despite extremely simple living conditions, the range of experiences they get at home is impressive. We have seen that at a young age, children learn about horticulture and the behavior and breeding of animals. They help raise their siblings, do housework, dye wool, spin, knit, warp, and weave intricate patterns into their clothes. They know how to fashion slings and propel stones into the distance to retrieve their animals and keep predators away. Children are also initiated into the use of natural medicine and learn about medical practices that are applied during the birth process and when disease strikes. They learn to organize fiestas and *faenas* (communal work), where they cooperate with family, neighborhood, and community.

Furthermore, children's initiation into the proper and logical sequence of rituals and ceremonies takes place as soon as they comprehend the ideology that respects all life. At an early age, children learn how to express gratitude and reciprocate the favors they receive from people and the deities. They gain knowledge about ecological processes and their spiritual and symbolic connotations. We have seen that on many occasions, especially when pasturing animals and watching over the community at night, children must be responsible, brave, and self-reliant. Work carries esteem and is considered as much fun as singing, dancing, inventing songs, and reciting poems and legends from ancient times. Creative and resourceful, sensitive and compassionate, these children know the value of the help they provide for their families and the community and the importance of an ideology that honors animals, every aspect of nature, and the spiritual life within all. This vast pool of experience furthers holistic thinking, which implies that no one in the chain of life may be forgotten and that all life is connected and deserves respect. Simultaneously, children establish a wide framework of knowledge that allows them to accommodate new experiences in an organized fashion.

The above issues receive little attention in the "modern" world, where respect for *all* life is seldom considered. But in the absence of a holistic framework children are left in a vacuum, unable to coherently organize the bits and pieces of knowledge and moral values they receive. The importance of the work children do at home and in the community, if any, is also largely ignored or underrated in Western society. Prize-winning New York educator John Taylor Gatto argues that "school takes our children away from any possibility of an active role in community life — in fact it destroys communities by relegating the training of children to the hands of certified experts — and by doing so it ensures our children cannot grow up fully human" (1992:14). Gatto refers to Aristotle, who taught long ago that "without a fully active role in community life, one could not hope to become a healthy human being." Peruvian anthropologist Oscar Núñez del Prado agrees with the above investigators, advising that children in remote communities should not have to sacrifice their traditional learning by spending all their time in school (personal communication). As we have seen in Chillihuani, working within the community not only facilitates children's smooth integration into adult life but also fosters abilities, such as mathematical skills, that are important wherever the children go.

Adolescents' Integration into Adulthood

In North America and other parts of the world, adolescence is considered a rather problematic stage in life. Emotional conflict and rebellion against parental authority are believed to be at the root of the problems, making life difficult for adolescents, their parents, and society at large. Innumerable books have been written about adolescence, its problems, and possible solutions. But the situation has not changed, and neither has the belief that adolescence is a time of great stress. Given this concern in North America and other parts of the world, why is the situation so different in Chillihuani, where the herders consider adolescence to be the best time of life?

Adolescents everywhere have much in common. They experience the same physical changes, the same surge in energy, and the same need for a harmonious and supportive yet challenging and adventure-filled social environment. In Chillihuani, the precarious physical environment is offset by a social sphere with little stress where young people work together in solidarity and joking, teasing, and laughter are always tempered by respect. Challenges and adventures are built into the herder children's daily existence. As they protect their herds from predators, ride their horses across the high mountains to help someone in distress, play music on a variety of instruments, sing ancient songs, invent new ones, dance at Pukllay amid thunder and lightning, weave intricate patterns into their clothes, and learn to become outstanding orators, they experience fulfillment in many forms as their incipient talents grow to greater perfection.

I witnessed the same kind of joy and fulfillment among adolescents while doing research in Peru's jungle regions. It is impressive to see these young people's elegant demeanor, strong sense of responsibility, generosity, and bravery despite great poverty in material terms. And there are other societies in the world where adolescents are neither stressed nor in emotional turmoil. In 1925, given great concern about adolescence in the United States, Margaret Mead (1967) took the advice of her mentor Franz Boas to test on the island of Samoa the widely accepted theory that the biological changes of adolescence are accompanied by a great deal of social and psychological stress. Mead discovered that in contrast to children in the United States, Samoan children experienced a much easier transition from adolescence into adulthood. She concluded that adolescence does not have to be a time of stress and strain, but that cultural conditions make it so. She attributed a variety of social and cultural factors to a child's easy integration into adolescence, some of which are similar to those encountered in Chillihuani. Thus, as is true for the Andean herders, Samoan children accepted responsibility at an early age. Before they reached adulthood, they knew their culture and the tasks they owed society. They were not pushed to become achievers, but were allowed to accomplish tasks when they were ready, and there was very little competition.

A good understanding and peaceful coexistence both among adolescents and between adolescents and adults are also seen in some African societies, where both genders are mild-mannered and non-competitive and childhood is marked by love, permissiveness, and respect (Gordon 1992, Turnbull 1983a and 1983b, and others).

"Modern" society penalizes its children in more than one way. Many families are dysfunctional due to a lack of time for their children and a lack of harmony, shared experience, or mutual respect. Regardless of the advice of knowledgeable educators (Gatto 1992, Healy 1990, Leach 1994, and others), most children are stuck in school from nine to four and then do homework and watch television. They have little chance to participate in community work, where they could accomplish relevant projects instead of being forced to absorb bits and pieces of information in a disjointed and mainly theoretical way. Many children are not in touch with nature, which could help soothe the spirit and instill creativity (see also Nabhan and Trimble 1994), but instead are forced into constant, stressful competition. Students who are not fast enough to follow a curriculum or are not ready for it fall behind, become depressed, give up, or engage in activities that are not beneficial to themselves or society. From decades of teaching and receiving outstanding awards, educator John Taylor Gatto found that "the unlikeliest kids kept demonstrating to me at random moments so many of the hallmarks of human excellence — insight, wisdom, justice, resourcefulness, courage, originality — that I became confused" (1992:xi).

When I asked the Chillihuani herders why adolescents and young adults feel so good about themselves and are so appreciated in the community, they confided that it is because these young people give and receive respect. As children learn about respect, they learn to be honest. We have seen that honesty is paramount in Chillihuani, not only at home, but also within and beyond the community. Thus, the elders of the village council make sure that decisions are never made behind closed doors. Community members are informed about all issues. In the course of their apprenticeships, adolescents and young adults are always present at village meetings, where they learn how to serve their community and how to become models themselves. Elders also stress that their children remain honest because there is no television in their village to teach them bad manners and crime. Teachers and people from other walks of life agree that the impact of television and action games on mainstream society has been devastating, causing children to behave badly and making them dull and lazy.[2]

The Chillihuani herders are impressed by some of the advances of modern science, but they shake their heads in disbelief when they hear that in mainstream societies adolescents and young adults must deal with fierce competition, greed, large-scale unemployment, crime, and an immensely uneven distribution of wealth. They cannot comprehend that people with vision are unable to put their societies on the right track. Nor can they understand why any society would penalize its children by offering them television programs, films, and video games that are violent and/or perverse, a disgrace to any society, an insult to people's intelligence, and a catalyst for crime. The elders asked me whether in efforts to avoid crime our young people protect our villages, fields, and animals as the young people do in their Andean villages.

Nor can the high-altitude herders comprehend why many "modern" societies show little concern for the future of their own children or for children elsewhere. They cannot grasp why one would poison the earth, the sacred Pachamama, or pollute the rivers and lakes. They notice that their own glaciers retreat, that mountain lakes and meadows dry up, inflicting suffering to all life. Global warming has hit the Andean region with great force.[3] It is difficult and embarrassing as one tries to answer their questions.

What Does It Take to Build a Society of Respect?

We need not travel as far as Chillihuani to discover how to build a society of respect. At least some of the building blocks that are required exist virtually everywhere. In every society certain individuals or groups of people are hard at work to instill respect, the catalyst to creating a dignified society. It is amazing to see that even in chaotic places, we find people who know how to respect *all* life. These people are models as they show compassion toward others, and like the Chillihuani herders they understand human nature and provide avenues for young children and adolescents to develop their personalities. These model adults allow children to discover new challenges for themselves and show them how to make life worthwhile for others. Jane Goodall's Roots and Shoots program is a prime example for such admirable efforts, and there are many more. Why do these positive attempts not draw wider circles to encompass society as a whole, to create a situation that is beneficial to all life within the cosmos, as is the case in Chillihuani?

In order to find the appropriate answers, we cannot directly compare the societies that have a vision with those in which things go wrong. There are a great many variables such as population size, degree of urbanization, remoteness from nature, and differing worldviews. Yet despite these variations, there are some issues that any society can address in an attempt to bring about positive change. A consideration of these issues will be decisive as to whether children must grow up in a society in trouble or can live in a society of respect.

When children learn to show respect for *all* life and treat all aspects of nature with sensitivity, they are well on their way to creating a society of respect. As respect becomes the very nature of a child, there will be no bullying of classmates, cruelty to animals, or destruction of the environment. Instead, a child will develop a holistic view of the world, where every part is connected and worthy of being treated with decency. It should be noted that the Quechua language has no word for respect. This is because respect is expected at all times. It is part of all thought and action and is never seen in isolation.

As long as "modern" society bombards its children with contradictory signals as to honesty, morals, and compassion, however, we can only expect confusion. What responsible parents may demonstrate to their children at home often stands in sharp contrast to what these youngsters experience outside their family or get through the media. And what they are taught in school might find no complement in the home. Where are the models our children can trust? Can children look to the adult world for guidance, or are they lost in a jumble of contradictions? What kinds of models engage in large-scale corruption or promote brutality through the media? The people of Chillihuani will never be able to comprehend how a society with vision can lend a blind eye and a deaf ear to the vast amount of destructive information that is piled on impressionable youth.

Some analysts predict that dishonesty, crime, and terrorism as we see it today will continue for decades to come. This means that generations of children might never experience a calm and serene atmosphere in their own country, let alone feel the beauty and excitement of foreign countries, with their many fascinating cultural and environmental attributes.

Yet to set the "modern" world on the right track is not impossible and may not even be difficult. The herders of Chillihuani, many of whom are illiterate, have shown us that to treat *all* life with respect, sensitivity, and compassion makes all the difference in creating a dignified and sustainable society of true *Homo sapiens sapiens,* people of wisdom. This is a clear signal, one that does not cause confusion. Is this so difficult to understand for highly educated "modern" societies?

I applaud the Chillihuani herders who allow their children to grow up in a dignified society. We can only hope that these people and their culture will survive, and that the extreme weather conditions caused by global warming and the infiltration of religious sects from different parts of the "modern" world will not destroy their physical and spiritual lives. Let us hope that they will continue in their wisdom and remain models for all those who strive to build a society of respect.

Introduction

1. Carlos Monge states in his studies on acclimatization that in the Andes, "people are born, live and reproduce at altitudes up to 17,000 feet above sea level" (1953:5).

2. *Tawa* means four; *suyu* means sector or quarter, and *ntin* implies "a unit of things that are inherently complementary or indivisible" (Wright 1984:51). Chillihuani elders told me that their village is also divided into two parts or moieties. Hatun Ayllu (the big *ayllu*) includes the *suyus* Chillihuani, Llaqto, and Qayara Chimpu. Huchuy Ayllu (the small *ayllu*) consists of the *suyu* Chullu. The church of Chillihuani houses a large statue of the saint Santiago on his horse that corresponds to the Hatun Ayllu, and a small statue of a mounted Santiago that corresponds to the smaller Huchuy Ayllu.

3. Villagers built and equipped most of these structures using communal labor. The latter two were financed with the help of friends, family, Change for Children in Edmonton, Malaspina University students, the German Red Cross, and the Landkreis Böblingen in Germany.

4. *Ayllu* can be translated as any political group with a local boundary; it also refers to the kin relatives of a person (Zuidema 1973:19–20). *Ayllu* also is "the basic social group into which Andean farmers and herders have traditionally been organized" (Flannery, Marcus, and Reynolds 1989:28–29). For a more detailed discussion on the *ayllu,* see Avila 1966 and 1983; Isbell 1977; Isbell and Roncalla Fernández 1977; Poole 1984; J. Rowe 1946; and Zuidema 1977.

5. Well-known ecologist Antonio Brack Egg notes that the total area of natural pastures in the high Andes is 18,800,000 hectares, which is almost 50 percent of the Sierra (1994:108). Of this area, 20 percent (3,600,000 hectares) is classified as excellent to good; 15 percent (2,800,000) is average; and the remaining 65 percent is poor and very poor.

6. For a detailed discussion of pastoral systems, see Browman 1990; Flannery, Marcus, and Reynolds 1989; and Orlove 1977. Regarding animal diseases, see McCorkle 1988.

7. I can understand why several of my students who were able to visit Chillihuani because they were not affected by high-altitude stress became fascinated by this village. I was surprised, however, when Ludwig, Prinz von Baden, then president of the German Red Cross, and his wife Marianne, Prinzessin von Baden, referred to Chillihuani as the highlight of their trip to Peru. They left their castle in Europe to come to Peru and visit the projects supported by the Red Cross. Despite the simplest living conditions within this herding society, they hope to return.

8. This applies only to Chillihuani and perhaps to other remote regions. Leaving valuables unattended in many other places is tempting fate.

9. Juan Núñez del Prado states: "Hanaqpacha, the Andean heaven, is a place of agricultural activity in which even children work, and its paradisiacal condition lies in the fact that lands are abundant and fertile and harvests are not subject to losses or calamities. This concept contrasts with the occidental concept of paradise, which is presented as a place of eternal leisure" (1985:250).

10. For an excellent description and analysis of the situation of the indigenous people of Peru, with a focus on the decades from 1900–1948, see Davies 1974.

11. See Acknowledgments for help received.

12. An interesting side effect of this grassroots development is the fact that the herders are treated with much more respect when they descend to the valley. The Yachaq group implemented a variety of grassroots projects in other villages as well.

13. *Coca* leaves (*Erythroxylum coca*) contain many elements necessary to supplement a meager diet. Peruvian obstetrician and biologist Sara Teresa Rivero Luque listed the elements in 100 grams of coca leaves (306 calories) as follows: proteins, 18.9 g; carbohydrates, 46.2 g; fat, 3.3 g; fiber, 14.2 g; water, 7.2 g; vitamin A, 14,000 iu; alpha carotene, 2.65 mg; vitamin B1, 0.68 mg; vitamin B2, 1.73 mg; vitamin B6, 0.58 mg; beta carotene, 20 mg; vitamin C, 53 mg; vitamin E, 44.10 mg; vitamin G, amount unknown; nicotinic acid, 5 mg; vitamin H, 0.54 mg; organic acids, 3.2 mg; natural alkaloids, 75 mg. The mineral content is: Al, 49 mg; C, 1.1 mg; P, 911.8 mg; Ba, 17 mg; Cr, 0.23 mg; Mg, 0.37 mg; B, 24 mg; Sr, 204 mg; Mn, 0.5 mg; Ca, 1,540 mg; Fe, 45.8 mg; K, 1.9 mg (1995:240–241).

Chapter 1

1. Obstetrician Teresa Rivero Luque, in her studies of other Andean regions, stresses the importance of parsley in attempts to space pregnancies (1998:8). She suggests several ways to achieve this: take one spoonful of juice made from parsley leaves for breakfast for three days following menstruation. Or take a cup of tea made from the crushed roots of parsley for breakfast during the days of menstruation, or take one cup of tea made from the leaves and the root of parsley only once right after birth. Rivero Luque also gives a list of recipes to space pregnancies that use other herbs.

2. See Rivero Luque 1998 and Saravia 1985 for similar issues in rural regions closer to mainstream society.

3. A healer from the Vilcanota Valley explained that formerly unmarried girls who lived in villages along the valley and who did not want the babies they had borne threw them into the river, despite their fears of the *twinti*. The story goes that the *twinti*, the soul of the child, cried. During nights of the full moon all the souls of the children who had ended up in the river danced in a circle, accusing their parents of the crimes they had committed. Within the last decade, though, the general attitude about raising a baby without a partner has changed, and one can see young unmarried girls proudly raising their babies themselves.

4. In Chillihuani, houses are built in *ayni*, which is aid given that is to be recipro-

cated in kind at a later time. In some other regions of the Andes, building a house with the help of extended family, neighbors, friends, or *compadres* is referred to as *minka*. See also Oscar Núñez del Prado 1973:30.

5. John Rowe quotes Bernabé Cobo's *Historia del nuevo mundo*, Book 13, Chapter 38: in Inca times "pregnant women were not supposed to walk in the fields but otherwise their work was not interrupted" ([1946] 1963:282).

6. See also Body Shop Team 1991:32 and Romney and Romney 1963 regarding beliefs about these issues in other parts of the world.

7. People from some villages in the valley below Chillihuani believe that a child will become an assassin when a knife is used or a thief when scissors are used to cut the umbilical cord. In other villages along the Vilcanota Valley, however, people believe that a child will be dull when the umbilical cord is cut with a tile and alert when it is cut with a sharp knife.

8. See Body Shop Team 1991:93 regarding the use of heat in other societies.

9. Liquid incense is a resin that is collected after the bark of the incense tree (*Styrax weberbaueri Perkins* [Brack Egg 1999:476]; or *Acacia senegal* [Tupayachi Herrera, personal communication]) has been removed. The resin solidifies when exposed to the air. As the incense is placed onto hot stones or charcoal, it melts and emits pleasant fumes. It is believed that when the *uraña wayra* hits a person, death follows quickly; when the *soq'a wayra* catches up with a person, she/he succumbs to a slow death unless a *curandero* is close by.

10. In Inca times women prayed at sacred sites asking for a safe birth (J. Rowe [1946] 1963:282, quoting Cobo 1890–1895, Book 14, Chapter 6).

11. The herders say that *qollpa*—ferrous sulfate or potash sulfate—is similar to saltpeter (*salitre,* Sp.), which is used in folk medicine and for other purposes.

12. Lefèber and Voorhoeve state: "Some indigenous customs of the South have already been taken over in the North such as the upright position of the women in labor" (1998:1).

13. Dra. Sara Teresa Rivero Luque asserts that in some regions the very effective herb *altamisa* or *markhu* (*Ambrosia peruviana* [Brack Egg 1999:28]) is poured into hot water with stems and leaves. The steam that rises is placed below the buttocks, thus helping dilation and accelerating the birthing process (1998 and personal communication). The people of Chillihuani do not know about this method.

14. This practice is known from other parts of the world as well. Lefèber and Voorhoeve (1998:20) write, "Indigenous midwives living in Mexico's central region use a technique called 'blanketing': a shawl or sheet is placed under the back of the woman, who is lying on her back. Then the midwife takes the two ends of the shawl and rubs rhythmically and slowly in the dorsal and iliac areas, going up and down various times."

15. Lefèber and Voorhoeve state that "from several countries in Latin America—Ecuador, Jamaica and Mexico—it has been reported that tea is especially recommended during pregnancy: tea laced with brandy, which is thought to bolster the strength of the

woman during labour and help speed delivery (Ecuador), bush teas flavored with bitter herbs which 'cool' the blood (Jamaica) and *té de manzanilla* (chamomile tea), believing that if it is false labour, the pains will go away, and if it is true labor, the pains will come stronger and harder (Mexico). Indigenous midwives in Colombia may give *agua de panela* (brown sugar) and *aguardiente* (rum) just before the delivery" (1998:20).

16. I was informed that when a baby does not cry, someone will blow into the baby's mouth and lightly slap the baby with an open hand around its mouth and cheeks. The birth attendant may also slap the soles of the baby's feet three times, holding the baby upside down. When mucus has collected in the nose or mouth of the newborn baby, warm water or mother's milk is used to clean it, sometimes with the help of a little stick. The mucus flows out more easily when the head of the baby is held lower than the rest of the body.

17. In Chillihuani only the healers and a few other villagers seem to be concerned about infections. In some other regions, the plant *arrayan* (*Sambucus peruviana* [Brack Egg 1999:48]) is used to disinfect the umbilical cord (S. T. Rivero Luque, personal communication).

18. Some people in Chillihuani assert that it can take on average between five minutes and one hour for the placenta to be expelled. When this is not the case, the new mother receives tea made of the herb *mamani alqa*. Some herders believe that the new mother must drink herbal tea with ashes from the stove to push out the placenta. Others assert that it may not take longer than twenty to thirty minutes for the placenta to be expelled. But most agree that after fifteen minutes, the umbilical cord must be burned with the stem of an *altamisa* plant for one minute. After another minute, pressure must be put on the rear of the uterus, which usually causes the entire placenta to be expelled.

19. The placenta can either be washed right after it emerges, by anyone attending the birth, or sometime during the next day. It must always be washed before it is burned. If the placenta is not washed, it is believed that the child will turn dark and the mother will have pains. After the placenta has been burned outdoors, the ashes are sprinkled over the animals for good luck, i.e., to enhance the fertility of the herd. Anyone who drinks the ashes of the placenta mixed with blessed water at the birth of a baby boy is believed to become immune to the effects of the malevolent wind. Not all people in Chillihuani seem to know the actual function of the placenta.

20. In villages below Chillihuani I was told that a cream made of the herbs *mapa, uñuka, chiri chiri* (*Grindelia boliviana*), and *romero* (*Rosmarinus officinalis*) is applied to the tear of the perineum. Others assert that the white membrane of the inside of an eggshell is used to cover the tear (S. T. Rivero Luque, personal communication).

21. The plants are finely ground and mixed with the fat of a sheep, chicken, or cow. The cream is used on the first, third, and fifth days after giving birth. It can be put on the hands of the new mother, which are then covered with a cloth. Sometimes the cream is rubbed over the whole body, including the head, and the woman is wrapped in blankets. During this treatment nettles are put on the navel and warm tiles are placed on the soles of the feet after rubbing them with a mixture of the cream plus chewed *coca*

and *romero*. This treatment is said to help considerably in the recuperation of a woman after birth.

22. See also Núñez del Prado Bejar 1975 and Saravia 1985:76–77 regarding beliefs about the birth of a girl among Andean pastoral and agricultural societies.

23. *Pito* (Sp.), *Hak'achu*, or *hak'akllu* (*Colaptes rupicola puna Cabanis*).

24. Lung is *bofé* (Sp.), *surq'a*, or *surq'an*. The lungs of a sheep are more effective than the lungs of a camelid. Since there are only a few cows in Chillihuani, people have never gotten into the habit of drinking milk, which is also expensive to buy. The milking of llamas and alpacas has never been practiced in the Andes. See Gade 1999:103–117 for an in-depth discussion of llamas and alpacas as unmilked animals.

25. The Chillihuani herders cannot afford to buy formula, and most do not know that it exists. Except for little Alan, who had a bottle with a broken lid, I have not seen baby bottles and was told that there are none in the village. Children are sometimes given herbal teas from a spoon or cup at a very young age.

26. See also Flores Ochoa 1979:43 regarding the omission of salt intake by new mothers in the department of Puno.

27. Carrying children in a bag close to the body is an indigenous custom that has been adopted in the north as well (Lefèber and Voorhoeve 1998:1).

28. *Unu* means water; *chakuy* means to throw. Or, the term *unuchakuy* is derived from *ch'akyay*, which means to acquire purity.

29. Formerly, by law names had to be taken from the almanac — a Catholic, civic, and astrological calendar. Now people are free to choose any name they like.

30. This sad reality exists not only in Chillihuani, but also in other parts of the high Andes. William Stein's research in Hualcán, in the department of Ancash in Peru, revealed that "infant mortality is high, but since most infant deaths are not reported, no reliable figures can be given" (1961:155). Paul Baker's 1968 study of population in the southern Peruvian highlands showed "high birth rates, high death rates, slow postnatal growth and unusually high female death rates postnatally as well as prenatally" (Flannery, Marcus, and Reynolds 1989:41, reporting on Baker's study). In Kaata, Bolivia, Joseph Bastien found that on the average four out of ten babies die during childbirth (1985:87). Other investigators, among them Catherine Allen (1988), also witnessed deaths during childbirth. A linguist I met in Cuzco who undertook studies in a high-altitude community nearby became dismayed with the frequent deaths of mothers and infants. When her landlady also died in childbirth, she left the Andes for good.

31. David Werner (1986) discovered during his far-reaching rural studies that women who are malnourished do not have the strength required to give birth and are likely to die.

32. Given these tragedies and others involving the deaths of mothers and infants, I organized a conference with the help of the Yachaq group in 1999 in the city of Cuzco. Together with invited experts from several disciplines, we sought solutions to the problems surrounding childbirth. On this occasion, the Yachaq healers were capacitated to

deal more adequately with childbirth and to discuss with their communities the most important issues relating to pregnancy and birth. The herders often reminded me that formerly, Chillihuani had excellent *paqos* (healers), both *pampamesayoq* and *altomesayoq*, the latter being the most advanced in the art and craft of healing physical and psychological ailments. Unfortunately, this knowledge has not been adequately perpetuated to new generations. For this reason, we were happy when our efforts to get a nurse for the health station in Chillihuani were finally successful. According to the healers and nurse, gestating mothers now visit the health station at appropriate intervals in the course of their pregnancies and deaths have declined considerably, although no precise statistics are available at the present time.

33. Black widow spiders are found in lower-altitude regions, not in Chillihuani.

Chapter 2

1. Of the various fiestas held for animals in the Andes, the people of Chillihuani celebrate Pukllay (carnival) in February/March in honor of alpacas and llamas. La Fiesta de San Juan, on June 24, is dedicated to sheep; la Fiesta de Santiago, on July 25 and 26, is celebrated in honor of horses; and Macho Pagaray, on August 1, honors male llamas and alpacas that carry loads to and from the fields. Other festivities for animals that are celebrated in some parts of Peru but not in Chillihuani are San Lazaro for dogs, San Marcos for cows, and San Antonio for pigs.

On October 4, 1931, in Europe, the anniversary of the death of Francis of Assisi was declared the Day of World Animal Protection. In 1962, April 24 was declared the International Day of the Experimental Animal (Ingeborg Livaditis, president of Tierrechte, Baden Württemberg, personal communication).

2. This and other customs have in recent years been re-introduced to Europe and North America (see Lefèber and Voorhoeve 1998).

3. In many other indigenous societies, such as the Mbuti of Zaire (Turnbull 1983a and 1983b) and the Ju/'hoansi of the Kalahari desert of Namibia and Botswana (Gordon 1992), young children are also in close contact with their mothers or other caregivers for most of their waking hours, receiving much affection and prolonged oral gratification.

4. When about six years old, boys begin to wear woven black pants (*wara*) that reach below the knees, a woven shirt (*aymilla*), and a jacket (*haguna*), over which they may wear a poncho. They also wear a knit hat (*ch'ullu*), sometimes with a felt hat on top. Girls wear skirts (*pullira*), a woven blouse (*aymilla*), a small jacket (*haguna*), a shawl (*lliklla*), and a flat hat with woolen fringes of different colors (*montera*, Sp.). Both sexes wear rubber sandals (*usuta*).

5. Flores Ochoa also noted that in Paratia there is a good deal of interaction between children and adults; therefore children reach social maturity at a very early age. "Nothing related to normal daily life is unknown to them; learning about sex, conception and birth is no problem" (1979:61).

6. Cutlery was seldom if ever used when I first came to Chillihuani in 1988. Now some families sometimes use forks and spoons. The Chillihuani herders started to use pots, pans, dishes, and cups made of modern materials only about 40 years ago. Elders informed me that in the past these items were made out of fired earth. They were bartered for wool, potatoes, or meat with the people from Pucara, close to Lake Titicaca, who still come to the valley below Chillihuani to sell their goods every year during the fiesta of the village saint, the Virgin Asunta.

7. Non-aggressive, gentle behavior has also been observed in both genders in other parts of the world. Haviland (1997:406) relates that in some New Guinean tribes neither males nor females are aggressive. This author further states that among the Ju/'hoansi of South Africa, both sexes are generally mild-mannered, energetic, and self-reliant, as is the case in Samoa (Mead 1967) and in Chillihuani. On the other hand, Whiting and Whiting (1975), in their studies of six cultures in different parts of the world, found that boys are significantly more aggressive than girls.

8. Santiago is a village saint that was brought to Peru by the conquerors. At the root of this fiesta, however, are ancient Andean beliefs in the mighty god of thunder and lightning. The thundering noise of galloping horses during the fiesta reminds the people of their powerful thunder god. (See Bolin 1998, Chapter 10.)

9. For *rimanakuy, casarakuy,* and the Fiesta de Santiago, see Bolin 1998, Chapters 8, 9, and 10.

10. Either a *madrina* or a *padrino* is chosen for the ceremony. The husband of the *madrina* or the wife of the *padrino,* although they do not figure directly in the ceremony, also becomes *comadre* or *compadre* and is thus part of the *compadrazgo* system. *Compadrazgo* is a ritualized spiritual co-parenthood in which fictive kinsmen are created to widen the network of rights and responsibilities between families. See also Babb 1998:132.

11. Joseph Bastien has an interesting explanation regarding the symbolic meaning of salt among the Qollahuaya people of Mt. Kaata in Bolivia. "Qollahuayas call unbaptized persons '*limbos*' when they are small, and '*ch'unchus*' when they are adults. According to Qollahuayas, *ch'unchus* are uncivilized lowland Indians who are naked, don't eat salt, and hunt with the bow and arrow which Qollahuayas consider inferior to agriculture and herding. The Yanahuayas, for example, interpret the putting of salt on the baby's tongue at baptism and the dressing with the baptismal robe to mean that the baby is no longer a *ch'unchu* but a Qollahuaya who eats salt and wears clothes" (1985:96–97). This belief is also common in the valley below Chillihuani, but the people of Chillihuani do not recognize this story.

12. The child's name and date of birth and the parents' names must now be registered within a month of a baby's birth.

13. In other regions, the First Haircut is also referred to as *rutuchikuy* or *chukcharutuchi* (*chukcha* means hair; *rutuy* or *rutukuy* means to cut). *Unuchakuy,* the Andean baptism that is held soon after the birth of a child, is normally followed by the Catholic baptism and *chukcha rutukuy,* the First Haircut. The sequence of these two ceremonies is not always the same, nor is there a fixed age for either of these rites of passage.

14. For this quotation ([1946] 1963:282), John Rowe used information written down by early Spanish investigators—Cobo (1890–1895, Book 14, Chapter 6); Gonzáles Holguín (1608); and Molina of Cuzco (1913:176)—about this Inca ceremony.

15. A First Haircut observed by Jorge Flores Ochoa in Paratia, Puno, contains some of the elements of ancient times. He writes, "The haircutting ceremony, *chujcharutu-chi* [same as *chukcha rutukuy*], takes place before the seventh birthday and sometimes coincides with the exchange of the *phalika* for skirt or pants. The godfather of the first haircutting gives alpacas to his godchild; these will form part of the godchild's future herd. If any of the animals die, it is the responsibility of the father to replace them. In this way, the child has animals that will multiply through the years and develop into a herd large enough so that he can support a wife and raise children. The *chujcharutuchi*, in which spiritual kinship bonds and friendship ties are established and strengthened, is always an opportunity for celebration" (1979:61).

16. As is true for baptism, the husband of a *madrina* or the wife of a *padrino* automatically becomes part of the ritual kinship network without being directly involved in the ceremony. In order to establish an ample network of kin during *unuchakuy* and First Haircut, pastoralists do not always select *compadres* from the village itself but sometimes from villages and towns in the valley.

17. In Quechua society children take the surname of their father followed by the surname of their mother. At marriage neither partner relinquishes their surnames. Thus, at birth the daughters in the Mamani household received the surname Mamani from the father and added the surname Illatinco from the mother. They do not change their name in marriage but keep it until death. The children of any of the four Mamani Illatinco daughters will use the name of their father, followed by Mamani, the paternal name of their mother. In the next generation, the surname Mamani will be lost, while the surname in the male lineage can continue indefinitely.

18. In making *chuño,* potatoes are sorted according to size and put on dry *ichu* grass spread out on the ground. Depending on the size of the potatoes and the degree of frost at night, they are left out for about ten days, exposed to the extreme cold at night and the drying sun during the day. Each morning some family members—sometimes the whole family—walk on the potatoes with their bare feet to squeeze out the moisture. The dehydrated potatoes become hard and turn a grayish-black color. They are then placed into a *taqe,* a cylindrical basket-like container made of straw, where they can be kept for up to ten years.

19. Between 1997 and 2002 the herds were depleted to such an extent that the herders wondered whether their way of life could continue.

20. Thanks to the funds we received from the Landkreis Böblingen in Germany, water has now been brought to the Mamani Illatinco household, which is a dream come true for this family and the patients who visit.

21. I was told that injections with *imicina* or *sillu sillu* can also cure the disease. For a detailed description of this disease, see McCorkle 1988:48–51.

22. Juan Mamani and Modesto Quispe joined the Yachaq group that I founded in 1992. Some time later, Ricardo Illatinco, Teresa Mamani, and Juan Braulio Quispe joined as well. In addition to the knowledge the healers have learned from their ancestors, they now learn from the healers of other regions and from physicians and other professionals in the Yachaq group. The Yachaq group members, in return, learn much from the Chillihuani healers.

23. Rodrigo Montoya, in his extensive research regarding poverty among the indigenous children of Peru, states: "In 1991 poverty has reached more than 5 million children, which is equal to 62% of the children of Peru. In rural areas, the proportion rises to 75% (Instituto Cuánto 1992:51). Between 1985 and 1992, critical poverty has risen more than 80 points (Peace 1994). In 1990 this index almost doubled due to the '*paquetazo*' or 'fuji-shock' which raised prices as never before in the history of Peru. A simple example: gas went up thirty-fold" (1995:72). Regarding the fuji-shock, see also Bolin 1991.

24. With funds received from Marianne, Prinzessin von Baden, Ludwig, Prinz von Baden, and Ingeborg Winker, the Yachaq group brought Luisita to a clinic in Cuzco, but she did not improve. She was then taken to Lima for examinations, but she could not be helped there either. Her condition finally improved a little during the course of therapy at the Colegio de Invidentes Nuestra Señora del Carmen, in San Jeronimo, Cuzco. She can now chew solid food and sit slightly upright in a stroller, moving her left arm. The family eventually moved to Cuzco to be close to this facility.

25. Children and young people who have died are dressed in white garments; married people who have died are dressed in black.

26. Sometimes caskets are used, but they are expensive. Also, it is becoming increasingly difficult to find space in the cemetery, where there is little soil.

27. The period of eight days has considerable significance in the high Andes. Many important events last for eight days, such as weddings and the Pukllay fiesta. Women are supposed to remain in bed or around the house for eight days after giving birth; eight days after a person dies, his/her spirit is sent off in ritual form.

28. *Soq'a* is also a disease that causes people to become very thin and die. Regarding *soq'a wayra*, see also McCorkle 1988:20. The Spanish word *alma* (soul) is used to describe the dead body that walks through the landscape harming people and animals.

29. Todos Santos consists of the Day of the Dead, on November 1, and the Day of the Living, on November 2. (In some regions these days are reversed.) On the Day of the Living girls receive bread dolls and boys receive bread horses. Not all people in Chillihuani can afford to buy bread. Given the scarcity of firewood, it is also difficult to bake it.

30. Peruvian anthropologist Jesús A. Cavero Carrasco, in his studies on the funerals of children, wrote, "The death of children in Andean villages is celebrated with happy fiestas" (1985:245). According to Cavero, people thank God for having called the child to him so his soul can remain white and clean and he will not suffer like the adults. Some people recall that in the past this kind of celebration was seen in Cusipata as well, but it was never seen in Chillihuani.

Chapter 3

1. People recount that until about forty years ago virtually all the items they used—cups, plates, bowls, pots, and pans—were made of clay. Now many of these utensils are made of aluminum or plastic, while pots and pans are made of iron. Few people use cutlery; instead they eat with their fingers. A large wooden spoon called *wislla* (*cucharon de madera*, Sp.) is used to ladle soup from the pot into the plates.

2. In some Andean regions, *coca* leaves are still used as a unit of exchange. These leaves are obtained in exchange for wool, *chuño*, meat, etc. Two pounds of *coca* leaves, for example, can be exchanged for one *arroba*, which equals 11.5 kg of potatoes in the marketplace.

3. Adults usually put *coca* leaves and sometimes money into their *unkuña* or *ch'uspa*. A *ch'uspa* is a small woven rectangular bag. A few people use a small narrow bag called *qolqe ch'uspa*.

4. Qoyllur Rit'i is a holiday that takes place one week before Corpus Christi; thus it can occur between May 20 and June 23 (Randall 1982:42).

5. See Jackson 1964 and Shoemaker 1964 for children's toys made from the natural environment in the jungle of Bolivia.

6. *Ukuku* is Quechua for bear. During the fiesta of Qoyllur Rit'i and other fiestas, men disguise themselves as *ukukus* using alpaca furs, masks, and other items with symbolic significance. (See also Flores Ochoa 1990 and Flores Lizana 1997.)

7. Three hundred thirty-three of these songs were published by these three investigators in a bilingual anthology called *Urqukunapa Yawarnin* (*la sangre de los cerros*, Sp., the blood of the mountain peaks).

8. See Payne 2000 for an interesting array of Quechua folktales.

9. According to the historical research by Philippe Ariès (1962), childhood in western societies has taken different forms throughout the centuries. Ariès found that in the medieval world there was little if any place for childhood. In the seventeenth century, on the other hand, children played the same games as adults and participated on an equal footing in celebrations. In the eighteenth century, however, the situation changed as children and adults were assigned separate status (Ariès 1962:99; Schwartzman 1978:11–14).

10. Pride in their work does not, however, apply to the forced labor Indians had to do on haciendas and in mines in colonial times or to the exploitative work many Indians are still forced to do today.

11. See also Bastien 1985:106–107 regarding the encouragement Andean children receive for the work they do.

12. For an in-depth discussion of the wool economy in Peru, see Orlove 1977.

13. See Cahlander, Zorn, and Rowe 1980 regarding sling braiding in the Andes.

14. When lightning strikes and kills a person or animal, an offering of *coca* leaves must be made right at the spot where the death occurred. Blowing on a *k'intu,* the thunder god is appeased with the words, *"Qhaqya, manan hamunkichu, chay k'intu pagamushaike"* (Striking force of the thunder god, I offer this *k'intu* so you never return). Animals are buried at the site where lightning struck; the bodies of people are brought home for the vigil and are usually buried in the cemetery, though some families bury the dead at the place where lightning struck.

15. I noticed that children who are out herding get some special items with the food they take whenever possible. Children receive the kind of food their families can afford. Stein's observations in Hualcán (1961:166), where children receive little food—often only scraps—and must steal, do not apply to Chillihuani.

16. For general information regarding condors, see Alford Andrews 1982.

17. Male alpacas carry on average three *arrobas* (Sp., one *arroba* equals 11.5 kg); male llamas carry on average five *arrobas.*

18. Early potatoes, called *papa maway,* are planted in August and harvested in February and March, during the early harvest (*ñawpa tarpuy* or *maway tarpuy*). Most potatoes are planted in September or October and harvested in May and June, during the big harvest (*chawpi tarpuy* or *hatun tarpuy*), when some of them are freeze-dried. Potatoes planted toward the end of October are harvested in July (*qhepa tarpuy,* last harvest).

19. Although children contribute considerably to the subsistence of a herding family and must work hard in cases where parents are sick or have died, this kind of work cannot be compared to child labor as it is performed in an exploitative way in many parts of the world. When harvests are destroyed due to extreme weather conditions, however, starting at around twelve years of age children must help their families survive by working in the houses or fields of landowners in valley towns, or, later, by logging or washing gold in the jungle regions of Madre de Dios. Overwork, poor nourishment, and diseases such as tuberculosis, malaria, ulcers, and the dreaded leishmaniasis frequently cause people to fall ill or die.

Chapter 4

1. The teachers lived in Chillihuani, where they taught every weekday from 8 a.m. to 4 p.m. and Saturdays from 8 a.m. to noon. They taught mathematics, reading, writing, language, the history of Peru, geography, sports, and art. All subject areas were taught in Spanish.

2. The situation in Chillihuani is reflective of Ronald Wright's statement, "In the Andes writing was—and still is—seen as something sinister, a tool of foreign domination. Atawallpa was killed because he rejected the invaders' holy book. Manku dismissed the Bible as 'painted sheets,' and the ordinary people found themselves cheated, drafted, jailed, and dispossessed by arcane paperwork" (1992:188).

3. People of the mestizo subculture do not adhere to traditional customs such as

wearing homespun clothes and chewing *coca* leaves, and often they will not speak the Quechua language.

4. For an insightful description of the abuses the Quechua Indians have endured in the first half of the twentieth century and the attempts made to improve their situation, see Davies 1974.

5. Teachers and investigators in Western societies have also recognized the importance of hands-on teaching. See Healy 1987 and 1990; Gatto 1992; Nabhan and Trimble 1994; and others.

6. See also Dickason 1997 regarding the importance of supporting self-confidence in native peoples.

7. The book *Manual del sistema agroecológico escolar* (*Handbook of the Agroecological System for Schools*), by Telésforo Velazco Gonzales and Pieter van Lierop Sips, published in 1995 by the Ministry of Education, delineates the Program of Ecological Education.

8. Signatures in the form of thumbprints are still accepted as long as a literate witness writes the person's name beside his/her thumbprint.

9. Jane Healy states: "Here in the United States boys consistently do better in mathematical reasoning (not necessarily computation); in one study they outpaced girls at age thirteen in the 'highly gifted' math category by thirteen to one. By tenth grade the majority of boys of normal IQ have passed most girls up in math. This differential could be related to their tendency to solve problems by touching and looking instead of 'talking' them through, since higher math requires a type of abstract reasoning based on relationships in the physical world" (1987:131). Recently, however, several U.S. schools and colleges have announced that girls are catching up to boys and sometimes overtaking them in mathematics, sciences, and other subject areas formerly dominated by boys.

10. See Flores Ochoa 1988:121–137 regarding the naming and classification of llamas and alpacas.

11. Full moon is *pura killa*, new moon is *musuq killa*, decreasing moon is *wañu killa*, and half moon is *chawpi killa*.

12. Chillihuani elders explain that sunrise is called *inti lloqsimuy* (*salida del sol*, Sp.). Noon is *chawpi p'unchay inti* (*medio dia*, Sp.). Sunset is *qhata inti* (*sol pendiente* or *puesta del sol*, Sp., sloping sun). Midnight is *kuska tuta* (*media noche*, Sp.). Solar eclipse is *inti wañuy*. *Inti q'ellumpay* is the reflection of the sun that is seen on the high parts of the mountain peaks when the sun has set. The time from sunrise to noon is called *wayna inti*—young sun. The time from noon to 5 p.m. is called *machu inti*—old sun. Stars and constellations are the subject of legends. I often heard the story of the three stars that represent the three lazy brothers. The story goes: A mother sent her three sons to the field to cultivate potatoes. The boys left, but instead of working, they only played. As they returned home, the mother asked, "Have you worked?" The boys answered, "Yes, we put in the seed." Weeks later, the mother asked, "Are you going to hoe your potatoes?" Yes, the boys answered, but they did not go to the field. Nor did they go to harvest the potatoes. The mother had to go to the fields to see for herself how the crop was standing and found

that nothing had been planted. The brothers were frightened and converted to stars. One became the evening star (*estrella de anochecer,* Sp.), the other the midnight star (*estrella de media noche,* Sp.), and the third became the morning star (*estrella de amanecer,* Sp.).

13. These women produced a fine, soft cloth of vicuña wool that resembled silk, referred to as *kumpi* (or *kunpi*) and destined for royalty. A much more rustic cloth made with coarser yarn, called *awasqa,* was woven and worn by the masses.

14. To dye the wool, Chillihuani herders put the coloring agent into hot water and stir until it is well mixed. Then the wool is added and the pot is set over the fire until the water reaches the boiling point. When the water has cooled down, the wool is taken out. Excess color is washed out, and the wool is put on stones to dry in the sun.

15. Peruvian anthropologist Dr. Jorge Flores Ochoa describes the wooden spindle and the way it is used: "The size of the spindle varies, depending on who uses it. Spindles are made of a rod of sanded wood inserted through the center of a wooden disc that serves as a counterweight. The disc also collects the thread and controls the speed. The tip of the spindle usually spins on a broken piece of pottery or fragments of pottery utensils. It is interesting to note that many individuals turn the spindle counterclockwise, while the mestizos spin in the opposite direction" (1979:97).

16. The number of threads that cross between the two horizontal stakes and the arrangement of their colors define the background for the patterns that will be woven into the warping.

17. Gary Urton states, "When the heddle is raised, the weaver selects or 'picks up' a predetermined patterned group of colored and white threads; the weft is then passed between the threads that were picked up and those that were not. After packing the weft snugly between what is now (after 'picking') a new set of upper and lower threads, the heddle is once again pulled up to establish the next upper and lower groups of working threads, and the appropriate pattern of the 'picking up' of threads is performed" (1997:117).

18. For a description of men's and women's clothing, see Bolin 1998:76.

19. For detailed discussions on spinning, weaving, and the meaning of woven motifs, see: Cereceda 1986; Desrosiers 1992; D'Harcourt 1974; Franquemont and Franquemont 1987; Franquemont, Franquemont, and Isbell 1992; Phipps 1992; A. Rowe 1987; Seibold 1992; Silverman 1988, 1991, and 1995; Stone-Miller 1994; Ulloa Torres and Gavilán 1992; Urton 1997; Zorn 1987; and others.

20. Christine and Edward Franquemont (1987) have described these stages for the agricultural community of Chincheros, in the department of Cuzco. Although children in Chillihuani also learn to weave in stages, certain activities and concerns of the Chincheros people, which are reflected in their weavings, differ from those of Chillihuani, where the herding way of life predominates and people are less involved in agriculture and market activities.

21. Christine and Edward Franquemont noted that in Chincheros, to make *chumpis,* a girl must concentrate to develop an understanding "of the visual rhythms, harmonies,

and symmetries of a few very specific and very complex traditional patterns. Her success and speed as a weaver depend on her ability to conceive of her work in a non-numerical, nonlinear way" (1987:66).

22. See also Urton 1997:125 for an analogy with typing. Apart from typing, other activities can also become automatic. A housewife may not have to use a scale or measuring cup to add the ingredients needed for a meal; she merely judges how much of each ingredient is required.

23. The Quechua word *pacha* stands for both space and time. *Kay pacha* simultaneously means this place, i.e., the world we live in, and this time or time period of our lives. See also Müller and Müller 1984:165. It is thus logical to assume that space/time is a concept that was known to the people of the Andes. The principle of space/time is also reflected in the way the Quechua tell time—by placing a vertical pole into the ground. As discussed above, the space where the shadow falls tells the time.

24. The Chillihuani herders maintain that they use only Inca motifs in their weavings and not colonial ones, which do appear in villages elsewhere. Most of the Chillihuani motifs are geometric designs that stand mainly for sacred places, animals, plants, and ideas. High mountain lakes figure prominently in the designs. Among them are T'ika Qocha (Flower Lake), Pampa Qocha (Plain Lake), and Sayaq Qocha (Upright Lake). Tawa T'ika Qocha (Four Flower Lake) is the most significant motif and is frequently seen in weavings in Chillihuani and other regions. Some Chillihuani weavers told me that the *t'ika* design can represent a flower or a snowflake. We know that mountain lakes are sacred and snowflakes are needed to replenish the water of a lake. The number *tawa* (four) is paramount—as in the four regions of Tawantinsuyu, the Inca Empire. Other motifs are Ñawpa Inca (ancient Inca), Yuraq Qenko (white zigzag line that stands for lightning), Puma Maki (the footprint of a puma), and Michi Ñawi (the eye of a catlike creature). The Chillihuani weavers also stress that the *t'inki* motif is very important because it stands for a chain that represents unity.

25. Regarding the *ceque* system, see Bauer 1998; Chávez Ballón 1970; Farrington 1992; J. Rowe 1980; Sherbondy 1982 and 1986; Zuidema 1964; and others. Gail Silverman (1995 and 1998) compares the logic involved in the weaving of motifs with that used in the *khipu* and *ceque* systems.

Chapter 5

1. In his studies among the Ndembu of Zambia, Turner found that rituals are "storehouses of meaningful symbols by which information is revealed and regarded as authoritative, as dealing with the crucial values of the community" (1969:2).

2. The raining season lasts from October to April. Pukllay is a movable fiesta. It can begin on any Sunday within the period from February 2 to March 6 (Urton 1993:125). The people from Cusipata say that Comadres Day always falls on a Thursday, one week after Compadres Day. Pukllay starts on the Sunday following Comadres Day and lasts

for eight days. It is celebrated in honor of alpacas and llamas; sheep have their day on June 24.

3. To make *chicha,* maize (corn) must be soaked in water for several days. It is then placed into a pot and covered with vegetable matter, such as *ichu* grass. After one or two weeks the maize sprouts, at which time the substance is referred to as *wiñapu,* or *jora* (Sp.). This substance contains the enzymes necessary to change starch into sugar. In order to prevent further germination, the *jora* must be dried in the sun. It is then ground on a millstone and mixed with water to form dough. Little by little the dough is mixed with boiling water, kept boiling for several hours, and then left in the pot overnight. The next morning it is boiled again, strained through a piece of cloth, and put into an *urpu,* a large jar, where it ferments for three days (Bolin 1998:233). The preparation of *chicha* is assigned to women in the belief that this sacred brew, already enchanting to the Inca ancestors, must have the female touch. As is common among pastoralists, girls around ten years of age start to help with this important activity.

4. Some people in Chillihuani maintain that Ch'uyaska and Ch'allaska are different terms for the same kind of activity. Others say that *ch'uyay* means to pour *chicha,* wine, or sugarcane alcohol (*trago*) onto the *enqaychu* (effigy in stone) or onto the four corners of an *unkuña* (small woven blanket for sacred items) or a *mesarumi* (altar of stone), while *ch'allay* means to sprinkle *chicha* into the air or onto the animals proper.

5. Regarding the *coca* leaf, see also this book's Introduction; Allen 1988; and Davis 1996.

6. *Coca* leaves have become expensive, and only small quantities can be bought through ENACO—Empresa Nacional de la Coca—in the city of Cuzco. I was told that ENACO buys *coca* leaves from the growers and sells them to stores at three or four times the price. Unless *coca* leaves are bought through ENACO or the stores it supplies, the leaves can be taken away from the native people by Peruvian authorities. *Coca* leaves and cocaine are two very different things.

7. See also Gow and Gow 1975:149 and Flores Ochoa 1977:214–215 regarding the secrecy of these rituals.

8. It is interesting to note that animal parts have been considered important in offerings in other regions of the world. Propp states that "parts of animals were the most ancient form of magical things" (1986:192). Ionesov, in his research on the Sapalli Proto Bactrian civilization in southern Uzbekistan from the eighteenth to the tenth century BC, argues that "the part replaced the entire animal as the notion replaced the shape of the image" (2000:48).

9. The Incas knew well how to preserve food that had been stored by individual families and also in storehouses (*qolqa*) throughout the empire. Now, people in the high Andes store their potatoes and other tubers in bins called *taqe,* made of *saylla* grass (*Festuca dichoclada Pilger*). The Inca distribution mechanisms within and between villages, districts, and regions that assured that no one went hungry are, sadly, no longer in place.

10. See also Flannery, Marcus, and Reynolds 1989:85–86 regarding the use of animal parts.

11. The processing of *moraya* is more complicated than that of *chuño*. High-quality *mallqu* potatoes are placed onto *ichu* grass and covered with more *ichu* for about six days and nights. Then, with their bare feet, people squeeze the moisture out of the potatoes, which in the process become flat and lose their skins and their acidity. In this state they are placed into a pond or rivulet, where they remain for about ten days before they are again put onto the ground and blanketed by *ichu* grass for another week. During all this time they are covered and thereby retain their whitish color. Finally they are squeezed again, dried, and stored in a container (*taqe*), where they can be kept for up to three years.

12. Dr. David Suzuki, preeminent Canadian scholar and environmentalist, states that global warming has caused an average increase in temperature of 0.5 degrees Celsius. By the time the temperature has risen an average of one degree, people living in the tundra and the high mountains of the world will be wiped out.

13. The people of Chillihuani thank the students of the Malaspina University College Anthropology Club, especially Bob Atwal, for collecting the much-needed funds to buy seed potatoes for the entire village.

14. The same belief exists among the native peoples of coastal British Columbia, Canada, who avert their eyes when offerings burn.

15. Qañiwa (*Chenopodium pallidicaule Aellen*) is similar to *quinoa*. The tiny *qañiwa* grains have a diameter of about one millimeter. The plant grows in Puno, Juliaca, and also in the high regions of the department of Cuzco.

16. After the ceremony, the flowers that are left in the pile are taken home for use as a tea, since they have properties that can ward off colds and other sicknesses.

17. Some herders mark animals by cutting small patterns into their ears.

18. Subsequently, White Cloud has given birth to Munay Suri, a beautiful white alpaca with silky *suri* wool. *Suri* alpacas share their name with the terrestrial bird *suri* (*Pterocnemia penata d'Orbigny*), the long feathers of which have been compared to the long shiny hair of the *suri* alpaca.

19. See Reinhard 1999 regarding children being dressed for sacrifices during Inca times. Catherine Allen wrote that on feast days saints are carefully dressed, reminiscent of the Incaic practice of clothing ancestral mummies (1988:65).

20. The desire to pay a sacrifice to the mountain gods is also strongly expressed during the spectacular pilgrimage to Qoyllur Rit'i, which takes place in Peru's Sinakara mountain range, where tens of thousands of people climb to the glaciers above 5,000 meters above sea level. They carry stones as gifts for the mountain gods. In exchange, people disguise as *ukukus,* (bears) chip off chunks of ice, and carry them downhill to heal the people of their villages. The rapid retreat of the glaciers in recent years has led to legislation that no longer permits this custom to continue (Bolin 2003).

21. *Cargo* is Spanish for "burden." The *cargo* system was introduced by the Spanish

conquerors. All men in an Indian community are expected to take part in the *cargo* system, a political-religious hierarchy without pay in which young men assume *cargos,* such as carrying messages through the village and cleaning the church or the offices of the village council. With time these youngsters climb up the ladder, eventually becoming village judges and/or presidents. These *cargos,* combined with the sponsoring of fiestas, lead to prestige but are financially draining.

Chapter 6

1. In Inca times, complete gender equality existed among commoners and the royalty. Martín Murúa, an early Spanish investigator, writes that the brave and beautiful queen Anahuarque—also called Ipavaco—governed the Inca Empire for a long time from the great city of Cuzco while her husband, the Inca Pachacutec Yupanqui, was away conquering other societies and tribal peoples ([1590] 1946:97).

2. See also Millones and Pratt 1990 regarding love and magic in a different region of the Andes.

3. Social scientists, among them A. R. Radcliffe-Brown (1952), argued that joking functions to channel, ritualize, and therefore neutralize hostile feelings in society. See also Schwartzman 1978:10.

4. The transition to womanhood is equally honored in other parts of South America. For example, Alan Ereira's research among the Kogi of Colombia revealed that the transition of a girl from childhood to womanhood "is created by the Great Mother, which we call nature. Every female is the Mother, every female is Nature herself. The onset of menstrual bleeding is a demonstration that nature has the power of fertility, and it is the careful management of that power which makes the world of the Kogi an ordered garden" (1992:92–93). The Kogi believe that menstrual blood is a powerful life energy, that "gold is menstruation, the pure blood of Mother Earth" whom they greatly respect. Regarding the Kogi, see also Gerardo Reichel-Dolmatoff 1978 and 1987, and Davis 1996.

5. *Mucocutaneous leishmaniasis,* or *Uta,* is a disease found in Peru caused by a species of *Leishmania* that is transmitted by sandflies (*Lutzomyia peruana*). This disease is usually contracted during work in jungle regions. Severe lesions affect the mucous membranes of the nose and mouth, eventually eroding part of the face. Death may occur due to infection or obstruction of airways or the food passage.

6. In agreement with shamans, village healers believe that it is best to cure a person at night, when it is easier to concentrate and give respect and appreciation to the Apus in a more direct and intimate way. The belief that Tuesdays and Fridays are not good days to make offerings to the Apus requesting their help is also still prevalent.

7. Every two years, in the General Assembly of Villagers (*asamblea general,* Sp.), a board of directors (*directiva,* Sp.) is elected to each level of the Rondas Campesinas. The board consists of a president, vice president, secretary, treasurer, three members at large (*vocales,* Sp.), and at least four guardians. Male members of the Rondas Campe-

sinas are referred to as *ronderos;* female members as *ronderas.* I will include both in the term *ronderos.* The term "Rondas Campesinas" derives from the word "*rondar*" (Sp.), which means "to go around to prevent disorders" or "to make the round of inspection."

8. The kind of punishment offenders have been subjected to by the General Assembly of the Rondas Campesinas has been successful in curbing re-offenses. First offenders are punished less severely than multiple offenders, who may have to be relegated to the district or provincial judge (*juzgado provincial,* Sp.). A thief who readily admits to having stolen an animal or having committed any other crime must return the stolen item or pay for it. If he also shows remorse, he is not ridiculed for the crime he committed. An offender who has been caught but does not admit to his crime is exposed to public shaming. This type of punishment has proven to be the best way to make offenders admit to their crimes and keep them from re-offending. During public shaming, an offender is sent into the river with or without clothes and sprayed with water. At a meeting in Paucarpata, a male offender had to run through the plaza wearing women's clothes. Female offenders must wear men's clothes. Offenders who have cleared their records often become part of the Rondas Campesinas.

9. See also Dickason 1984 regarding the severe damage caused to native North American cultures by missionary activities.

Chapter 7

1. Regarding Kogi ideology, see also Davis 1996; Ereira 1991 and 1992; and Reichel-Dolmatoff 1978 and 1987.

2. When I talked to people from various villages, they felt that although some television programs are good, the bad ones stick more with the children, since they contain issues that are new to them.

3. It has been predicted that within ten to fifteen years the small glaciers that supply 80 percent of the fresh water in the Andes will have melted due to global warming (Bolin 2003). The rest of the world will not be in much better shape.

Note: Words of Spanish origin are designated by the notation "Sp." All other words are Quechua. Alternate spellings are in parentheses.

ahijado/a (Sp.): godson, goddaughter.

akawara: diaper.

alcalde (Sp.): mayor.

alqo kiska: plant (*Xanthium catharticum*) used to prevent conception.

altamisa or *markhu:* an herb (*Ambrosia peruviana*) used to dilate during the birthing process.

altomesayoq (*altomesayuq, altomisayoq*): diviner of the highest level.

ama llulla, ama suwa, ama qella: don't lie, don't steal, don't be lazy. An Inca greeting.

amaru: large snake, serpent, deity. Also perceived as a symbol standing for a variety of concepts such as water, wisdom, revolution, and revolt.

antara (*zampoña,* Sp.): indigenous Andean musical instrument; panpipes.

Antisuyu: eastern quadrant of the Inca Empire.

añu or *isañu* or *maswa:* Andean tuber (*Tropaeolum tuberosum*).

apacheta (Sp.): sacred cairn consisting of stones that were deposited by worshipers for the spirit guardians of a particular place; *apachita* in Quechua.

Apu: powerful mountain deity or other powerful sacred place; lord.

aqha (*aha*): fermented beverage; see *chicha* (Sp.).

arariwa: guardian of agricultural fields.

arpa (*arpay*): offering; sacrifice of a llama or alpaca.

awana: the stage at which accomplished weavers produce *llikllas,* ponchos, etc.

awki: protective ancestral spirit and mythical personage living in the highest mountain peaks.

awkicha: grandfather.

awkilla or *hatun qoyacha:* great-grandmother.

awkillo or *hatun awkicha:* great-grandfather.

ayllu: kin group, lineage, or indigenous community with a territorial base and members who share a common focus.

aymilla: a woven blouse worn by girls.

ayni: balanced reciprocity; aid to be reciprocated in kind.

ayranpu (*ayrampo*): a cactus-like plant (*Opuntia soehrensii*) used for medicinal purposes. The dark-red seeds are used as a dye.

capuli: native Andean tree (*Prunus serofinal*) with fruits similar to cherries.

cargo (Sp.): literally, "burden"; a duty Indian community members take on within the political-religious hierarchy to serve their community.

carguyoq: a person who holds a *cargo* (Sp.); e.g., the sponsor of a fiesta.

casarakuy: church wedding. In some places, wedding is referred to as *runachakuy* or *warmichakuy.*

ceques: imaginary lines that connected sacred places in Inca times.

chakitaklla: foot plow from Inca times.

chakra (chacra): agricultural field.

Ch'allaska (Ch'uyaska, Ch'uyasqa): the ritual of spraying water or *chicha* over the herd animals in a gesture of symbolic purification.

chanaku: the last child to be born to a family.

chansanakuy: having a good time while joking together.

ch'arki: dried llama or alpaca meat. The English word "jerky" is derived from *ch'arki.*

chaski (chasqui): runner who carried messages and goods in Inca times.

chaskiqkuna: young men who perform rituals of respect and learn the tasks of village authorities. Includes the positions of *arariwa, cobrador* (Sp.), and *agentes policiales* (Sp.).

chicha (Sp.): fermented beverage made out of corn or *quinoa; aqha* in Quechua.

chikchi wasi (casa de la granizada, Sp.): house of the hail.

Chinchaysuyu: northern quadrant of the Inca Empire.

chukcha rutukuy: First Haircut (also referred to as *rutuchikuy* or *chukcharutuchi* or *chukcha rutuy*).

ch'ullu: knit hat with colorful symbols worn by men.

chullumpi: honorable address for llamas during rituals.

chumpi: woven belt. Also refers to the stage when children know how to weave belts.

ch'unchu: dancer at Qoyllur Rit'i representing indigenous people from the jungle regions.

chuño (ch'uñu): freeze-dried potatoes.

chushllu: honorable address for alpacas during rituals.

ch'uru: seashell; see also *mullu.*

ch'uspa: small woven bag men use to carry *coca* leaves and money.

coca (kuka): leaves of the *coca* plant (*Erythroxylon coca*) that when chewed with the ash of certain other plants (*llipht'a*) act as a mild stimulant and alleviate fatigue, hunger, and thirst. A dietary supplement as well as a central ingredient in all ritual offerings to the deities, *coca* leaves are central to social interactions.

coca k'intu: see *k'intu.*

coca mukllu (kuka mukllu): coca seed.

Collasuyu: see Qollasuyu.

comadre (Sp.): co-mother; godmother.

compadrazgo (Sp.): ritual-fictive kinship.

compadre (Sp.): co-father; godfather.

compadres (Sp.): godparents.

condenado (Sp.): soul of the condemned that must do penance; *kukuchi* in Quechua.

curandero/a (Sp.): male or female healer.

cuy (Sp.): guinea pig; *qowe* or *qowi* in Quechua.

despacho (Sp.): offering to the gods.

enqa: life force contained in the *enqaychu.*

enqaychu: a small, natural, or slightly worked stone, usually resembling an animal but sometimes resembling a human or an object, believed to contain life force and the power to promote fertility, happiness, and luck.

faena (Sp.): communal obligatory work party.

garbanzo (Sp.): chickpea; they are nutritious and thus considered one of the best foods in an offering to the deities.

hach'u (kuka hach'u or *khullu):* wad of chewed *coca* leaves.

hach'u p'anpay: ritual burial of chewed *coca* leaves.

hacienda (Sp.): landed property or estate.

haguna: a small jacket worn by boys and girls.

hallpay: to chew *coca* leaves.

hampiq (curandero, Sp.): healer.

Hanan Cuzco (Hanan Qosqo): upper part of Cuzco.

hanan pacha: upper world; the Andean heaven where the spirits reside.

Hawkaypata (Haucaypata) (Plaza de Armas, Sp.): the principal plaza in Cuzco.

haywa: ritual offering; see also *pago* (Sp.), *despacho* (Sp.), and *ofrenda* (Sp.).

Hurin Cuzco (Urin Qosqo): lower part of Cuzco.

ichu (ichhu, stipa ichhu): favored high-altitude grass for llamas and alpacas that can be used for a variety of purposes.

illa: see *enqaychu.*

Illapa: god of thunder and lightning; see also Qhaqya.

Inti: sun; sun god.

iphiña: everyday corral for camelids and sheep.

irpay (irpa): ceremony of marking alpacas, llamas, or sheep. In Chillihuani, also considered a ritual wedding of young animals.

iskaymanta: weaving technique that uses two contrasting colors to produce motifs that appear on only one side of a cloth.

kanti (huso, Sp.): spindle.

kantunka: belt with woolen tassels that is worn by men during Pukllay.

kay pacha: this world; the world where we live.

kehuiña (qewña, keuña): native Andean tree (*Polylepis incana*) that grows between approximately 3,000 and 4,800 meters above sea level.

kero (qero): vase-shaped container used for drinking.

khipu (quipu): a knotted string device on which the Incas kept record. It consists of a thick cord to which thinner cords of various colors and sizes are attached.

khipukamayoq: keeper of the *khipu.*

killa: moon; moon goddess.

kinsamanta: weaving technique that uses two contrasting colors in addition to white to produce motifs in reverse on both sides of a cloth.

k'intu: offering, usually of three perfect *coca* leaves placed green side up in a bouquet.

kishwar (kiswar): indigenous Andean tree (*Buddleia incana*).

k'uchi taka: agility game.

Kuntisuyu (Cuntisuyu): western quadrant of the Inca Empire.

leishmaniasis (Eng.): disease caused by protozoan parasites, genus *Leishmania.*

llanp'u: powder obtained by grinding soft white stone, believed to purify and keep evil spirits away.

llant'a: firewood.

llaqta: town, village, community.

lliklla: woven shawl with symbols used by Andean women from Inca times to the present.

llipht'a: compressed ash of certain plants, chewed with *coca* leaves to release alkaloids.

lloqhetaku: paint obtained from red earth that is used on the fur of animals in a marking ceremony.

lloq'esqa: the act of twisting threads toward the left side to fabricate strings used to keep away misfortune.

llulluch'a or *qochayuyu:* algae from mountain lakes that makes up an important part of the highland Indians' diet.

mach'ay: burial cave.

machu: old one, ancient one. Can refer to an ancient spirit that can be either benevolent or malevolent.

machula: grandfather.

madrina (Sp.): godmother of a child.

Mama: mother of a child and sister of a child's mother.

mamani alqa: herb (*Ouricia chamaedrifolia Benth*) used to facilitate labor and help expel the placenta.

mama q'epe (*mama q'epi*): bundle consisting of various ritual paraphernalia wrapped into a colorful *lliklla*.

Manqo Qhapaq (Manco Capac): first mythical Inca.

mapa: medicinal plant (*Senecio rhyzomatosus Rushby*) used to soothe tears after giving birth.

markachana: small cave in the ceremonial corral used to burn an offering; see also *q'oyana*.

mashwa (*maswa;* also called *añu* or *isañu*): an important food staple (*Tropaeolum tuberosum*) in the sierra.

mayu: river; the Milky Way.

mesarumi: table of stone; altar where sacred rituals take place. (Literally, *mesa* (Sp.) for table and *rumi* for stone.)

minka: work arrangement between different parties, e.g., in house construction.

misti (*mestizo,* Sp.): person of mixed Indian and Spanish descent.

montera (Sp.): flat hat with fringes.

moraya: dehydrated potatoes; similar to *chuño*.

mullu: large seashell used in rituals; sometimes referred to as *ch'uru* or *qocha*.

murmuntu: dark edible algae found in lakes and springs.

muyukancha: corral used during sacred rituals.

ñawi: eye.

ñawin aqha: eye of the *chicha*, i.e., the first cup of *chicha* offered to the deities from a vessel.

niwa: long-stemmed grass (*Cortaderia quila*) used to make the festive hats worn by
  men during Pukllay and other festivities.

ofrenda (Sp.): sacred offering; also referred to as *despacho* (Sp.), *pago* (Sp.), or *haywa.*

oqa (*oca*): tuber that serves as one of the food staples in the *puna* region of the Andes
  (*Oxalis tuberosa*).

oqhe qora: plant to prevent conception (*Descurainia titicacensis Walp*).

pacha: time; earth; space; universe.

pacha tira: remote, uninhabited, and dangerous places.

Pachakuteq Inca Yupanqui (Pachakuteq Inka Yupanki, Pachacuti Inca Yupanqui): the
  ninth Inca emperor, who made many changes within the empire, earning him
  the name "transformer of the world."

pachakuti (*pachacuti*): reversal of the world.

Pachamama: Mother Earth, the Great Mother.

padres de familia (Sp.): a parent organization.

padrino (Sp.): godfather.

pampamesayoq: less important shaman than *altomesayoq.*

paqo: diviner; specialist in ritual activities. See also *altomesayoq* and *pampamesayoq.*

paka paka pukllay: hide and seek.

partera (Sp.): midwife.

partero (Sp.): male counterpart to midwife.

phalika (*kulis*): rectangular woven cloth worn by children under six years of age. It is
  wrapped around the body and tied at the waist with a woven belt.

phallcha: sacred flowers (genus *Gentiana*) and symbols of fertility used during
  Pukllay's Ch'allaska ceremony.

phallchay or *phallchakuy:* ritual of sprinkling *phallcha* blossoms over the herds.

phukuy: the act of blowing across *coca* leaves in a ritual offering to the deities.

pochero (Sp.): most festive meal at Pukllay; *t'inpu* in Quechua.

pollera (Sp.): woman's skirt.

Pukllay (Puqllay): literally, "play" or "game." A major festivity in the Andes, also
  referred to as Carnavales (Sp.), or Carnival Week.

pukuchu: bag made of the fur of an alpaca that was aborted as a fetus, was born dead,
  or died immediately after birth.

puna: high-altitude region with tundra-like grasslands.

puru (*poro*): drinking vessel made of gourds from tropical regions used during rituals.

qañiwa: nutritious indigenous Andean plant (*Chenopodium pallidicaule Aellen*) with
  tiny seeds; similar to *quinoa.*

q'apachi (*incienso,* Sp.): incense.

qarawi: pre-Hispanic songs.

qayara (*Puya herrerae*): bromeliad that reaches about 1.5 meters in height and is used
  as fodder for some animals. Its roots are used as fuel.

Qellwaqocha: mountain peak and high mountain lake in Chillihuani.

q'eperina, q'eprina, q'epina: woven carrying cloth for women and men.

qespe rumi: sharp quartz stones children play with.

Qhaqya: Andean god of thunder and lightning; see Illapa and *rayo* (Sp.).

qhashwa (*qhaswa*): circular dance of Inca origin. Also the name of an organization in
    Chillihuani in which young people have a chance to meet one another.

qocha (*cocha; laguna,* Sp.): tarn; high mountain lake or lagoon.

qochayuyu (*cochayuyu*): algae that is a part of the highland Indians' diet. See also
    llulluch'a.

Qollasuyu (Collasuyu): southern region of the Inca Empire.

qollpa: Powder of a white mineral used to keep away evil spirits.

qolqa (*collca*): storage area for food; storehouse.

qolqe lazo: threads of silver-colored yarn used in ritual offerings.

qolqe libro: thin slices of silver-colored paper used in ritual offerings.

qoncha (*setas,* Sp.): mushrooms.

Qorikancha (Coricancha): the Temple of the Sun in Cuzco.

qori lazo: threads of gold-colored yarn used in ritual offerings.

qori libro: thin slices of gold-colored paper used in ritual offerings.

qoya (*coya*): queen; sister/wife of the Inca.

qoyacha: grandmother (*hatun qoyacha* means great-grandmother).

q'oyana: see *markachana.*

qoyllur: star.

Qoyllur Rit'i: object of a pilgrimage to the high, snow-covered mountains of the
    Sinakara range.

Quechua: native language of the Incas, still the predominant indigenous language of
    the Andes.

quinoa (Sp.) (*kiwina*): nutritious, high-protein grain (*Chenopodium quinoa*) with
    small white seeds grown at high altitudes in the Andean highlands.

rayo (Sp.): thunderbolt; lightning flash; Andean god of thunder and lightning. See
    Illapa and Qhaqya.

rimanakuy: marriage in the traditional Andean way.

rit'i: snow.

ronderos/as (Sp.): derived from the Spanish word "*rondar,*" meaning "to go around to
    prevent disorders" or "to make the round of inspection." *Ronderos* are members
    of the Rondas Campesinas.

roq'a: plant of the cactus family (*Colletia spinosa*) used in folk medicine.

ruda (Sp.): herb (*Ruta graveolens L.*) used to cure various ailments; also used to
    prevent conception.

runa: human being, referring to an indigenous Andean person; plural is *runakuna.*

runasimi: the language of the people, i.e., Quechua.

ruphasqa haywa (*ofrenda quemada,* Sp.): burnt offering.

rutuchikuy: ritual First Haircut ceremony. The practice is of pre-Spanish origin.

senq'apa: the first stage when children learn to weave narrow strips of cloth.

sierra (Sp.): highlands.

soq'a: disease caused by the malevolent wind.

soq'a waya: malevolent wind.

soq'ana: wool sling used to throw stones; also used as a whip in dances during Pukllay.
    See *warak'a.*

suroqch'i (*soroche*, Sp.): mountain sickness.

susto (Sp.): ailment that mainly befalls children when severely frightened. Can result in diarrhea, fever and sometimes death. *Mancharisqa* or *q'aqcha* in Quechua.

sususka: method called "blanketing" used to bring a baby into the right position for entering the birth canal.

suyu: region; division; territory.

takanakuy or *k'uchi taka:* an agility game where children push against one another with their shoulders without using their hands.

taqe: bin made of reeds where freeze-dried potatoes are stored.

Tawantinsuyu (Tahuantinsuyu): land of the four quarters; the Inca Empire.

tayta: father of a child and brother of a child's father.

tenientes escolares (Sp.): assistants to the *padres de familia* (Sp.).

t'inka: libation or toast for the deities made by flicking drops of a beverage into the air using thumb and forefinger.

t'inpu (*pochero,* Sp.): elaborate meal for Pukllay.

trago (Sp.): sugarcane alcohol.

tullu ruki: weaving tool made from the femur bone of a camelid.

Tusuna Q'asa Pata: site above a ravine between high mountain peaks where dances take place during Pukllay. There are several of these sites in Chillihuani.

uchu (*aji,* Sp.): chili (*Capsicum sp.*).

ukhu pacha: world below; underworld.

ulluku or *lisas:* high-altitude tuberous food plant (*Ullucus tuberosus*).

ukuku: bear dancer seen mostly during Qoyllur Rit'i. Some investigators believe that *ukukus* represent alpacas.

unkuña (*unkhuña*): small woven cloth used to hold *coca* leaves and in rituals and dances.

untu: pure fat from the chests of alpacas and llamas.

unuchakuy: baptism Andean-style only days after birth.

uñuka: medicinal plant used to soothe tears after giving birth (scientific name unknown).

uraña wayra: terrible wind believed to cause severe stomach pains, vomiting, and *susto,* a state of extreme fear.

urpu: earthen container for *chicha.*

usuta: rubber sandal.

uywa: animal.

vara (Sp.): staff.

varayoq: literally, "with staff"; the one who possesses the staff of office. A member of the indigenous civil-religious hierarchy of an Andean community.

víspera (Sp.): eve.

waka (*huaca*): sacred place or divinity.

waltha: swaddling cloth.

walthasqa: a treatment using the herbs *chiri chiri, romero, mapa,* and *mutuy* against hemorrhaging.

Waqraqocha: literally, "horn lake;" sacred high-altitude lake in Chillihuani.

warak'a: woolen whip used to throw stones; see *soq'ana.* Also used in some dances and
    as a weapon in Inca times.

wari: hybrid between llama and alpaca.

Wari (Huari): pre-Inca culture characterized by urban settlements, such as Pikillacta
    near Cuzco, with large buildings for administration, storage, military, and other
    purposes.

wawa: baby, from birth to about two years of age.

wayñu (huayno): folkloric Inca music and dance.

wayra: wind.

wayruru (huayruru): brilliantly colored beans used in rituals and as love charms.

yana uyakuna: blackfaces (*yana* means black; *uya* means face; *kuna* denotes plural).

yapuy (barbecho, Sp.): ploughing of the land.

Academia Mayor de la Lengua Quechua
1995 *Diccionario Quechua-Español-Quechua*. Qosqo, Peru: Municipalidad del Qosqo.

Acosta, José de
[1589] 1962 *Historia natural y moral de las Indias*. Mexico City: Fondo de Cultura
     Económica.

Alford Andrews, Michael
1982 *The Flight of the Condor: A Wildlife Exploration of the Andes*. Boston: Little,
     Brown and Company.

Allen, Catherine
1988 *The Hold Life Has: Coca and Cultural Identity in an Andean Community*.
     Washington, D.C.: Smithsonian Institution Press.

Arguedas, José Maria, and Ruth Stephan
1957 *The Singing Mountaineers: Songs and Tales of the Quechua People*. Austin:
     University of Texas Press.

Ariès, Philippe
1962 *Centuries of Childhood: A Social History of Family Life*. Trans Robert Baldick.
     New York: Vintage Books.

Arriaga, Father Pablo Joseph de
[1621] 1968 *The Extirpation of Idolatry in Peru*. Trans. and ed. L. Clark Keating.
     Lexington: University of Kentucky Press.

Ascher, Marcia, and Robert Ascher
1981/1997 *Mathematics of the Incas: Code of the Quipu*. Mineola, N.Y.: Dover
     Publications, Inc.

Aveni, Anthony F.
1989 *Empires of Time: Calendars, Clocks, and Cultures*. New York: Basic Books.
2000 *Between the Lines: The Mystery of the Giant Ground Drawings of Ancient Nasca,
     Peru*. Austin: University of Texas Press.

Avila, Francisco de
[1598] 1966 *Dioses y Hombres de Huarochirí*. Translated from the Quechua by José
     María Arguedas. Lima: Museo Nacional de Historia and Instituto de Estudios
     Peruanos.
[1598] 1983 *Hijos de Pariya Qaqa: La tradición oral de Waru Chirí*. Spanish translation
     from the Quechua by Jorge L. Urioste. Latin American Series no. 6. Syracuse,
     N.Y.: Maxwell School of Citizenship and Public Affairs, Syracuse University.

Babb, Florence
1998 *Between Field and Cooking Pot: The Political Economy of Market Women in Peru.*
    Austin: University of Texas Press.

Baker, Paul
1968 *High Altitude Adaptation in a Peruvian Community.* Occasional Papers in
    Anthropology, no. 1. University Park: Department of Anthropology,
    Pennsylvania State University.

Banco de Crédito del Peru
1984 *Panorama del Departamento del Cuzco,* Junio.

Bastien, Joseph W.
1985 *Mountain of the Condor: Metaphor and Ritual in an Andean Ayllu.* Prospect
    Heights, Ill: Waveland Press, Inc.

Bauer, Brian S.
1998 *The Sacred Landscape of the Inca: The Cusco Ceque System.* Austin: University of
    Texas Press.

Bauer, Brian S., and David S. P. Dearborn
1995 *Astronomy and Empire in the Ancient Andes: The Cultural Origins of Inca Sky
    Watching.* Austin: University of Texas Press.

Beyersdorff, Margot
1984 *Léxico agropecuario Quechua.* Cuzco: Centro de Estudios Rurales Andinos
    "Bartolomé de las Casas."

Body Shop Team
1991 *Mamatoto: A Celebration of Birth.* London: Virago Press.

Bolin, Inge
1987 The Organization of Irrigation in the Vilcanota Valley of Peru: Local Autonomy,
    Development and Corporate Group Dynamics. Ph.D. diss., University of
    Alberta, Canada.
1990a The Hidden Power of Women: Highland Peru and West Sumatra Compared.
    Development and Cooperation 1:12–13.
1990b Upsetting the Power Balance: Cooperation, Competition, and Conflict along an
    Andean Irrigation System. *Human Organization* 49(2):140–148.
1991 The "Big Shock" in Peru—August 1990. *Latin American Anthropology Review*
    3(1):42–43.
1992 Achieving Reciprocity: Anthropological Research and Development Assistance.
    Practicing Anthropology 14(4):12–15.
1994a Health for the Poor: Grassroots Medicine in Peruvian Villages. *Development and
    Cooperation* 5/6:18–20.
1994b Levels of Autonomy in the Organization of Irrigation in the Highlands of Peru.
    In *Irrigation at High Altitudes: The Social Organization of Water Control Systems
    in the Andes,* ed. William P. Mitchell and David Guillet, pp. 141–166. Society for
    Latin American Anthropology Publication Series, vol. 12. Jeffrey David

Ehrenreich, General Editor. Washington, D.C.: American Anthropological
Association.

1996 Reviving Traditional Medicine in the Peruvian Andes. *Practicing Anthropology*
18(2):6–9.

1998 *Rituals of Respect: The Secret of Survival in the High Peruvian Andes.* Austin:
University of Texas Press.

1999 Survival in Marginal Lands: Climate Change in the High Peruvian Andes.
Development and Cooperation 5:25–26.

2001 When Apus Are Losing Their White Ponchos: Environmental Dilemmas and
Restoration Efforts in Peru. *Development and Cooperation* 6:25–26.

2003 Our Apus Are Dying: Glacial Retreat and Its Consequences for Life in the Andes.
Paper presented at the American Anthropological Association annual meeting,
Chicago, November 19, 2003.

2004 The Power of the *Enqaychu* and the Cosmos of Andean Pastoralists. Paper
presented at the 12th Latin American Symposium, Museum of Man, San Diego,
Calif., March 6, 2004.

Bolin, Inge, and Greg Bolin
2003 A Solar Cooker's Odyssey on Three Continents. *Solar Cooker Review* 9(3):4.

Bolton, Ralph, and Enrique Mayer, eds.
1977 *Andean Kinship and Marriage.* Special Publication of the American
Anthropological Association, no. 7. Washington, D.C.

Brack Egg, Antonio
1994 La sierra del Peru: Pobreza y posibilidades. *Allpanchis* 43/44:87–116.
1999 *Diccionario enciclopedico de plantas utiles del Peru.* Cuzco: Centro de Estudios
Regionales Andinos "Bartolomé de las Casas."

Browman, David L.
1974 Pastoral Nomadism in the Andes. *Current Anthropology* 15(2):188–196.
1990 High Altitude Camelid Pastoralism of the Andes. In *The World of Pastoralism:
Herding Systems in Comparative Perspective,* ed. John G. Galaty and Douglas L.
Johnson, pp. 323–352. New York and London: The Guilford Press.

Brush, Stephen
1976 Man's Use of an Andean Ecosystem. *Human Ecology* 4(2):147–166.
1977 *Mountain, Field and Family: The Economy and Human Ecology of an Andean
Valley.* Philadelphia: University of Pennsylvania Press.

Burchard, Roderick E.
1992 Coca Chewing and Diet. *Current Anthropology* 33(1): 1–24.

Cáceres Ch., Efraín
1986 El agua como fuente de vida: Traslación y escape en los mitos andinos.
Allpanchis 28:99–122.

Cahlander, Adele, with Elayne Zorn and Ann Pollard Rowe
1980 *Sling Braiding of the Andes.* Weaver's Journal Monograph IV. Boulder: Colorado Fiber Center Inc.

Cavero Carrasco, Jesús Armando
1985 El Qarawi y su función social. *Allpanchis* 25: 233–270.

Cereceda, Verónica
1986 The Semiology of Andean Textiles: The Talegas of Isluga. In *Anthropological History of Andean Polities,* ed. John Murra, Nathan Wachtel, and Jacques Revel, pp. 149–173. Cambridge: Cambridge University Press.

Chávez Ballón, Manuel
1970 Ciudades Incas: Cuzco, capital del imperio. *Wayka* 3:1–15.

Cieza de León, Pedro
[1551] 1943 *Del señorío de los Incas.* Buenos Aires: Ediciones Argentinas Solar.

Cobo, Bernabé
[1653] 1956 *Historia del Nuevo Mundo.* In *Obras del P. Bernabé Cobo de la compañía de Jesús,* ed. P. Francisco Mateos. Biblioteca de Autores Españoles, vols. 91 and 92. Madrid: Ediciones Atlas.
[1653] 1964 *Historia del Nuevo Mundo.* In *Obras del P. Bernabé Cobo de la compañía de Jesús,* ed. P. Francisco Mateos. Biblioteca de Autores Españoles, vols. 91 and 92. Madrid: Ediciones Atlas.
1890–1895 *Historia del Nuevo Mundo.* 4 vols. Ed. Marcos Jiménez de la Espada. Seville: Sociedad de Bibliófilos Andaluces.
1990 *Inca Religion and Customs.* Trans. and ed. Roland Hamilton. Austin: University of Texas Press.

Comisión Coordinadora Nacional de Rondas Campesinas.
2003 Proyecto de Reglamento de la Ley 27908 — Ley de Rondas Campesinas. Lima, February 7, 2003.

Crumrine, N. Ross, and Alan Morinis, eds.
1991 *Pilgrimage in Latin America.* New York: Greenwood Press.

Cusihuamán G., Antonio
1976 *Diccionario Quechua Cuzco Collao.* Lima: Ministerio de Educación, Instituto de Estudios Peruanos.

Custred, Glynn
1979 Symbols and Control in a High Altitude Community. *Anthropos* 74:379–392.

Dauncey, Guy, with Patrick Mazza
2001 *Stormy Weather: 101 Solutions to Global Climate Change.* Gabriola Island, British Columbia: New Society Publishers.

Davies, Thomas M., Jr.
1974 *Indian Integration in Peru: A Half Century of Experience, 1900–1948.* Lincoln: University of Nebraska Press.

Davis, Wade
1996 *One River: Explorations and Discoveries in the Amazon Rain Forest.* New York: Simon and Schuster.
2001 *Light at the Edge of the World: A Journey through the Realm of Vanishing Cultures.* Vancouver: Douglas and McIntyre.

Desrosiers, Sophie
1992 Las técnicas del tejido ¿tienen un sentido? Una propuesta de lectura de los tejidos andinos. *Revista Andina* 10(1):7–46.

D'Harcourt, Raoul
1974 *Textiles of Ancient Peru and Their Techniques.* Seattle and London: University of Washington Press.

Dickason, Olive Patricia
1984 *The Myth of the Savage.* Edmonton: University of Alberta Press.
1997 *Canada's First Nations: A History of Founding Peoples from Earliest Times.* Toronto: Oxford University Press.

Dover, Robert V. H., Katherine E. Seibold, and John H. McDowell
1992 *Andean Cosmologies through Time: Persistence and Emergence.* Bloomington: Indiana University Press.

Duviols, Pierre
1971 *La Lutte contre les religions autochtones dans le Pérou colonial: L'extirpation de l'idolâtrie entre 1532 et 1600,* Documentary appendix. Lima and Paris: Institut Français d'Etudes Andines.

Eisner, Eliot
1988 The Ecology of School Improvement. *Educational Leadership* 5:24–29.

Eliade, Mircea
1965 *The Two and the One.* London: Harvill Press.

Ereira, Alan
1991 *From the Heart of the World.* A film produced by the BBC, directed by Alan Ereira, distributed by Mystic Fire Video, 524 Broadway, Suite 604, New York, N.Y. 10012.
1992 *The Elder Brothers.* New York: Alfred A. Knopf.

Escalante Gutiérrez, Carmen, and Ricardo Valderrama Fernández
1992 *Nosotros los Humanos—Ñuqanchik Runakuna. Testimonio de los Quechuas del siglo XX.* Cuzco: Centro de Estudios Regionales Andinos "Bartolomé de las Casas."

Farrington, Ian S.
1992 Ritual Geography, Settlement Patterns and the Characterization of the Inka Heartland. *World Archaeology* 23(3):368–385.

Fischer, Eva
2002 Las categorías del tiempo y el concepto de temporalidad: El caso de Upinhuaya. *Revista Andina* 35:167–190.

Fisher, Lillian Estelle
1966 *The Last Inca Revolt, 1780–1783.* Norman: University of Oklahoma Press.

Flannery, Kent V., Joyce Marcus, and Robert G. Reynolds
1989 *The Flocks of the Wamani: A Study of Llama Herders on the Punas of Ayacucho, Peru.* San Diego: Academic Press Inc.

Flores Lizana, Carlos
1997 *El taytacha Qoyllur Rit'i: Teología India hecha por comuneros y mestizos Quechuas.* Sicuani, Peru: Instituto de Pastoral Andina.

Flores Ochoa, Jorge A.
1977 Enqa, Enqaychu, Illa y Khuya Rumi. In *Pastores de puna: Uywamichiq punarunakuna,* comp. Jorge A. Flores Ochoa, pp. 211–237. Lima: Instituto de Estudios Peruanos.
1979 *Pastoralists of the Andes: The Alpaca Herders of Paratía.* Trans. Ralph Bolton. Philadelphia: Institute for the Study of Human Issues.
1986 The Classification and Naming of South American Camelids. In *Anthropological History of Andean Polities,* ed. John V. Murra, Nathan Wachtel, and Jacques Revel, pp. 137–148. Cambridge: Cambridge University Press.
1988 Mitos y canciones ceremoniales en comunidades de puna. In *Llamichos y paqocheros, pastores de llamas y alpacas,* ed. Jorge A. Flores Ochoa, pp. 237–251. Cuzco: Centro de Estudios Andinos.
1990 *El Cuzco: Resistencia y continuidad.* Cuzco: Centro de Estudios Andinos.

Franquemont, Christine, and Edward M. Franquemont
1987 Learning to Weave in Chinchero. *Textile Museum Journal* 26:55–78.

Franquemont, Edward M., Christine Franquemont, and Billie Jean Isbell
1992 Awaq Ñawin: El ojo del tejedor—La práctica de la cultura en el tejido. *Revista Andina* 10(1):47–80.

Gade, Daniel
1975 *Plants, Man and the Land in the Vilcanota Valley of Peru.* The Hague: Dr. W. Junk B. V.
1999 *Nature and Culture in the Andes.* Madison: The University of Wisconsin Press.

Galaty, John G., and Douglas L. Johnson, eds.
1990 *The World of Pastoralism: Herding Systems in Comparative Perspective.* New York and London: Guilford Press.

Garcilaso de la Vega, El Inca
[1609] 1966 *The Incas: Royal Commentaries of the Incas and General History of Peru, Parts I and II.* Trans. Harold V. Livermore. Austin: University of Texas Press.

Gatto, John Taylor
1992 *Dumbing Us Down: The Hidden Curriculum of Compulsory Schooling.*
Philadelphia and Gabriola Island, British Columbia: New Society Publishers.

Gavilán Vega, Vivian, and Liliana Ulloa Torres
1992 Proposiciones metodológicas para el estudio de los tejidos andinos. *Revista Andina* 10(1):107–134.

Gay, John, and Michael Cole
1967 *The New Mathematics and an Old Culture: A Study of Learning among the Kpelle of Liberia.* New York: Holt, Rinehart, and Winston.

Gelles, Paul
1985 Coca and Andean Culture: The New Dangers of an Old Debate. *Cultural Survival Quarterly* 9(4):20–23.

German Agency for Technical Cooperation Ltd.
1978 *Utilization of Vicugnas in Peru.* Eschborn: GTZ.

González Holguín, Diego
[1608] 1952 *Vocabulario de la lengua general de todo el Peru llamada lengua Qquichua, o del Inca.* Corregido y renovado conforme a la propiedad corte sana del Cuzco. Lima.

Gordon, Robert J.
1992 *The Bushman Myth: The Making of a Namibian Underclass.* Boulder, Colo.: Westview.

Gow, David, and Rosalinda Gow
1975 La alpaca en el mito y el ritual. *Allpanchis* 8:141–174.

Guamán Poma de Ayala, Felipe
[1615] 1956 *La nueva crónica y buen gobierno.* Trans. into modern Spanish by Luis Bustíos Gálvez. 3 vols. Lima: Editorial Cultura.
[1615] 1980 *El primer nueva crónica y buen gobierno.* Ed. John V. Murra and Rolena Adorno. Translated from the Quechua by Jorge L. Urioste. 3 vols. Mexico, Madrid, and Bogota: Siglo Veintiuno Editores.

Harris, Olivia
1978 Complementarity and Conflict: An Andean View of Women and Men. In *Sex and Age as Principles of Differentiation,* ed. Jean Sybil La Fontaine, pp. 21–40. London: Academic Press.

Harrison, Regina
1989 *Signs, Songs, and Memory in the Andes.* Austin: University of Texas Press.

Haviland, William A.
1997 *Anthropology,* 8th ed. Fort Worth, Tex.: Harcourt Brace College Publishers.

Healy, Jane M.
1987 *Your Child's Growing Mind: A Parent's Guide to Learning from Birth to Adolescence.* Garden City, N.Y.: Doubleday & Company.

1990 *Endangered Minds: Why Children Don't Think—and What We Can Do About It.* New York: Simon & Schuster.

1998 *Failure to Connect: How Computers Affect Our Children's Minds—for Better or Worse.* New York: Simon & Schuster.

Heise, Maria
1989 Los niños Asháninka. *Amazonia Indígena,* 9(18):172–178.

Hemming, John
1970 *The Conquest of the Incas.* New York: Harcourt, Brace, Jovanovich.

Henry, J., and Z. Henry
[1944] 1974 *Doll Play of Pilagá Indian Children.* New York: Vintage/Random House.

Hochachka, Peter
1992 Principles of Physiological and Biochemical Adaptation: High-Altitude Man as a Case Study. In *Physiological Adaptations in Vertebrates—Respiration, Circulation, and Metabolism,* ed. Stephen C. Wood, Roy E. Weber, Alan R. Hargens, and Ronald W. Millard, pp. 21–35. New York: Marcel Dekker, Inc.

Hochachka, Peter W., C. Stanley, G. O. Matheson, D. C. McKenzie, P. S. Allen, and W. S. Parkhouse
1991 Metabolic and Work Efficiencies during Exercise in Andean Natives. *Journal of Applied Physiology* 70(4):1720–1730.

Instituto Cuánto and UNICEF
1992 *Mujeres y niños del Perú: Situación social.* Lima: Instituto Cuánto.

Ionesov, Vladimir I.
2000 The Ritualization of Conflict within Post-primitive Societies. In *The Nature and Function of Rituals: Fire from Heaven,* ed. Ruth-Inge Heinze, pp. 37–57. Westport, Conn., and London: Bergin & Garvey.

Isbell, Billie Jean
1977 Kuyac: Those Who Love Me: An Analysis of Andean Kinship and Reciprocity within a Ritual Context. In *Andean Kinship and Marriage,* ed. Ralph Bolton and Enrique Mayer, pp. 81–105. Special Publication of the American Anthropological Association, no. 7. Washington, D.C.

1985 *To Defend Ourselves: Ecology and Ritual in an Andean Village.* 3rd ed. Prospect Heights, Ill.: Waveland Press, Inc.

Isbell, Billie Jean, and Fredy A. Roncalla Fernández.
1977 The Ontogenesis of Metaphor. *Journal of Latin American Lore* 3(1):19–49.

Jackson, Evangelyn
1964 Native Toys of the Guarayu Indians. *American Anthropologist* 66:1153–1155.

Julien, Catherine
2000 *Reading Inca History.* Iowa City: University of Iowa Press.

Kern, Stephen
1983 *The Culture of Time and Space, 1880–1918.* Cambridge, Mass.: Harvard University Press.

Lancy, David F.
1996 *Playing on the Mother Ground: Cultural Routines for Children's Development.* New York and London: Guilford Press.

Leach, Penelope
1994 *Children First: What Our Society Must Do—and Is Not Doing—for Our Children Today.* London: Michael Joseph.

Lefèber, Yvonne, and Henk W. A. Voorhoeve
1998 *Indigenous Customs in Childbirth and Child Care.* Assen, Netherlands: Van Gorcum & Comp.

Lira, Jorge A.
1968 *Diccionario Kkechuwa-Español.* Cuzco: Edición Popular.

Lorenz, Konrad
1976 Psychology and Phylogeny. In *Play: Its Role in Development and Evolution,* ed. J. Bruner, A. Jolly, and K. Sylva, pp. 84–95. New York: Basic Books.

Lyon, Patricia J., ed.
1985 *Native South Americans: Ethnology of the Least Known Continent.* Prospect Heights, Ill.: Waveland Press, Inc.

MacCormack, Sabine
1991 *Religion in the Andes: Vision and Imagination in Early Colonial Peru.* Princeton, N.J.: Princeton University Press.

Malengreau, Jacques
1972 Les limites de la communauté à Cusipata, un village des Andes péruviennes. Ph.D. diss., Université Libre de Bruxelles.

Mayer, Enrique
1985 Production Zones. In *Andean Ecology and Civilization: An Interdisciplinary Perspective on Andean Ecological Complementarity,* ed. Shozo Masuda, Izumi Shimada, and Craig Morris, pp. 45–84. Tokyo: University of Tokyo Press.

McCorkle, Constance
1988 *Manejo de la sanidad de rumiantes menores en una comunidad indígena andina.* Lima: Comisión de Coordinación de Tecnología Andina CCTA.

Mead, Margaret
1967 *Coming of Age in Samoa.* New York: William Morrow and Co.

Meyerson, Julia
1990 *Tambo: Life in an Andean Village.* Austin: University of Texas Press.

Millones, Luis

1975 Economía y ritual en los Condesuyos de Arequipa: Pastores y tejedores del siglo XIX. *Allpanchis* 8:45–66.

1992 *Actores de altura: Ensayos sobre el teatro popular andino.* Lima: Editorial Horizonte.

1993 Representando el pasado: Desfiles y disfraces en los Andes. In *El mundo ceremonial andino,* ed. Luis Millones and Yoshio Onuki, pp. 275–288. SENRI Ethnological Studies no. 37. Osaka: Museo Nacional de Etnología.

Millones, Luis, and Tomoeda Hiroyasu, eds.

1982 *El hombre y su ambiente en los Andes Centrales.* SENRI Ethnological Studies no. 10. Osaka: Museo Nacional de Etnología.

Millones, Luis, and Mary Louise Pratt

1990 *Amor Brujo: Images and Cultures of Love in the Andes.* Foreign and Comparative Studies/Latin American Series 10. Syracuse, N.Y.: Maxwell School of Citizenship and Public Affairs, Syracuse University.

Mishkin, Bernard

1963 The Contemporary Quechua. In *Handbook of South American Indians,* ed. Julian H. Steward, 2(143):411–470. New York: Cooper Square Publishers, Inc.

Mitchell, William P.

1991 *Peasants on the Edge: Crop, Cult, and Crisis in the Andes.* Austin: University of Texas Press.

Mitchell, William P., and David Guillet, eds.

1994 *Irrigation at High Altitudes: The Social Organization of Water Control Systems in the Andes.* Society for Latin American Anthropology Publication Series, vol. 12. Jeffrey David Ehrenreich, General Editor. Washington, D.C.: American Anthropological Association.

Molina, Cristóbal de

[1575] 1913 Relación de las fábulas y ritos de los Incas, ed. T. Thayer Ojeda. *Revista Chilena de Historia y Geografía* 5:117–190.

[1575] 1916 *Relación de las fábulas y ritos de los Incas.* Lima: Imprenta y Librería Sanmartí y Ca.

Monge, Carlos M.

1984 *Acclimatization in the Andes.* Baltimore: John Hopkins University Press.

1953 Biología general y humana: Características de los seres aclimatados en el altiplano: Revista de conjunto sobre la función respiratoria del andino. *Peru Indígena* 4(9):4–21.

Montoya, Rodrigo

1995 Los niños indígenas en el Perú: Entre la exclusión histórica y la promesa de una ciudadanía étnica. *América Indígena* 53(3):67–103.

Montoya, Rodrigo, with Luis and Edwin Montoya

1987 *Urqukunapa yawarnin: La sangre de los cerros (Antología de la poesía quechua que se canta en el Perú. Edición bilingüe de 333 canciones).* 2 vols. Lima: Mosca Azul Editores, Centro Peruano de Estudios Sociales (CEPES), y Universidad Nacional Mayor de San Marcos.

Morinis, Alan, and N. Ross Crumrine
1991 La Peregrinación: The Latin American Pilgrimage. In *Pilgrimage in Latin America,* ed. N. Ross Crumrine and Alan Morinis, pp. 1–17. New York: Greenwood Press.

Müller, Thomas, and Helga Müller
1984 Cosmovisión y celebraciones del mundo andino. *Allpanchis* 23:161–176.

Murra, John V.
1962 Cloth and its Functions in the Inca State. *American Anthropologist* 64(4):710–728.
1965 Herds and Herders in the Inca State. In *Man, Culture and Animals,* ed. A. Leeda and A. P. Vayda, pp. 185–215. American Association for the Advancement of Science Publications, 78. Washington, D.C.
1986 The Expansion of the Inka State: Armies, War, and Rebellions. In *Anthropological History of Andean Polities,* ed. John V. Murra, Nathan Wachtel, and Jacques Revel, pp. 49–58. Cambridge: Cambridge University Press.

Murúa, Martín de
[1590] 1946 Historia del origen y genealogía real de los reyes incas del Perú. Ed. Constantino Bayle, S. J. Madrid: C. Bermejo, Impresor. J. García Morato.

Nabhan, Gary Paul, and Stephen Trimble
1994 *The Geography of Childhood: Why Children Need Wild Places.* Boston: Beacon Press.

Nachtigall, Horst
1975 Ofrendas de llamas en la vida ceremonial de los pastores. *Allpanchis* 8:133–140.

Nash, June, and Helen I. Safa, eds.
1985 *Women and Change in Latin America: New Directions in Sex and Class.* South Hadley, Mass.: Bergin and Garvey Publishers.

Niles, Susan A.
1987 *Callachaca: Style and Status in an Inca Community.* Iowa City: University of Iowa Press.

Núñez del Prado, Juan Víctor
1985 The Supernatural World of the Quechua of Southern Peru as seen from the Community of Qotobamba. In *Native South Americans: Ethnology of the Least Known Continent,* ed. Patricia J. Lyon, pp. 238–251. Prospect Heights, Ill.: Waveland Press, Inc.

Núñez del Prado, Oscar
1973 *Kuyo Chico: Applied Anthropology in an Indian Community.* Chicago and London: University of Chicago Press.
1983a Una cultura como respuesta de adaptación al medio andino. In *Q'ero, el último*

ayllu inka, ed. Jorge A. Flores Ochoa and Juan V. Núñez del Prado, pp. 14–28. Cuzco: Centro de Estudios Andinos.

1983b La vivienda Inca actual. In *Q'ero, el último ayllu inka,* ed. Jorge A. Flores Ochoa and Juan V. Núñez del Prado, pp. 82–86. Cuzco: Centro de Estudios Andinos.

1983c El hombre y la familia: Su matrimonio y organización politico-social en Q'ero. In *Q'ero, el último ayllu inka,* ed. Jorge A. Flores Ochoa and Juan V. Núñez del Prado, pp. 106–130. Cuzco: Centro de Estudios Andinos.

Núñez del Prado Bejar, Daisy Irene
1975 El poder de decisión de la mujer quechua andina. *América Indígena* 35(3):623–630.

Oliart, Patricia, and Patricia Ames
1998 Notas de campo: El trato a los niños y niñas en la Sierra Rural. *Cuestión de Estado* 22:34–38.

Orlove, Benjamin
1977 *Alpacas, Sheep and Men: The Wool Export Economy and Regional Society in Southern Peru.* New York: Academic Press.

Palomino Díaz, Julio
1994 *Intiwatanas y numeros.* Qosqo: Municipalidad del Qosqo.

Pantigozo de Esquivel, Dina, comp.
1995 *Yachasun: Experiencias en medicina tradicional andina.* Publicado por YACHAQ, Qosqo. Cuzco: Editorial Mercantil.

Payne, Johnny, ed. and trans.
2000 *She-Calf and Other Quechua Folk Tales.* Albuquerque: University of New Mexico Press.

Peace, Henry
1994 La pobreza no espera, política social ahora. *Diario La República,* March 27, Lima.

Phipps, Elena
1992 Response to Sophie Desrosiers' article "Las técnicas de tejido ¿tienen un sentido?" *Revista Andina* 10(1):39–40.

Poole, Deborah
1984 Ritual-Economic Calendars in Paruro: The Structure of Representation in Andean Ethnography. Ph.D. diss., University of Illinois, Urbana.

Preuss, Fritz
1997 Tier und Mensch—Gedanken zu Tieren, Tierquälerei, Tierversuchen. Tierversuchsgegner Berlin und Brandenburg, e.V.

Propp, V.
1986 *Istoricheskie korni volshebnoj skazki.* Leningrad: Izdatelstvo Leningrad Skogo Universiteta.

Radcliffe-Brown, A. R.
1952 *Structure and Function in Primitive Society.* New York: Free Press.

Randall, Robert
1982 Qoyllur Rit'i, an Inca Fiesta of the Pleiades: Reflections on Time and Space in the Andean World. *Bulletin de l'Institut Français d'Etudes Andines* (Lima) 11(1–2):37–81.
1987 Del tiempo y del río: El ciclo de la historia y la energía en la cosmología incaica. *Boletín de Lima* 9(54):69–95.

Rastogi, Nina
2002 Living As If the World Mattered: Choosing to live Simply and Responsibly. M.A. thesis, Pacific Oaks College, Pasadena, California.

Reichel-Dolmatoff, Gerardo
1978 The Loom of Life: A Kogi Principle of Integration. *Journal of Latin American Lore* 4(1):5–27.
1985 Funerary Customs and Religious Symbolism among the Kogi. In *Native South Americans: Ethnology of the Least Known Continent,* ed. Patricia Lyons, pp. 289–301. Prospect Heights, Ill.: Waveland Press, Inc.
1987 The Great Mother and the Kogi Universe: A Concise Overview. *Journal of Latin American Lore* 13(1):73–113.

Reinhard, Johan
1999 Children of Inca Sacrifice Found Frozen in Time. *National Geographic* 196(5):36–55.

Rivero Luque, Sara Teresa
1995 Coca. In *Yachasun: Experiencias en medicina tradicional andina,* comp. Dina Pantigozo de Esquivel, pp. 240–241. Publicado por YACHAQ, Qosqo. Cuzco: Editorial Mercantil.
1998 *Planificación familiar con plantas medicinales en el Cuzco.* Cuzco: República del Peru, Región Inka, Departamento del Cuzco.

Rivero Luque, Víctor
1990 *La Chakitaqlla en el mundo andino.* Lima: Herrandina Proyecto de Herramientos e Implementos Agrícolas Andinos.

Robinson Finnan, Christine
1982 The Ethnography of Children's Spontaneous Play. In *Doing the Ethnography of Schooling: Educational Anthropology in Action,* ed. George Spindler, pp. 356–380. Prospect Heights, Ill.: Waveland Press, Inc.

Romney, Kimball, and Romaine Romney
1963 The Mixtecans of Juxtlahuaca, Mexico. In *Six Cultures: Studies of Child Rearing,* ed. Beatrice B. Whiting, pp. 541–691. New York: John Wiley.

Rostworowski de Diez Canseco, María
2001 *Pachacutec Inca Yupanqui.* Lima: Instituto de Estudios Peruanos.

Rowe, Ann Pollard
1987 *The Junius B. Bird Andean Textile Conference.* Washington, D.C.: Textile Museum.
1992 Response to Sophie Desrosiers' article "Las técnicas de tejido ¿tienen un sentido?" *Revista Andina* 10(1):40–42.

Rowe, John
1946/1963 Inca Culture at the Time of the Spanish Conquest. In *Handbook of South American Indians,* ed. Julian H. Steward, 2(143):183–330. New York: Cooper Square Publishers Inc.
1980 Relación de las guacas del Cuzco (1653). In *An Account of the Shrines of Ancient Cuzco,* trans. and ed. John H. Rowe. *Ñawpa Pacha* 17:2–80.

Sallnow, Michael J.
1987 *Pilgrims of the Andes: Regional Cults in Cusco.* Washington, D.C.: Smithsonian Institution Press.
1991 Dual Cosmology and Ethnic Division in an Andean Pilgrimage Cult. In *Pilgrimage in Latin America,* ed. N. Ross Crumrine and Alan Morinis, pp. 281–306. New York: Greenwood Press.

Saravia A., Pilar
1985 Familia campesina andina y la reproducción biológica: Un estudio de caso en los Andes Centrales. *Allpanchis* 25:65–80.

Schwartzman, Helen B.
1978 *Transformations: The Anthropology of Children's Play.* New York and London: Plenum Press.

Seed, John, Joanna Macy, Pat Fleming, and Arne Naess
2000 *Thinking Like a Mountain.* Philadelphia: New Society Publishers.

Seibold, Katharine
1992 Textiles and Cosmology in Choquecancha, Cuzco, Peru. In *Andean Cosmologies through Time,* ed. Robert V. H. Dover, Katharine Seibold, and John H. McDowell, pp. 166–201. Bloomington: Indiana University Press.

Sharon, Douglas
1978 *Wizard of the Four Winds: A Shaman's Story.* New York: Free Press.

Sherbondy, Jeanette
1982 *The Canal System of Hanan Cuzco.* Ann Arbor, Mich.: University Microfilms.
1986 Los ceques: Código de canales en el Cuzco incaico. *Allpanchis* 27:39–73.

Shoemaker, Nola
1964 Toys of Chama (Ese'ejja) Indian Children. *American Anthropologist* 66:1151–1153.

Silverblatt, Irene
1978 Andean Women in Inca Society. *Feminist Studies* 4(3):37–61.
1987 *Moon, Sun, and Witches: Gender Ideologies and Class in Inca and Colonial Peru.* Princeton, N.J.: Princeton University Press.

Silverman, Gail P.

1988 Weaving Technique and the Registration of Knowledge in the Cuzco Area of Peru. *Journal of Latin American Lore* 14(2):207–241.

1991 Iskay Manta/Kinsa Manta: La técnica de tejer y el libro de la sabiduría elaborado en el Depto. del Cuzco. *Boletín de Lima* 74:49–66.

1995 *The Cusco Area Textile Tradition.* Awana Wasi del Cusco Series, vol. 4. Cusco: Awani Wasi del Cusco.

1998 *El tejido andino: Un libro de sabiduría.* Trans. Javier Flores Espinoza and Mariana Pease Mould. Mexico: Fondo de Cultura Económica.

Stein, William W.

1961 *Hualcán: Life in the Highlands of Peru.* Ithaca, N.Y.: Cornell University Press.

Stilwell, Barbara, Matthew R. Galvin, and S. Mark Kopta

2000 *Right vs. Wrong: Raising a Child with a Conscience.* Bloomington and Indianapolis: Indiana University Press.

Stone-Miller, Rebecca

1994 *To Weave for the Sun: Ancient Andean Textiles in the Museum of Fine Arts, Boston.* New York: Thames and Hudson Inc.

Suzuki, David

1998 *Earth Time.* Toronto: Stoddart Publishing Co.

Troll, Carl, ed.

1968 *Geo-Ecology of the Mountainous Regions of the Tropical Americas.* Bonn: Ferd Dummlers Verlag.

Tupayachi Herrera, Alfredo

1993 *Forestales nativos andinos en frutos.* Cuzco: Universidad Nacional de San Antonio Abad del Cuzco.

Turnbull, Colin M.

1983a *The Human Cycle.* New York: Simon & Schuster.

1983b *The Mbuti Pygmies: Change and Adaptation.* New York: Holt, Rinehart and Winston.

Turner, Victor

1968 *The Drums of Affliction: A Study of Religious Processes among the Ndembu of Zambia.* Oxford, U.K.: Clarendon Press.

1969 *The Ritual Process.* Chicago: Aldine Publishing Co.

Ulloa Torres, Liliana, and Vivian Gavilán

1992 Proposiciones metodológicas para el estudio de los tejidos andinos. *Revista Andina* 10(1):107–134.

Urton, Gary

1993 Moieties and Ceremonialism in the Andes: The Ritual Battles of the Carnival Season in Southern Peru. In *El mundo ceremonial andino,* ed. Luis Millones and

Yoshio Onuki, pp. 117–142. SENRI Ethnological Studies no. 37. Osaka: Museo
Nacional de Etnología.

Urton, Gary, with Primitivo Nina Llanos
1997 *The Social Life of Numbers: A Quechua Ontology of Numbers and Philosophy of
Arithmetic.* Austin: University of Texas Press.

Velazco Gonzales, Telésforo, and Pieter van Lierop Sips
1995 *Manual del sistema agroecológico escolar: Programa de educación ecológica.* Lima:
Ministerio de Educación.

Walker, Charles
1991 La violencia y el sistema legal: Los indios y el estado en el Cusco después de la
rebelión de Tupac Amaru. In *Poder y violencia en los Andes,* comp. Henrique
Urbano, ed. Mirko Lauer, pp. 125–147. Cuzco: Centro de Estudios Regionales
Andinos "Bartolomé de las Casas."

Werner, David
1986 *Where There Is No Doctor: A Village Health Care Handbook.* Palo Alto, Calif.: The
Hesperian Foundation.

Weyl, Hermann
1952 *Symmetry.* Princeton, N.J.: Princeton University Press.

Wheeler, Jane C.
1984 On the Origin and Early Development of Camelid Pastoralism in the Andes.
In *Early Herders and Their Flocks of Animals and Archaeology,* vol. 3., ed.
J. Clutton-Brock and C. Grigson, pp. 395–410. Oxford, U.K.: BAR International
Series 202.
1995 Evolution and Present Situation of the South American Camelidae. *Biological
Journal of the Linnean Society* 54:271–295.

Whiting, Beatrice B., ed.
1963 *Six Cultures: Studies of Child Rearing.* New York: John Wiley.

Whiting, Beatrice B., and John W. M. Whiting
1975 *Children of Six Cultures: A Psycho-Cultural Analysis.* Cambridge, Mass.: Harvard
University Press.

Whiting, John
1961 Socialization Process and Personality. In *Psychological Anthropology,* ed. Francis
Hsu, pp. 355–399. Homewood, Ill.: Dorsey Press.

Winterhalder, Bruce
1994 The Ecological Basis of Water Management in the Central Andes: Rainfall and
Temperature in Southern Peru. In *Irrigation at High Altitudes: The Social
Organization of Water Control Systems in the Andes,* ed. William P. Mitchell and
David Guillet, pp. 21–67. Society for Latin American Anthropology Publication

Series, vol. 12. Jeffrey David Ehrenreich, General Editor. Washington, D.C.: American Anthropological Association.

Wolf, Eric R.
1955 Types of Latin American Peasantry. *American Anthropologist* 57(3):452–471.

Wright, Ronald
1984 *Cut Stones and Crossroads. A Journey in the Two Worlds of Peru.* New York: Viking Press.
1992 *Stolen Continents: The "New World" through Indian Eyes since 1492.* Toronto: Viking Press.

Zimmerer, Karl S.
1994 Transforming Colquepata Wetlands: Landscapes of Knowledge and Practice in Andean Agriculture. In *Irrigation at High Altitudes: The Social Organization of Water Control Systems in the Andes,* ed. William P. Mitchell and David Guillet, pp. 115–140. Society for Latin American Anthropology Publication Series, vol. 12. Jeffrey David Ehrenreich, General Editor. Washington, D.C.: American Anthropological Association.

Zorn, Elayne
1987 Un análisis de los tejidos en los atados rituales de los pastores. *Revista Andina* 5(2):489–526.

Zuidema, R. Tom
1964 *The Ceque System of Cuzco.* Leiden, Netherlands: E. J. Brill.
1973 Kinship and Ancestor Cult in Three Peruvian Communities. Hernández Príncipe's Account of 1622. *Bulletin de l'Institut Français d'Etudes Andines* 2(1):16–33.
1977 The Inca Kinship System, a New Theoretical View. In *Andean Kinship and Marriage,* ed. Ralph Bolton and Enrique Mayer, pp. 240–281. Special Publication of the American Anthropological Association, no. 7. Washington, D.C.
1982 Bureaucracy and Systematic Knowledge in Andean Civilization. In *The Inca and Aztec States 1400–1800,* ed. George A. Collier, Renato I. Rosaldo, and John Wirth, pp. 419–459. New York: Academic Press.

Zuidema, R. Tom, and Gary Urton
1976 La constelación de la llama en los Andes peruanos. *Allpanchis* 9:59–119.

Zuloaga, Elsa, Alejandro Rossel, and Laura Soria
1993 *Los niños del Peru: Pautas y prácticas de crianza.* Lima: Desco, UNICEF.

Adolescence, xi, xii, 15, 135–149; as a cherished state in life, xi, 136–137, 149, 157; games throughout, 67, 68; learning adult activities during, 137, 143, 149; love and romance during, 136; as recalled by elders, 137; and stress, 141, 142, 156, 157; in the U.S., xii, 157

Adolescents: and bravery, 142; and cargo system, 145; and community learning, 144, 145, 146, 147, 148, 158; and competition, 140; defending rights of, 148; in an egalitarian society, 149; feeling at ease, 149, 157, 158, 159; and gender, 138; importance of, to society, 144; integration of, into adulthood, 156; joining organized groups, 144, 146, 147, 148; learning about healing, 143, 144 (see also Healing knowledge); learning about metaphors, 136; in other countries, 156, 157, 158; personality traits of, 47, 142–143, 156; physical changes in, 138–139, 157; and the *qhaswa*, 144, 145; respect and responsibility received by, 138, 141, 158; roles of, during Pukllay, 110, 132–134; and Rondas Campesinas, 147–149; sensitivity in, 47, 140; and stress, 141, 157; and stylized joking (*chansanakuy*), 136–137; and work ethics, 138

Agriculture/horticulture, 5; finding work in, 12; learning about, 70, 155; plowing the soil (*yapuy, barbecho,* Sp.), 79; subsistence on, 2, 58; without chemicals, 138

Alford Andrews, Michael, 171n16

Allen, Catherine, 16, 137, 165n30, 175n5, 176n19

Alpacas. *See* Camelids

Ama llulla, ama suwa, ama qella (Inca greeting), 7, 71

Andean cultigens, 176n15

Andean glaciers, 65, 178n3

Animals: days in honor of, 166n1; in play activities, 65; respect and compassion for, 1, 33–36; treatment of, in "modern" societies, 35–36. *See also* Camelids; Condors; Foxes; Horses; Pumas; Sheep

Apu Ausangate, 3, 28, 35; and animal sacrifice, 119, 120, 128; as protector, 119; in rituals, 123, 125; songs about, 133

Arariwa, 145

Archaeological evidence. *See* Chillihuani

Ariès, Philippe, 170n9

Aristotle, 153, 156

Arpay, 119–120

Ascher, Marcia, and Robert Ascher, 105, 107

Avila, Francisco de, 161n4

Ayllu, 5, 144; definition of, 161n4

Ayni (reciprocal work relationship), 17, 82, 162n4

Babb, Florence, 167n10

Baker, Paul, 31, 165n30

Banco de Crédito del Peru, 90

Baptism, Andean (*unuchakuy*), 14, 27–29, 47

Baptism, Catholic, 48–49; meaning of salt used in, 167n11

Bastien, Joseph W., 16, 23, 24, 38, 165n30, 167n11, 170n11

Bauer, Brian S., 107, 174n25

Body Shop Team, 163nn6,8

Bolin, Inge, 12, 16, 17, 42, 45, 47, 68, 70, 72, 83, 95, 97, 101, 109, 110, 117, 119, 129, 134, 135, 136, 144; and Greg Bolin, 12

Bolivia, x, 10
Brack Egg, Antonio, 9, 22, 161n5, 163nn9,13, 164n17
Browman, David L., 161n6

Cáceres, Ch., Efraín, 94
Cahlander, Adele, with Elayne Zorn and Ann Pollard Rowe, 100, 170n13
Camelids (alpacas and llamas), 5–6, 10; attacks on, by condors, 77, 78; attacks on, by pumas, 77; capacity of, to carry loads, 171n17; classification of, 94, 172n10; death of, 114, 119, 121; herders' ideology of, 34; herding of, 74–78, 93–94; and high-altitude stress, 31; in historical perspective, 10; marking of, 127, 176n17; in metaphoric context, 42, 64, 65, 67, 95, 97, 117, 118, 126; respect, love, and compassion for, 33–36; respectful address of, 64, 126; rituals in honor of, 35, 110–128; sacrifice of, 35, 119–120; as unmilked animals, 165n24; used in subsistence, 5, 6, 100
Cargo system, 132, 140, 145, 176n21
Casarakuy. See Wedding, Catholic
Cavero Carrasco, Jesús Armando, 139, 169n30
Ceque system, 105, 174n25; defined, 107
Cereceda, Verónica, 173n19
Chakitaklla (foot plow), 72, 79
Ch'allaska, 115, 122–128, 175n4
Chávez Ballón, Manuel, 174n25
Chicha, 115, 117, 123, 125, 126, 128; making, 175n3
Childbirth, 14, 19–24; beliefs about, 20; and beliefs about conception, 23–24; blanketing during, 21, 163n14; breathing problems in, 164n16; death during, 18, 29–30, 79; diet and nutrition following, 24–25, 165nn24,26; help in, 18; infections in the course of, 164n17; knowledge of the past about, 21; medicinal plants used after, 164nn20,21

(*see also* Medicinal plants); stillbirths, 18; placenta in, 164nn18,19; problems of mother during, 165nn31,32
Childhood, xi, 14, 43; beliefs of elders about, 47; chores in the course of, 138, 171n19; diseases of, 30–32; early years of, 18, 33–61; happiness in, 150, 151, 152; lack of, xii; in other societies, 158; and rituals, 109; and unhappiness, 43
Child rearing, 6, 7, 15, 146; and achieving obedience, 38–40; adaptive patterns of, 37, 83, 150; benefits of, xi; in cities, 86; emphasis on respect in, 152; enculturation and socialization in, 36–43; excellence through, xii; focus on competition in, lack of, 47; gender issues in, 46–47; learning compassion through, 33–36, 42, 45; and learning history, 45; in other societies, 152–156; permissive attitude in, 14, 37–40, 43, 63; perpetuating values through, 1; in poverty, 1–2
Children at work, 71–81, 152, 155
Children's games, 67–69; of daring, 68; gender differences in, 69; hide and seek (*paka paka* pukllay), 67; joking (*chansanakuy*), 68, 137; lacking aggression, 68; and mathematics, 93; and non-competitive attitude, 68; pushing (*takanakuy*), 67; soccer, 68
Chillihuani, the community of: archaeological evidence about, 4, 10; climate of, 2–3, 12, 17; development projects in, 11–12; ecological zones of, 5; field work in, 6–10; living conditions of, 2–5, 17; location of, 2–5; number of inhabitants of, 2; village structure of, 144–146
Chillihuani healers (*hampic, curanderos*, Sp), 10; attending to patients, 121; concern of, 43, 56, 121; knowledge of, 16, 17, 31, 32, 82, 144, 177n6; knowledge of, about childbirth, 21–22; learning new concepts, 82; as participants in Yachaq

Runa, 12, 169n22; spinning wool, 99;
teaching adolescents, 143
Chuño. See Potatoes
Cieza de León, Pedro, 107
Clothing, 6, 36, 101, 103, 104, 114; festive, 129, 136, 166n4, 173n18; from Inca
times, 114, 115
Cobo, Bernabé, 163nn5,10, 168n14
Coca k'intu, 28, 125; for deities, 20, 34, 51,
52, 97, 116, 118, 131; for funeral, 60
Coca leaves, 116, 175nn5,6; in barter,
115, 170n2; in the birth process, 20;
carried in *unkuñas* and *ch'uspas,* 170n3;
chewing of, x, 13; and cocaine, 13;
ingredients in, ix, 13, 116, 162n13; as
intermediaries, 116; and lightning,
171n14; misconceptions about, 116;
ritual use of, 28, 51, 73, 116, 125; sacred
to the Incas, ix; in social and economic
interactions, ix, 13, 116, 129
Coca seed (*mukllu*), 97
Compadres, 168n16. *See also* Godchildren
(*ahijada, ahijado*) and godparents
(*madrina* and *padrino*)
Compassion of Chillihuani herders, 1, 2,
32, 33, 35, 43, 56, 61, 84, 136, 151, 155
Competition: children winning, 90; in
city schools, 86; positive and negative
approachs to, 154; and stress, 158. *See
also* Non-competitive attitude
Condors, 2, 34, 77–78, 101
Conflict, resolution of, xi
Co-parenthood (*compadrazgo*): definition of, 167n10; godchild (*ahijada,
ahijado*), 48–52; godmother of child
(*madrina*) and godfather of child
(*padrino*), 27–28, 48–52, 168n16; rights
and duties of, 27–28, 48–52
Corral: daily (*iphiña*), 64; sacred (*muyukancha*), 64, 118, 123, 127–128
Creativity, x, 1, 14, 33, 88, 89; instilled by
nature, 158; in play, 62, 96
Curandero. See Chillihuani healers

Cusihuamán G., Antonio, 9
Cuzco, 3, 10, 11, 53, 56, 90, 91, 95, 107, 144

Dances, for children and adults, 43, 45,
67, 69–70; and contests, ix, 90; during Pukllay, 112, 121, 128, 129, 132–134;
slings used in, 100, 101
Davies, Thomas M., Jr., 162n10, 172n4
Davis, Wade, 175n5, 177n4, 178n1
Death, 6, 12, 16, 32, 59, 60, 70, 141,
169nn25,26,28,30; of animals, 11, 35,
121; in childbirth, 18, 21, 29, 30; by
lightning bolts, 32; and Pachamama,
29; of a shaman, 29; spirits honored
after, 61
Desrosiers, Sophie, 173n19
D'Harcourt, Raoul, 173n19
Dickason, Olive Patricia, 172n6, 178n9
Disease: in animals, 54, 74, 119, 121, 126,
127; in childhood, 30–32; children
learning about, 155; and disability, 57–
59; extreme weather and, 30, 54; in
metaphoric context, 18, 19, 28, 102,
127; research on, 16; due to stress, 141;
tropical, 12. *See also* Hypoxia
Division of labor, 53–56, 73, 79, 80, 81
Dual forces, 128

Egalitarian society, ix, xii, 53, 87, 149, 153
Eisner, Eliot, 84
Enqa (life force, vital energy, fertilizing
power), 65, 110, 114, 117, 121, 126
Enqaychu: of a condor, 94; defined, 65,
117; and rituals, 117, 125, 126
Ereira, Alan, 13, 116, 177n4, 178n1

Faena (communal work party), 7, 11, 72,
73, 82, 155
Farrington, Ian S., 174n25
Fertility: rituals for deities requesting, 17,
23, 110–134, 138, 139; symbols of, 95,
115, 123
Fiesta de Santiago: baptism during the,

48, 49, 51; definition of, 109, 167n8; horse race during, 68, 140, 154; and thundergod, 109
Fiestas: adolescents' participation in, 136, 142, 145; in August, 110; bartering food for, 46; calendar of, 96; generosity during, 97; learning to dance during, 70; learning organizational skills during, 15, 70, 73, 155; Macho Pagaray, 64; mathematical challenges during, 97; old people's memories of, 47; Peru's Day of Independence, 110; Pukllay, 13, 14, 110–134; songs sung during, 69. *See also* Fiesta de Santiago
First Haircut (*chukcha rutukuy*), 48, 50–52, 167n13; in Inca times, 50, 168n15; and kinship ties, 50–52
Fischer, Eva, 96
Fisher, Lillian Estelle, 144
Flannery, Kent V., Joyce Marcus, and Robert G. Reynolds, x, 8, 10, 31, 161nn4,6, 165n30, 176n10
Flores Lizana, Carlos, 170n6
Flores Ochoa, Jorge A., 38, 40, 65, 139, 165n26, 166n5, 168n15, 170n6, 172n10, 173n15, 175n7
Flowers: *phallcha* as symbols of fertility, 115, 123, 126; as raw materials in play, 63, 65; in rituals, 35, 64; songs about, 45
Food plants, 5–6, 63, 73, 122, 176
Foxes, 40, 54, 77, 101
Franquemont, Christine, and Edward M. Franquemont, 173nn19,20,21
Franquemont, Edward M., Christine Franquemont, and Billie Jean Isbell, 173n19
Funeral, 59, 60, 61, 70, 169n30

Gade, Daniel, 5, 9, 165n24
Games. *See* Children's games
Garcilaso de la Vega, El Inca, 107
Gatto, John Taylor, 154, 156, 158, 172n5
Gay, John and Michael Cole, 153

Gender: and absence of competition, 140, 153; of an animal, 94; and complementarity and cooperation, 138, 139; no difference regarding, 36, 91, 108, 139, 153; and firstborn, 23; and godparents, 28; and parallel roles, 146; and work, 79, 153
Godchildren (*ahijada, ahijado*) and godparents (*madrina* and *padrino*): and baptism, 27–28, 48–49; and death of godchild, 59; and First Haircut, 50–52; and guiding, 129; mountains as, 14, 28; and newlyweds, 129; rights and duties of, 27–28, 48–52; selection of, 48. *See also* Co-parenthood
González Holguín, Diego, 168n14
Gordon, Robert J., 158, 166n3
Gow, David, and Rosalinda Gow, 175n7
Guaman Poma de Ayala, Felipe, 102
Guinea pigs, 5

Hail, 5, 76, 85, 101, 114, 120, 131; house of (*chikchi wasi*), 29
Haviland, William A., 154, 167n7
Healers (*curanderos*). *See* Chillihuani healers
Healing knowledge, 56, 144; of children and adolescents, 143; exchange of, 12
Healy, Jane M., 84, 91, 94, 96, 158, 172nn5,9
Heaven (*hanan pacha*), 29, 60, 138; definition of, 7, 162n9; perception of Andean people about, 138
Heise, Maria, 87
Herders. *See* Pastoralists
High-altitude pressure, 18, 31
Hochachka, Peter, 31
Horses, 53, 64, 65, 73, 109, 110, 157
Hypoxia, 31

Ichu grass, 17, 53, 94, 119
Inca Empire (Tawantinsuyu), 5, 10, 11, 136; conquest of, 70; four quarters of, 136; learning the oral history of, 70;

parallel hierarchies in, 136; remembering life in, 70, 136; rituals reminiscent of, 136; song about, 133

Inca rulers: Atawallpa, 171n2; Mama Anahuarque, 177n1; Pachakuteq Inca Yupanqui, 4, 177n1

Incas: achievements of, 10–11; agricultural practices dating back to, 79, 80, 81; architecture, 10; beliefs of, 19, 95; *ceque* system of, 107; child rearing among, 70; coca leaves held sacred by, 116; First Haircut among, 50; food preservation and distribution of, 175n9; gender equality among, 177n1; greeting of, 7, 71; history of, 11, 45, 70; khipus used by, 105, 107; male/female power among, 136; mathematics among, 105, 107; memories and beliefs going back to, 10, 12, 95, 133; metaphoric world of, 63, 94; mother of (*qoya*), 95; myth of origin of, 94; origin of, 10; and pre-Inca remains, 4, 10; puberty rites among, 139; rituals and fiestas among, 110, 121, 134, 135, 136; sacrifice of children among, 176n19; sling (*warak'a*) and insignia of, 75, 101, 102; songs and sung legends from times of, 133, 136; space/time among, 105; unwritten language of, 9; weaving going back to, 98, 105; work ethics of, 138

Inheritance, 78–79

Instituto Cuánto and UNICEF, 169n23

Inti. See Sun

Ionesov, Vladimir I., 175n8

Isbell, Billie Jean, 161n4

Isbell, Billie Jean, and Fredy A. Roncalla Fernández, 161n4

Jackson, Evangelyn, 170n5

Kacharpari (farewell), 128, 134

Khipu, 105–107, 174n25; definition of, 105; and use at conquest, 107

Khipukamayuq (keeper of the *khipu*), 105

Kinship, fictive. *See* Co-parenthood

K'intu. See Coca k'intu

Kogi Indians of Colombia, 19, 151, 177n4, 178n1

Labor: in the care of infants, 36; division of, in accordance with gender, 53, 73

Lake Titicaca, 10, 67, 127

Lancy, David F., 153, 154

Leach, Penelope, 153, 154, 158

Learning by observation, xi, xii, 36, 37, 46, 73, 137, 150, 153; about dancing, 70; in an integrated fashion, 84; about plants and animals, 84; about playing instruments, 46, 70; about rituals, 123; about spinning and weaving, 99–105

Learning oral history, 8, 70, 95, 133

Lefèber, Yvonne, and Henk W. A. Voorhoeve, 20, 163nn12,14,15, 165n27, 166n2

Leishmaniasis, 140, 177n5

Libations for deities, 118, 131

Lightning: asking deities for protection from, 126; fear of, 32; frequent deaths by, 32, 76; in metaphorical context, 131; stress caused by, 141; thundergod causing, 76

Lira, Jorge A., 9

Llamas. *See* Camelids

Llulluch'a (*qochayuyu*), 5, 73

MacCormack, Sabine, 10

Macho Pagaray. *See* Fiestas

Mamakuna, 98

Mama q'epe (bundle with ritual items), 116

Mathematics: challenges in, 97; contests of, 90; culture as springboard for learning, 93–98; excelling in, xii, 15; as favorite topic, ix, 83, 90, 91, 155; and gender, 91, 108; in *khipu* and *ceque* system, 105–107; and knowledge of spatial relationships, 94; in the U.S., xii, 91, 172n9; stimulating concentration through, 97; and weaving, 98–105

McCorkle, Constance, 161n6, 168n21, 169n28

Mead, Margaret, 152, 154, 157, 167n7

Meals, festive Andean, *t'inpu* or *pochero* (Sp), 109, 114–115, 122, 129

Medicinal plants, 16, 17, 19, 20, 22, 24, 54, 163n13, 163–164nn15,17,18,20,21; to heal tears caused in birth process, 22; to help expel placenta, 19; to prevent conception, 16–17; to rub body, 22; to speed up birth process and cleanse body, 19; to stimulate flow of milk, 24

Mesarumi (altar of stone), 51, 123, 125, 127, 131

Mestizo culture, 87, 88, 94, 171, 172n3

Metaphors: and abstract reasoning, 96; and adolescents, 136; and animals, 34, 126; in the cosmos, 94, 95, 108; fiestas full of, 15, 135; guiding people's lives, 7; learning about, 15; North American native societies and, 34; and numbers, 97, 98; people's worldview and, 149; *qañiwa* seeds as, 97; slings as, 101; *ukukus* as, 42; and winds, 20

Midwife, 18, 21, 30; equipment required by, 19

Millones, Luis, and Mary Louise Pratt, 177n2

Minka, 82

Molina, Cristóbal de, 168n14

Monge, Carlos M., 161n1

Montoya, Rodrigo, 43, 69, 87

Montoya, Rodrigo, with Luis and Edwin Montoya, 69

Moon, 172n11; and agricultural activities, 95; as deified mother of the *Qoya* (Inca empress), 95; and *kukuchi,* 40; as perceived in conception and birth, 24

Moraya. See Potatoes

Mother Earth. *See* Pachamama

Müller, Thomas, and Helga Müller, 96, 174n23

Murúa, Martin de, 177n1

Music: gender issues relating to, 46–47; learning to sing and play, xii, 46, 70, 132, 137, 145; and Pukllay, 112, 116. *See also* Songs

Musical instruments, 46, 112–113, 116, 131, 132; learning through observation, 46

Muyukancha. See corral

Myths and legends, 63, 69, 70, 71, 94, 114, 133, 156

Nabhan, Gary Paul, and Stephen Trimble, 158, 172n5

Newborn, 22–32; baby formula for, 24; baptism of, 27–29; clothing for, 25–27; hypoxia in, 31; mortality of, 18, 31, 165n30; naming of, 28, 165n29; nursing of, 25; origin of soul of, 29; at risk, 18; rituals for, 14, 34, 35; sickness of, 18, 31; weight of, 22–23

El Niño/La Niña, 30, 119

Non-aggressive demeanor, 68, 141, 142, 167n7

Non-competitive attitude, ix, xi, xii, 80, 107, 154, 155, 157, 167n7; between age categories and gender, 140; during horse races, 68; and games, 68; in other countries, 153, 154, 157; in school children, 86; success of children despite, 90

Núñez del Prado, Juan Victor, 162n9

Núñez del Prado, Oscar, 40, 84, 162–163n4

Núñez del Prado Bejar, Daisy Irene, 97, 165n22

Oliart, Patricia, and Patricia Ames, 87

Oral history, 70

Organizational strategies and skills, ix, 15, 82, 108, 112, 147, 149

Orlove, Benjamin, 161n6, 170n12

Pachakuteq Inca Yupanqui. *See* Inca
  rulers
Pachamama (Earth Mother and Goddess): and birth, 21; bond of, with
  females, 78, 139; and death, 29, 32,
  59–60; giving spiritual life, 29; giving
  thanks to, 51, 54, 56; honor and appease, 6, 120, 129, 131; honor to work
  with, 78, 139; offerings for, 31, 33, 34,
  51, 52, 118, 139, 145
Pampamesayoq. See Ritual specialists
Pantigozo de Esquivel, Dina, 12
Paqo. See Ritual specialists
Pastoralists (herders): and continuation of lifeways, 121; definition of, 6;
  and distrust of strangers, x; fieldwork
  among, 6–10; ideology of, x, 2, 6–
  7, 151; in Inca and pre-Inca times, x;
  negative stereotype of, ix, xi, 8, 87;
  and organizational skills, 82–83, 149;
  personality traits of, 47, 142–143; respectful demeanor of, x, 7; subsistence
  strategies of, 5–6
Payne, Johnny, 69, 170n8
Peace, Henry, 169n23
Personality traits of herders (pastoralists), 47, 142–143, 156
Peru: conquest of, 10, 98; Day of Independence, 97, 110, 135; and Shining
  Path, 9, 12; stereotype of native population, 87; and war of Independence
  from Spain, 10
Phalika, 114
Phallchay/phallchakuy, 115
Phipps, Elena, 173n19
Phukuy, 51, 116, 123
Plants. *See* Flowers; Food plants; *Ichu*
  grass; Medicinal plants; Trees
Play activities: and adult tasks, 15, 62–67,
  81; and Andean religious ideology, 65;
  building miniature homesteads and
  irrigation systems, 63–65; differences
  in, 62; and make-believe play, 67; and

math, 97; in metaphorical context, 63
  (*see also* Metaphors); and work, 152
Pleiades, 95
Poole, Deborah, 161n4
Potatoes: and barter, 114; crop destruction, 120–121; early crop of, 171n18;
  freeze-drying (to make *chuño* and *moraya*) of, 29, 51, 53–55, 114, 119, 168n18,
  176n11; planting and harvesting of,
  79, 122, 171n18; and play, 63, 65; and
  rituals, 119, 120; seed, 121
Poverty: among indigenous children,
  169n23; in a marginal environment, x–
  xi, 1–2; and positive thinking, 8, 150;
  and school, 87; and stress, 141, 150
Power of concentration (mental power),
  expressed during rituals, 97, 117, 121,
  125–126
Pregnancy, 14, 16–19; beliefs about, 18–
  19; diet during, 18, 24; prevention of,
  16–17; unplanned, 142; work during,
  18, 25
Preuss, Fritz, 34
Propp, V., 175n8
Pukllay, x, 110–134, 174n2; central issues
  of, 110, 114; and cosmos, 134; and
  dances, 131; dual forces of, 128; falling
  in love during, 134; festive clothes
  for, 129; generosity during, 121; and
  Kacharpari, 128, 134; music and songs
  during, 46, 112, 116, 121, 133; preparations for, 114; stylized joking on, 68;
  Suyay Ch'isin rituals during, 115–119,
  128
Pukuchu. See Ritual items
Pumas, 2, 54, 77, 95

Qhaswa, 144
Quespe rumi (quartz stones) used in play,
  67
Qochayuyu (llulluch'a), 5, 73
Q'oyana (markachana), and offerings, 64,
  118, 126

Qoyllur Riti, 65, 170nn4,6, 176n20
Quechua language (*runasimi*): definition
    of, 9; lack of children's songs and
    stories in, 69, 70; meaning of space/
    time (*pacha*) in, 96; officially acknowl-
    edged, 144

Race track on Oqhe Q'asa Pata, 131
Radcliffe-Brown, A. R., 177n3
Rainbow (*k'uychi*), 132
Randall, Robert, 95, 97, 118, 170n4
Reciprocity, xii, 2, 60, 61, 122; between
    the dead and the living, 60; coming
    full circle, 126; and the cosmos, 15,
    126; as hallmark of Andean life, 152; in
    rituals, 125; and survival, 2
Reichel-Dolmatoff, Gerardo, 19, 177n4,
    178n1
Reinhard, Johan, 176n19
Religious sects, 12, 13, 149, 160
Respect: in addressing others, x, 2, 42,
    43; in ancestral times, xii, 13, 14; for
    animals, 2, 33–36, 64, 126, 128; as a
    catalyst for dignified living, 150, 158,
    159; in children's lives, x, xi, 32, 33, 43,
    86, 89, 108, 125, 129, 139, 141, 142, 147,
    149; for the deceased, 59; for deities
    and cosmic forces, xi, 7, 13, 33, 95, 123,
    126, 139; for the disabled, 140; between
    elders and adolescents, 135, 136; equally
    expressed for both genders, 139; and
    horse race, 68, 140; in Inca times, 121;
    instilled in new generations, 14; joking
    with, 137, 157; as key value, xi, 33, 138;
    lack of, 36, 88, 114, 141, 149, 153, 158; for
    all life, 2, 7, 13, 33, 42, 61, 134, 150, 151,
    159; in offering meals, 54; in rituals,
    expressed, xi, 110, 116, 123, 125; in social
    cohesion, 1, 8; from suitors, expected,
    17; for teachers, 86; and work ethics,
    62
Responsibilities of children, 52, 53, 79, 88,
    108, 135, 136, 138, 145, 147, 150, 156, 157
Rituals: and animals, 35, 64 (*macho paga-*

ray), 115, 127 (*irpay*); burning offerings
    in, 126; and ceremonies, 15, 109–134,
    174n1, 175n8; in childbirth, 20; and
    death, 60; differences among, 109;
    at different levels of society, 84, 109;
    doubt about, 142; involving elders and
    adolescents, 136, 145; and fertility, 119–
    121; among Incas, x, 110; ingredients
    and items used in, 13, 97, 114, 117–118,
    123; key values of, 109, 114; gaining
    knowledge and skills from, 15, 97, 126;
    for the newborn, 14; and numbers,
    97; and power of concentration, 97,
    117, 121, 125–126; secrecy of, 175n7; and
    symbols and metaphors, 97, 108, 136
Ritual items, 97, 115–118
Ritual specialists—*paqo* (*altomesayoq*
    and *pampamesayoq*) and shamans, x,
    28, 29, 32, 127, 143–144, 156–166n32,
    177n6
Rivero Luque, Sara Teresa, 162nn1,2,13,
    163n13, 164nn17,20
Robinson Finnan, Christine, 69
Romney, Kimball, and Romaine Romney,
    163n6
Rondas Campesinas, 147, 148, 149, 177n7,
    178n8
Rowe, Ann Pollard, 173n19
Rowe, John, 16, 19, 101, 139, 161n4,
    163nn5,10, 168n14, 174n25

Sallnow, Michael J., 11, 144
San Martín, José de, 144
Santiago. *See* Fiesta de Santiago
Saravia, Pilar, 162n2, 165n22
Scholastic abilities: of Chillihuani chil-
    dren, xi, 2, 82, 90, 155; eagerness to
    learn and, 86; impact of poverty and
    sickness on, 87; with regard to mathe-
    matics, 90–93
School: attendance by gender in, 85, 86;
    built, 11; and chores at home, 84, 86;
    competitive attitude in city, 86; and
    new curriculum—an articulation pro-

gram, 88–90; with focus on ecology, 89, 172n7; importance of, 85; indigenous children elsewhere and, negative impact of, 87, 156–160; in other societies, 152, 153; parent representation in, 146; program fostering self-esteem, decision making, etc., 88–90; and solar lighting, 12; stress in, 141; teachers, 85

Schwartzman, Helen B., 170n9, 177n3

Seibold, Katharine, 173n19

Shamans. *See* Ritual specialists

Sharon, Douglas, 125

Sheep: diseases of, 54, 119; *enqaychu* of, 65; herding of, 54, 55, 74, 77, 78, 93; in metaphoric context, 64, 67, 117; as prey, 77, 78; and subsistence, 5, 6, 24, 25, 27, 59

Sherbondy, Jeanette, 174n25

Shining Path (Sendero Luminoso), 9, 12

Shoemaker, Nola, 170n5

Silverblatt, Irene, 98

Silverman, Gail P., 100, 105, 173n19, 174n25

Sling. *See* Warak'a (*soq'ana*)

Snow blindness, 76

Songs, 170n7; about animals and flowers, 45; for children and adults, 43, 69–71; and competition, 90; about conquest of Inca Empire, 133; honoring Apu Ausangate, 133; inventing of, 46, 112, 129, 156, 157; about love, 33, 45, 46, 136; in metaphoric context, 19; *qarawi*, 139; *wayñus* (Inca love songs), 136

Space and time (space/time), Andean perceptions of, 96, 105, 114, 174n23

Spinning, 99, 173n15; and learning through observation, 53, 98, 99; as practiced by both sexes and all ages, 99

Stars: in constellations, 95; counted by children, 93, 95; telling time by, 96

Stein, William W., 38, 137, 165n30, 171n15

Stone-Miller, Rebecca, 98, 104, 105, 173n19

Sun, fertilizing rays of in metaphoric context, 115, 117; in horticulture and agriculture, 53, 54, 84; as perceived in Inca times, 50, 95; and telling time, 95–96; temple of the, 107; Virgins of the, 98; worship of, 117

Surnames, in Quechua society, 168n17

Susto, 31

Suyu, 5

Symbols: relating to animals, 118; of camelids, 118; engraved in rock, 4; of fertility, 95, 115, 123; from the Incas past, 136; metaphors and world view, 108, 149; and numbers, 97; power of, 98; of prosperity, 118; and rituals, 136; weaving designs and, 98; of women and life, 139

Tawantinsuyu. *See* Inca Empire

Thundergod (*Illapa, qhaqya*), 131, 171n14; and Fiesta de Santiago, 109; sending hail, 76 (*see also* Hail); causing lightning, 76 (*see also* Lightning); rituals to honor and appease, 117, 118, 145

T'inpu (*pochero,* Sp). *See* Meals, festive Andean

Teachers, x, 171n1; and children's problems, ignoring, 87; and Chillihuani children, 85–93; and Independence Day festivities, 135; and math, 91, 93; mestizo, 88; and new curriculum, 89, 90; opinion of, on impact of TV, 158; parents cooperating with, 146; of the past, 85

Time, Andean perceptions of, 95, 96, 172n12. *See also* Space and time

Todos Santos (All Saints Day), 60–61, 169n29

Torrential rains and landslides, 13, 53, 76, 85, 110, 119, 129

Toys: ceramic, 67; food items used as, 63; made from natural substances, 62, 63, 67, 170n5; parent's tools used as, 62; stones used as, 63–67

Trees, 5–6
Tullu ruki (weaving tool), 6
Tupac Amaru/Micaela Bastides, 11, 144
Tupayachi Herrera, Alfredo, 163n9
Turnbull, Colin M., 150, 151, 154, 158, 166n3
Turner, Victor, 8, 109, 174n1

Ukukus, 67; definition of, 170n6
Ulloa Torres, Liliana, and Vivian Gavilán, 173n19
Unkuña. See Ritual items
Unuchakuy. See Baptism, Andean
Urton, Gary, 105, 173nn17,19, 174nn2,22

Velazco Gonzales, Telésfora, and Pieter van Lierop Sips, 172n7
Vicuña, 2

Waqraqocha, 47, 57, 95
Warak'a (sojana) (sling): blade of grass as metaphor of, 65; braiding of, 100–103, 170n13; in dances and ceremonies, use of, 100–101; in herding animals, use of, 101; Incas' use of as insignia and chief hunting weapon, 101; and judging distance, 94; in metaphoric context, 101; workings of, 75
Wari (a pre-Inca civilization), 4, 10
Warping, 98, 100, 173n16
Weather conditions, extreme, 1, 11, 56, 76, 85, 112, 114, 119, 120, 129. *See also* Hail;

Lightning; Thundergod; Torrential rains and landslides; Winds
Weaving, 98–107, 173nn16,17,19,20,21, 174n22; in accordance with age and gender, 99–104; for communicating, 98, 105; and conquest, 98; by Inca women, 173n13; investigators on the art of, 173n19; and key cultural symbols, 98; learned through observation, 99, 100, 104; and manual dexterity, 103; motifs and symbols in, 173n19, 174n24; patterns in, xii; as stimulant for mathematical thinking, 98–107; techniques used, 104–105; tools used in, 99–100
Wedding, Andean (*rimanakuy*), 16, 17, 49
Wedding, Catholic (*casarakuy*), 17, 49, 129
Werner, David, 21, 165n31
Weyl, Hermann, 105
Whiting, Beatrice B., and John W. M. Whiting, 167n7
Winds, 18, 20, 28, 47, 59, 84, 141; malevolent spirits in, 18, 141, 163n9; as metaphors, 20
Work ethic, 2, 7, 62, 72, 81, 138
Wright, Ronald, 161n2, 171n2

Yachaq Runa, 11, 12, 82, 83, 169n22

Zorn, Elayne, 173n19
Zuidema, R. Tom, 107, 121, 161n4, 174n25